Software Project Management

FOR DUMMIES®

by Teresa Luckey, PMP, MBA, and
Joseph Phillips, PMP

WILEY

John Wiley & Sons, Inc.

Software Project Management For Dummies®

Published by
John Wiley & Sons, Inc.
111 River Street
Hoboken, NJ 07030-5774
www.wiley.com

Copyright © 2006 by John Wiley & Sons, Inc., Hoboken, New Jersey

Published by John Wiley & Sons, Inc., Hoboken, New Jersey

Published simultaneously in Canada

For general information on our other products and services, please contact our Customer Care Department within the U.S. at 877-762-2974, outside the U.S. at 317-572-3993, or fax 317-572-4002. For technical support, please visit www.wiley.com/techsupport.

Wiley publishes in a variety of print and electronic formats and by print-on-demand. Some material included with standard print versions of this book may not be included in e-books or in print-on-demand. If this book refers to media such as a CD or DVD that is not included in the version you purchased, you may download this material at http://booksupport.wiley.com. For more information about Wiley products, visit www.wiley.com.

Library of Congress Control Number: 2005935165

ISBN 978-0-471-74934-9 (pbk); ISBN 978-0-470-08513-4 (ebk); ISBN 978-1-118-08481-6 (ebk)

10 9 8 7 6 5 4 3 2

1B/RZ/QZ/QW/IN

WILEY

About the Authors

Teresa Luckey was born in Indianapolis, Indiana, the eighth of twelve children. She earned the degree of Bachelor of Science from the University of Southern Indiana, with a major in Education. She earned her teaching endorsements in Computer Education and Mathematics from the University of Indianapolis and thoroughly enjoyed teaching (and learning from) junior high students for several years. After deciding to expand her horizons beyond the teaching profession, she pursued her interests in information systems and project management while working at hospitals in Indianapolis, and then moved on to a consulting firm, where she now works as a manager implementing health-care systems. Teresa earned her Master of Business Administration degree from Indiana Wesleyan University, where she served as co-class president with her husband, David. She is just shy of completing her Master of Science in New Media at Indiana University School of Informatics. One of these days — soon — she hopes to finish that degree so that she can maintain her reputation as a life-long learner.

Teresa earned her Project Management Professional Certification through the Project Management Institute in 2001 and continues to maintain her certification. She enjoys contributing to the field of project management, particularly with regard to healthcare software.

Teresa takes pleasure in spending time with her family — especially her husband David and their children, Amanda, Sara, and Adam. Being a firm believer in the axiom that there's more to life than work, Teresa and her family are passionate about traveling and exploring all types of music.

Joseph Phillips, PMP, Project+, is the Director of Education for Project Seminars. He has managed and consulted on projects for various industries, including technical, pharmaceutical, manufacturing, and architectural, among others.

Phillips has served as a project management consultant for organizations creating project offices, maturity models, and best-practice standardization.

As a leader in adult education, Phillips has taught organizations how to successfully implement project management methodologies, information technology project management, risk management, and other courses. Phillips has taught courses at Columbia College, University of Chicago, Indiana University, and others. He is a Certified Technical Trainer and has taught over 10,000 professionals. Phillips has contributed as an author or editor to more than 30 books on technology, careers, and project management.

Phillips is a member of the Project Management Institute and is active in local project management chapters. He has spoken on project management, project management certifications, and project methodologies at numerous trade shows, PMI chapter meetings, and employee conferences. When not writing, teaching, or consulting, Phillips can be found behind a camera or on the working end of a fly rod. You can contact Phillips through www. projectseminars.com.

Dedication

I dedicate this effort to David, Amanda, Sara, and Adam Luckey.

Authors' Acknowledgments

Teresa Luckey: Thanks to Kevin Kirschner, Editorial Manager, for his confidence in me and for providing me with this opportunity. I appreciate Katie Feltman, Acquisitions Editor, for her diligence in bringing this book to fruition and for her patience in gracefully answering all of my questions. Nicole Haims, Project Editor, provided a great deal of guidance and support to me and I am grateful to her for her efforts. Ed Kirschner, thanks for your ideas and input, and most of all thank you to David, Amanda, Sara, and Adam Luckey for your unrelenting support throughout this and all endeavors.

Joe Phillips: Books, like projects, are never done alone.

Thank you to Teresa Luckey for her hard work and incredible input on this project. A humongous thank you to Katie Feltman and all the folks at *For Dummies* for their patience and persistence. I would also like to thank the hundreds of folks who have attended my PMP Boot Camps. Your questions, conversations, and recommendations have helped me write a better book.

Finally, thank you to Elizabeth Lee, Rick Gordon, Scot Conrad, Phil Stuck, and my son, Kyle.

Both authors would like to recognize and thank Cynthia Snyder and Karen Scott for being conscientious and thorough while reviewing this book.

Publisher's Acknowledgments

We're proud of this book; please send us your comments through our online registration form located at `http://dummies.custhelp.com`.

Some of the people who helped bring this book to market include the following:

Acquisitions, Editorial, and Vertical Websites

Project Editor: Nicole Haims

Acquisitions Editor: Katie Feltman

Technical Editors: Cynthia Snyder and Karen Scott

Editorial Manager: Jodi Jensen

Vertical Websites Manager: Laura VanWinkle

Editorial Assistant: Amanda Foxworth

Sr. Editorial Assistant: Cherie Case

Cartoons: Rich Tennant (`www.the5thwave.com`)

Composition Services

Project Coordinator: Jennifer Theriot

Layout and Graphics: Claudia Bell, Carl Byers, Lauren Goddard, Lynsey Osborn, Heather Ryan, Julie Trippetti

Proofreaders: David Faust, Jessica Kramer, Aptara

Indexer: Aptara

Publishing and Editorial for Technology Dummies

    Richard Swadley, Vice President and Executive Group Publisher

    Andy Cummings, Vice President and Publisher

    Mary Bednarek, Executive Acquisitions Director

    Mary C. Corder, Editorial Director

Publishing for Consumer Dummies

    Kathleen Nebenhaus, Vice President and Executive Publisher

Composition Services

    Debbie Stailey, Director of Composition Services

Contents at a Glance

Table of Contents

Part IV: Controlling Your Software Project...................263

Chapter 13: Managing Changes to the Software Project 265

Chapter 14: Using Earned Value Management in Software Projects 281

Introduction

Welcome to *Software Project Management For Dummies;* we hope you enjoy the ride as we take you through scenic highways dotted with the hues and shades of software project management concepts, project team development, and various descriptions of fascinating new terminology.

We're two experienced software project managers, and we wrote this book because we want you to benefit from the lessons we've learned through years of experience. You don't have to suffer to be a success. You just have to follow our example.

About This Book

The purpose of this book is to assist you in understanding and using software project management concepts. We want to pique your curiosity about some of the project management topics and processes and provide you with some tips on communicating project information to team members, executives, clients, and other important stakeholders. With the help of this book, you can develop high-performing project teams who complete projects on time and under budget. Not only that, with the help of *Software Project Management For Dummies,* we hope that you'll cultivate high-performing teams who respect your authority and believe in your abilities, even though you sometimes make them work overtime.

This book isn't intended to be a complete reference for discovering *everything* there is to know about software project management. It's also not intended to be your sole source of information if you're preparing for your PMP certification (for that you might want to check out *PMP Certification For Dummies* by Peter Nathan Gerald Everett Jones and published by our friends at Wiley).

We're ambitious, but not unrealistic, and we know that project management of any type is a little bit of an art and involves a lot of practice. There is so much more to know that this book would have ended up being as big as, well, as big as something that's really big. It's not that we necessarily excluded anything from this book, but we touched on some topics at a high level for the sake of practicality. We discuss quality management for example, but volumes upon volumes have been written on just that one topic, so we couldn't give you every bit of information — just the information you need to get the job done and get on to the next task.

To find out more about software project management and project management in general, or to study for your PMP certification, you may want to check out *Software Project Management Kit For Dummies* by Greg Mandanis and Allen Wyatt. We also personally reread many times *PMP: Project Management Professional Study Guide,* 3rd Edition, by Kim Heldman (Wiley). Although Heldman's book is written in a different format and follows a different flow than the PMP bible, *Guide to the Product Management Body of Knowledge* (PMI), it contains the same information and it's a good companion to the *Guide to the PMBOK.*

Who Should Read This Book?

So you've just picked up this treasure in the bookstore and you're looking it over trying to decide whether it's the book for you. Well, this book is definitely for you if you are

- ✔ An experienced software project manager who is interested in improving your skills and finding out a little bit more from other experienced software project managers' perspectives.

- ✔ An experienced general project manager who is moving into software project management (or maybe you've been thrust into software project management without a lot of time to prepare).

- ✔ Just starting to get to know the discipline of project management and deciding whether you should move in the direction of software project management.

- ✔ An ambitious project team member who has become an *ad-hoc* project manager because your boss isn't showing enough leadership.

- ✔ Not involved in a project management career at all, but contemplating software project management as an alternative.

So, whether or not you are currently a project manager or software project manager, actively working on a project team, or completely in the dark about this mysterious field, this book has something for you. If you're experienced, you're bound to discover a new method for handling a situation, and if you're deciding whether or not to delve into the field of software project management, this book may help you make that significant decision.

How This Book 1s Organized

This book contains six major parts. Each part contains several chapters. Look at the Table of Contents and decide which areas are of most interest to you. Or skim through the index for a keyword or term that you want information about.

This book was written in a format that coincides with the natural progression of a software project, from planning stages until the very end. However, it's not absolutely imperative that you read all of the chapters in order. Feel free to skip to and fro. All projects move at their own pace and have their own unique challenges, so some chapters might have more relevant information for you right now than others. We do think you should start at Chapter 1 before you move forward, and if you never deal with creating software project budgets, you can safely skip Chapter 9. If you're not working with vendors or contracts, you could also safely skip Chapter 12. Some project managers on smaller projects might not have to worry about earned value management, so skip Chapter 14 with a clear conscience if you don't need to know about this topic.

Part 1: Starting Your Software Project

Part I introduces you to those elements of software project management that are the foundation upon which you construct the remaining phases of your software project. All the other chapters in the book are based on the concepts contained within Part I.

Part 11: Planning Your Software Project

Part II introduces you to the basic concepts and essential elements of creating your software project plans. You discover how to

- Document your scope statement
- Comprehend the importance of project communication
- Develop a risk management plan and understand why that's so crucial to your project's success
- Create a quality management plan
- Recruit the appropriate members for your software project team
- Generate top-notch schedules and budgets

Part III: Executing Your Software Project Plan

Part III introduces you to your next steps after planning your software project. You can create the most fantastic software project plan your stakeholders have ever set eyes on, but if you don't know how to execute the project plan, what's the point? That would be like going bear hunting with a BB gun.

Amaze your friends and flabbergast your competition by discovering how to

- Work the software project plan you've created
- Ensure that your software project plan contains all of the required quality aspects to make it a huge success
- Understand different personality types on your team and develop a high-performance project team
- Get a feel for some of the different types of contracts

Part IV: Controlling Your Software Project

Part IV introduces you to the concept of putting controls on your software project after it gets started. You can figure out how to develop change control processes and you can discover the importance of following these processes the easy way (discovering this on your own, the hard way, can be pretty brutal, believe us).

After reading Part IV, you'll understand how to be proactive in determining whether your project is under or over budget, ahead of or behind schedule, and whether the project scope is creeping up on you. You can also be aware of how to track and communicate your project performance.

Part V: Closing Your Software Project

Part V introduces you to the steps that you must complete in order to bring your project to a successful closing. You'll find out about all the fun things you get to do at the end of your project such as

- Helping your project team members with their next steps
- Taking care of vendors and contracts

✔ Documenting your lessons learned (which of course you started documenting at the start of your project planning)

✔ Completing audits and quality control

✔ Celebrating your successes

Part VI: The Part of Tens

In this part, you get some important tips on what to do, and what not to do, if you want to make your software project a huge success. You get pointers on project team leadership and communicating the good — and not so good — news that routinely comes up when you're managing a big project. Find out once and for all how to run flawless and effective meetings so that everyone remains focused and productive.

Appendix

Read the appendix to find out more about resources offered by the Project Management Institute. You can also find out about the coveted Project Management Professional Certification exam.

No matter what area of project management you enter, you should become thoroughly familiar with the Project Management Institute. It's an enormously helpful resource.

Icons Used in This Book

In this book, we use a few graphical icons to help point out especially vital information. Don't skip these icons — they offer shortcuts to software project management success.

This icon provides you with some tricks of the trade, enabling you to benefit from our experiences and mistakes. No need to thank us.

Take special notice of items marked with this icon. You may need this information later.

Duck! If you don't heed the information highlighted by the Warning icon, your software project may be in jeopardy.

We use this icon to point out real-life examples, scenarios that we've encountered, or hypothetical situations to which you can apply the tools and techniques we're describing.

This icon informs you that we're providing you with some technical information that may not be especially important to you. You can skip this information if you would rather not let your inner geek roam free.

Where to Go from Here

Take a gander at the Table of Contents to decide where you want to begin your software project management extravaganza. Then you may want to begin with Chapter 1 for an introduction to project management, or you may prefer to dive right into the deep end and read about procuring goods and services. It's all good. As you read through the material, if you have any questions or comments, please feel free to e-mail TMLuckey@yahoo.com.

Good reading and good luck. We hope you enjoy the exhilarating world of software project management as much as we do.

Part I

Starting Your Software Project

"The engineers lived on Jolt and cheese sticks putting this product together, but if you wanted to just use 'cola and cheese sticks' in the Users Documentation, that's okay too. We're pretty loose around here."

In this part . . .

Part I provides an overview of software project management and introduces you to some of the jargon used in this field. Don't miss these chapters — they form the foundation for all remaining chapters in the book.

Chapter 1

Examining the Big Picture of Project Management

*H*ere's a tough decision for you: Manage a project to create a new piece of software that can make or break your entire organization, or jump from an airplane with a parachute that may — or may not — function. For some project managers the decision is the same either way.

But not for you. At least you're on the right track to capture, improve, and successfully lead your projects to completion.

The adrenaline rush in skydiving (and in project management) may not be at the same level, but the butterflies in your stomach definitely are. There's really one secret to skydiving and it's the same secret to successful project management. (No, it's not "don't do it.") The key to successful software project management and skydiving is preparation.

Many projects fail at the beginning rather than the end. After you do the prep work, you must execute your plan, take control of your project, and ultimately bring it to its natural (and successful) conclusion.

Defining Software Projects

Software project management is a type of project management that focuses specifically on creating or updating software. Just as there are billions of ice cream flavors, there are billions of types of software. Project managers, effective ones, can lick them both.

A project, technically, is a temporary endeavor to create a unique product or service. For some people, everything is a project; for others, projects are special, lofty activities that occur infrequently. A project is a unique entity. In other words, the creation of a new application is unique, whereas the maintenance and day-to-day support of an existing application is not so unique. Projects can have many attributes:

- They change or improve environments in organizations.
- They get things done.
- They are unique from other work.
- They have a defined start and end date.
- They require resources and time.
- They solve problems.
- They seize opportunities.
- They are sometimes challenging.

Defining Software Project Management

For some people, *project management* is just a stack of work doled out to a group of people by a goober called the project manager. For other folks, project management is a foggy, scary science directed by a different goober with a slide ruler. And for others still, a project manager is a goober that touts formulas, certifications, and facts without ever really getting things done.

But in effective project management there ain't no room for goobers. Effective project management centers on the serious business of getting work done on time and within budget while meeting customer expectations. Effective project management is about accomplishment, leadership, and owning the project scope. It's an incredible feeling to sign off on the project and know that you and your project team contributed to the project's success.

Management is concerned with one thing: results.

Project management involves coordinating people, vendors, and resources. Project management requires excellent communication skills, a strong will to protect the project scope, and leadership skills to enforce quality throughout the project work.

According to the Project Management Institute (www.pmi.org), the defining resource on all things related to project management, project management is centered on nine *knowledge areas*. Events in each knowledge area affect what happens in the other eight knowledge areas. Table 1-1 gives you the lowdown.

Table 1-1	The Nine Project Management Knowledge Areas
Knowledge Area	*What It Does*
Project Scope Management	Controlling the planning, execution, and content of the project is essential. You need to pay special attention to both project and product scope so that the software you end up with is what you intended to make in the first place.
Project Time Management	Managing everything that affects the project's schedule is crucial. Who wants tax software that comes out on April 16?
Project Cost Management	Projects cost money, and this knowledge area centers on cost estimating, budgeting, and control.
Project Quality Management	No project is a good project if the deliverable stinks. Quality doesn't happen by accident, so this knowledge area works to ensure that the product you are producing is a quality product that meets customer expectations.
Project Human Resources Management	The members of the project team must get their work done. Hiring or assigning people who are competent and managing them well are at the center of this knowledge area.
Project Communications Management	Project managers spend 90 percent of their time communicating. Communications management focuses on who needs what information — and when.

(continued)

Table 1-1 *(continued)*

Knowledge Area	What It Does
Project Risk Management	This knowledge area is about avoiding doom. The focus is on how to anticipate risks, handle them when they arise, and take advantage of the opportunities that can help a project.
Project Procurement Management	Sometimes during the course of your software project, you may be required to work with vendors to purchase goods and/or services. You may even be the vendor that someone else is contracting for their project. This knowledge area is concerned with the processes to create vendor contracts and to purchase goods and services.
Project Integration Management	What happens in one knowledge area affects attributes of the other knowledge areas. The ninth knowledge area is fan-freakin-tastic because its purpose is to ensure the coordination of all the other knowledge areas.

Comparing Projects and Operations

There is a distinct difference between projects and operations. *Operations* are the day-to-day activities that your organization does. For example, a car manufacturer makes cars. An airline flies people from one city to another. A help desk supports technical solutions. Within each of these companies reside various departments working on projects that enable operations to function. A project at an automobile manufacturer might be to design a new sports car. The car manufacturer's operations involve manufacturing that design again and again.

Software creation is special. Imagine you have customers around the world who want you to create a piece of software that helps them keep track of sports statistics. This is your new business — you create sports stat software and you're a gazillionaire.

Each flavor of the software you create could be a separate project; your company has software for baseball stats, football stats, soccer stats, field hockey stats, and everyone's favorite sport, water polo stats. Each project has its own requirements, its own purpose, its own budget, and its own project manager and project team. Each project has its own resources, schedule, budgets, and goals.

Your day-to-day support of the software, the sales of the software, the credit card purchases, and the delivery of millions in cash to your bank account are all part of operations.

Some companies have changed their approach to business by treating all of their operations as projects. This microscale of their enterprise, where every activity is part of a project and all projects contribute to the betterment of the organization, is called *management by projects*.

Examining Project Constraints

A *constraint* is anything that restricts the project manager's options. Constraints are requirements, confines, or, if you're a glass-is-half-empty kind of person, prison walls. Constraints can include

- Resource constraints such as a team member being assigned to too many concurrent projects
- Tight deadlines
- Budgetary limitations
- Government regulations
- Limitations of software
- Scope limitation, such as being required to use a particular existing interface
- Hardware requirements
- Anything else that restricts your options

Understanding Universal Constraints (Time, Cost, and Scope)

The three universal project constraints you will *always* face are

- **Time:** Time constraints may range from a reasonable schedule to an impossibly short timeframe that can't budge because the product simply *must* be on shelves by September 15 (never mind that September 15 was last week).

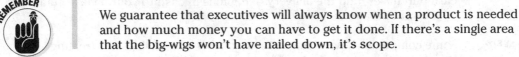

✔ **Cost:** Cost constraints are the usual budgetary restrictions that you expect. ("Here's a nickel. Make it happen.")

✔ **Scope:** Sometimes scope is a no-brainer (you're working on the 700th rev of Acme Wizware to fix a bug). On the other hand, scope can be a bit trickier if you're dealing with an executive who isn't sure what he wants.

We guarantee that executives will always know when a product is needed and how much money you can have to get it done. If there's a single area that the big-wigs won't have nailed down, it's scope.

These three constraints make up what we affectionately refer to as the somewhat inflexible-sounding nickname the *Iron Triangle of project management.* Check out Figure 1-1. Each side of the Iron Triangle represents one of the triple constraints. For a project to be successful, each side must remain in balance with the other two. You will read more about project constraints in Chapter 3.

In order to achieve quality in the project deliverable, and in the management of the project, the Iron Triangle must remain balanced.

Figure 1-1:
The Iron Triangle describes constraints that all projects must face.

For example, say your boss decides to add more stuff to the project scope (now instead of simply fixing a mathematical bug in your Wizware accounting software, you have to create a whole new feature in the software that edits photos and home movies). Even though your boss has changed the scope, you have to deliver more stuff within the same amount of time and with the same amount of cash, as Figure 1-2 depicts. You'll need more time, more money, or both for the triangle to remain equilateral.

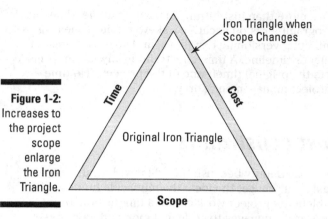

Figure 1-2:
Increases to the project scope enlarge the Iron Triangle.

Managing time constraints

Time constraints are simply deadlines. You have a project to create a new piece of software within six months. Or there's an opportunity in the marketplace for a new application, but the window of opportunity is small, so you have no time to waste. Time can also be calculated as labor: Working or billable hours, processor speed, database consistency, and even network latency issues can be used to estimate time constraints.

Introducing the law of diminishing returns

Time is time. Don't be fooled into thinking you can buy more time — no one can. You can buy more labor if you think it will help your team do more work faster, but that's not the same thing as adding time to a project. The *law of diminishing returns* dictates that adding labor doesn't exponentially increase productivity; in fact, at some point productivity can even go backwards (is that antiductivity?). When that happens, you've hit a plateau, and then everyone is sad because you just can't do more with the labor you have.

For a real-life example of the law of diminishing returns, consider that you may have two hardworking, experienced programmers working on a section of code. In your quest to finish the project on time, you add one more programmer to the mix. Now the programmers may be completing the code more quickly, and you're so excited that you decide to add six more programmers so that you can finish even sooner. You soon realize that although adding one programmer increased your productivity, adding six more only created chaos, with programmers stepping on each other's toes, inadvertently neutralizing each other's code, and creating a contentious environment. You reached the point of diminishing returns when you added six programmers.

Time constraints require more than just hitting a target deadline. Unavailable resources (your ace programmer is on vacation), skewed milestone targets within the project, conflicting versioning deadlines, and so on, all present constraints on the project's timeline. A time constraint is any factor or issue that changes or impacts the original timeframe of the project. (No time machines allowed in project management, sorry.)

Managing cost constraints

Cost constraints are easy to identify because they deal with cash money. Well, it's not always cash, but you get the idea; the miniscule funds in your project budget to complete the project work create a unique constraint. Your costs include computers and languages to code in, labor, and anything else you need to buy in order to get the job done.

For some folks the funds are *blue dollars,* departmental dollars that shift from one department to another based on the project costs. For other people the budget is a very real number in dollars and cents: Customers hire you to complete work for them; then they give you a satchel full of cash.

Projects almost always cost somebody something. Be sure to factor in hidden costs for labor, resources, computers, pizza, celebrations, training, bribes, and more. Just kidding about the bribes part. As far as you know.

Managing the scope

The third part of the Iron Triangle is the scope. There are two scopes within project management:

- **Product scope:** The product scope describes, lists, and categorizes all the features and components of the finished deliverable. This is what the customers see in their minds' eye.

- **Project scope:** This is where you focus. The project scope is all the required work, and only the required work, to create the project deliverable. The project scope focuses on work, activities, and progress to achieve the product scope. The project scope must be protected from unapproved changes because it dictates what the project team will do and what the end result of the project will be.

The product scope and the project scope are in love. The product scope kisses details in the project scope and the project scope returns the favor. It's romantic. Each scope depends on the other, and what happens in either scope affects the other. If there is disharmony between these two scopes, trouble is brewing.

Delivering what's promised (and *only* what's promised)

In the Iron Triangle the project manager's concern is on the project scope — the project work. The project manager must direct the project team to do the required work, nothing more or less, to deliver exactly what the product scope calls for.

Nothing more? Shouldn't the project manager and the project team always deliver more than what was promised? No, no, no! This may shock you, but the job of the project manager and the project team is to deliver exactly what you and the customer have agreed to create.

Let me write that again so you don't think it's a typo: The project manager should deliver exactly what the customer expects.

You and the project stakeholders should define everything the project should deliver as soon as possible. When value-added changes are made after the project scope has been created, the analysis of these changes takes time and money and may impact the schedule.

We're not saying the project manager should hold back good designs, ideas, and incredible features that the customer may want and can use. We're saying that neither the project manager, nor any stakeholder, can arbitrarily add features to the software because doing so would be to change the project scope.

Controlling Scope Creep

Changes to the project scope can affect cost and time constraints, melting your Iron Triangle. The Iron Triangle is a key tool in project management and is ideal for negotiations with stakeholders. For example, if your stakeholder insists on adding software functionality to your project scope, you can use the Iron Triangle as a tool to explain that when you increase one side of the triangle (the scope side) the triangle is no longer in balance. To change the scope, you must change the cost or the schedule (or both) to keep the triangle balanced. The Iron Triangle is also a terrific tool to use in discussions with the project team, and to keep your own duties as project manager in alignment (see "Understanding Universal Constraints (Time, Cost, and Scope)," earlier in this chapter).

Unplanned changes to the project scope, sometimes called *scope creep,* are the little extras that expand the scope without reflecting the changes in the cost and time baselines. You'll notice from the graphic that with scope creep, the lines of the Iron Triangle are no longer even. See Figure 1-3.

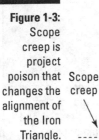

Figure 1-3: Scope creep is project poison that changes the alignment of the Iron Triangle.

The reason scope creep is so poisonous is because it can happen so easily, and so innocently. And yet, it can be so deadly. When the scope goes off track, time and funds are stolen from the original baselines. It's not as if extra money and time are magically added to the project to handle all the little extras. Balancing the three sides of the triangle ensures a high-quality final product.

Changes to the project scope should be controlled and managed through a *change control system,* which you can find out more about in Chapter 13. In essence, a change control system accommodates a process for documenting requested changes and requires obtaining appropriate approval for all requested project changes. The key is to avoid changes that are not directly approved or requested by the customer.

Making Sense of Project Success (Or Failure)

Most projects start with an optimistic attitude about creating a deliverable, keeping the customer happy, and making this the best software project ever. And then things (bad things) happen. The good projects end on time and as planned. Ah, paradise. We'd wager that these projects have three things in common:

- ✔ A leader who knows what he or she is doing
- ✔ A tight change control system (see Chapter 13)
- ✔ Team members who understand what the project is supposed to deliver and can therefore get results

Commonly, projects limp to the finish line, late, overbudget, and after crushing the morale of everyone involved. Done, but maybe not done well. These projects typically have three attributes:

- ✔ Poor requirements from the project customers
- ✔ Poor communications through the project manager
- ✔ Poor morale from the project team

The saddest of projects are the ones that never make it to the finish. This bunch misses deadlines, blows budgets, or experiences a radical change of scope so often that no one (not even the PM) knows exactly what the project should be creating anymore. Failed projects usually have some, if not all, of these attributes:

- ✔ No clear vision of what the project priorities are
- ✔ Lack of leadership from the project manager and/or sponsor
- ✔ A timid project manager
- ✔ Lack of autonomy for the project manager
- ✔ New resumes being typed in unison

Starting and Finishing Software Projects

All projects, from your software creations to building the bridge over the River Kwai, pass through five process groups as defined by the Project Management Institute. A *process group* is a mini life cycle that moves the project one step closer to completion. Process groups are cycles because the processes don't just happen once; they are repeated throughout the project as many times as needed.

Figure 1-4 demonstrates a sequence for process groups; the processes flow organically, in the order that best suits the needs of the project. Although we hope you don't have to keep repeating some of these stages, if your project isn't going according to plan you will have to do just that.

All projects, software and otherwise, go through these project management processes. Each of these project management processes has its nuances. We describe them in more detail in Chapter 2.

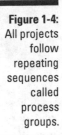

Figure 1-4:
All projects
follow
repeating
sequences
called
process
groups.

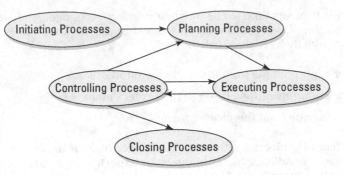

- ✔ **Initiating:** That's really where you are now. The project is in the process of getting selected, sponsored, funded, and launched.

- ✔ **Planning:** As you can see in Figure 1-4, planning is an *iterative* process. Planning basically determines how the project work will get accomplished.

- ✔ **Executing:** After you get a plan, your project team does the work.

- ✔ **Controlling:** Your project team does the work, but you control them.

- ✔ **Closing:** Ah, paradise. After the project work has been completed, you tie up loose ends and close out the software project.

Understanding What Makes Software Project Management So Special

There's nothing special about software project management that changes the Iron Triangle or the five process groups. What is special about project management, however, is the nature of the work.

Just as the particulars of designing a new warehouse, building a house, or creating a prototype for a remote controlled airplane are unique, so is the creation of software:

- ✔ Software development is weird and requires a specialized skill set to do it well.

- ✔ Software creation is tough.

- ✔ Software development can be boring, routine, and mind numbing.

- ✔ Software creation can create challenges within the development of the code.

Breaking Moore's Law

A long time ago, in 1965, Gordon Moore wrote a scientific paper called "Cramming More Components onto Integrated Circuits." The synopsis of his paper is that the number of transistors per integrated circuit could double every two years. The press loved it. The theory became known as Moore's Law. And he's been pretty accurate on his prediction.

The importance of Moore's Law in software project management is that more transistors per circuit mean faster processors. Faster processors mean more elaborate software. More elaborate software means we need faster processors. And on and on the cycle goes.

Because information technology (IT) drives many businesses today, there is a direct connection between the speed of technology and an organization's bottom line. Between the two is the software the organization relies on. Consequently, businesses demand software that's reliable, secure, and scalable. Your organization's profitability, stability, and ability to attract new customers rely on you and your project team.

Although businesses rely on technology to remain competitive, many software project managers miss this key point: It's not about the technology. Software project management is about the business. It's about helping your company, your colleagues, and even the stockholders of your organization to be successful.

If you're an IT guru you may easily fall in love with the bits and bytes of day-to-day software development. However, if you're a project manager, you *cannot.* Your focus should be on one thing: getting the project done — on time and on budget.

Dealing with Moore

As your project moves towards completion, chances are there will be leapfrogs in the technology you're dealing with. There'll be new versions of operating systems, service packs to address problems in versions of software your software relies on, and more. Part of software project management is to have a plan to address these potential changes. Every (yes, every) software project manager should have an allotment of time added to the project schedule specifically for planning and responding to Moore's Law. You're saying, "My customers and management won't give me more time just for planning and responding. My customers and management barely give me enough time to complete my project if everything goes perfectly." Notice that we said you "should" have more time. That doesn't mean you will. After all, time is money.

So what do you do? By relying on historical information, you can help your project adjust to Moore's Law. If you have documented instances of past projects that failed because of a lack of time to respond to changing technology, use it. If you have records of your past projects, you can show how the project would have, or at least could have, been more successful with this allotment of time.

This is a good time to remind you to save your project documentation so that you and other software project managers can use it for the same purpose in the future. Check out Part V of this book for more on documentation.

Documented instances are your best argument. We're not saying it's a slam-dunk, but we'd wager dollars to donuts you'll at least have a meaningful conversation about the extra time allotment for planning. Ask your customer or management to try it one time and see what happens. And then document, document, document to prove your point.

If you don't have these project records, well, there's good news and bad news. The bad news is that it's hard to argue for additional time for planning without proof of why the time will be needed. The good news is that you can start now. Without the additional time allowed for your project, here's what we recommend:

- ✔ **Do a thorough risk assessment.** Document how the risks due to changes in technology could contribute to failure.

- ✔ **Document lost time.** Document any lost time tied to technical changes (research, team training, subject matter experts, and so on).

- ✔ **Document lessons learned.** Begin your lessons learned documentation, a document that highlights all the lessons learned, with attention to technology changes, at the start of the project, and as your software project progresses, complete your lessons learned documentation.

- ✔ **Communicate proactively.** Communicate to your stakeholders when changes to technology enter and influence your project.

As a technology professional, it's your job to have your finger on the pulse of change in your industry. You don't want to be blindsided by some major technological event, and you never want to withhold information to your stakeholders that could affect the longevity of a software product. The most important thing you can do is balance cost effectiveness and profitability.

Dealing with the first-time, first-use penalty

One of the most common questions when it comes to software project management is, "How can we tell how much this'll cost or how long this'll take if it's never been done before?"

This is the *first-time, first-use penalty.* The penalty is that you just don't know. It may cost thousands, even millions, if the technology has never, ever been done before. And time? Well, that's even more difficult to grasp.

You've experienced this. The first time your project team develops code in a new language, productivity slides. The first time an end user loads and uses your application, there's a learning curve.

TIP

Leading versus managing

When you think of *leadership* you probably think of positive attributes; a leader is honest, inspiring, and motivating. All true. And when you think of a manager you probably have thoughts like work-centric, accountability, and results-oriented. Also true.

A project manager has to be both a leader and a manager. A leader aligns, motivates, and directs people towards accomplishments. A leader is interested in what others want and what others need. A leader can empathize, inspire, and help others reach their goals. A leader cares.

A manager is concerned about one thing: results. A manager needs the team members to deliver on their promises. A manager needs to see progress and accomplishment. A manager may care about the project team, but not as much as he cares about the project team's ability to get the work done.

A truly effective project manager, regardless of the situation, organizational structure, or technology the project focuses on, must be a leader and a manager. You have to be both.

Take note. If you've got any skills at all and you're just starting out in this business, you are probably either a good manager or a good leader, but not yet both. You'll soon find out which category you fall into. Remember, not everyone has to like you, but everyone has to respect you. If team members refer to you as Mussolini when they're standing around the water cooler, you're probably overdoing the management part of your job. If they call you "all talk and no action," you may need to beef up those management skills and lay off the motivational seminars. As you evolve as a PM, you'll find the right balance between these two extremes.

The first time you stretch your teams, you face challenges with deadlines, cost, and even attitude. Productivity slides, but eventually productivity should curve beyond current levels to a new plateau. At least that's the theory. Actual mileage may vary.

Chances are your team has worked with the programming language before. Chances are you've done a similar project before. Chances are you have a gut feeling for the time, cost, and feasibility of the project. Chances are, based on your experience, you have some idea of how the project is going to go.

Of course, out here in the real world, you can't go on hunches. Even though it's not feasible to expect these things, your customers, your boss, and your stakeholders want just the facts, only the most definite answers, and the most exact time and cost figures possible.

This is where an *acceptable range of variances* must be introduced. A range of variance is a cushion based on your estimates. No, we're not talking about bloating your estimates, but establishing a level of confidence in the estimates you give. A range of variance is the +/– percentage, time, or cost you append to your estimates. See Figure 1-5.

Figure 1-5:
The ideal
baseline,
the
accepted
range of
variance,
and the
actual
results for a
typical
software
project can
vary wildly.

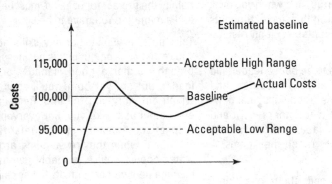

Chapter 2

Initiating a Software Project

- -

In This Chapter

▶ Determining what the project's purpose is

▶ Handling the various organizational entities

▶ Studying the project's feasibility

▶ Determining which plan works best

▶ Recognizing problems in your software project

- -

Projects, big and small, have to be *initiated*. All initiation really means is that everyone acknowledges that the project has a purpose (and that everyone agrees on what that purpose is): to solve a problem, to grasp an opportunity, or to meet demand for a new piece of software.

Software projects, all software projects, have one thing in common: They attempt to provide something for someone else, whether it's the organization or the customer. The goal, from a project manager's perspective, is to solve the problem to satisfy the demand.

Identifying the Project Purpose

Before you, the project manager, or your organization can go about the business of satisfying the demand you're fulfilling with your software product, you must take care of a few formalities. Yes, formalities. In some organizations, perhaps yours, the only formality of initiating a project is a shopping list of demands thrown onto your desk.

You have our sympathy.

Successful projects, and, by default, successful project managers, have to start by ironing out a few details. Make sure these questions are asked and successfully answered:

- **Why is the project being initiated?** You first have to know the project purpose.

- **Does everyone agree on this purpose and goals?** There must be consensus on what the project will create. There must be consensus on the goals of the project. If not, you can count on trouble before the project is complete.

The project purpose is just a fancy way of understanding the background of why the project is being initiated. If you don't have enough background information, you won't be able to ask the right questions to create a solution that solves the problem, grabs the opportunity, or improves the organization.

Your fundamental purpose, at this point in the project life cycle, is to understand why the project is being initiated. But another crucial element to successful project management is to be in tune with the structure of your organization.

Talking to the stakeholders

When a project is being initiated, you want to capture as much information as possible about the project goals. Without a clear picture of what the project is to capture, it's going to be challenging to plan and prepare for your software project.

Stakeholders, from your customers to senior management, will have different concepts about what signifies that a project is complete. You need to know what their expectations are so you can reach the project completion with few surprises (or headaches). Here are five questions every project manager should ask stakeholders:

- **What are the factors for completion?** You should ask this key question *far* in advance of starting the project work. As a project manager you need to know what the project will accomplish and be able to plan how to get there. If the qualifications for completion are unknown or fuzzy at best, you're not ready to get to work. Starting a project without knowing what the end result should be is like building a house without blueprints.

- **What is the goal of this project?** Knowing the project's goal helps you and the team plan. For some projects the goal will be to win new customers, or to make internal processes more efficient, or to solve a problem. Other projects may be financially based. For example, the goal may be to create this essential transition to VoIP without spending more than $235,000.

✔ **What are the areas of the organization that this project will affect?** The answer to this question tells you who you need to communicate with. It also brings to attention that there may be stakeholders who aren't attending meetings and should be. Although it's easy to identify the end-users of your software, there may be "hidden stakeholders" to consider: accounting, security personnel, government agencies, a training team, and so on.

✔ **What is the project priority?** Chances are good you'll be managing more than one project at a time, and there are equal chances that your project team members will be on multiple projects as well. When you consider these odds it's best to know your priorities so you know where to spend your energy. Consider your software conformance to the Sarbanes-Oxley Act versus a feature to search a database through a Web browser. Both may be important, but you'll need to determine which takes priority. Refer to *Sarbanes-Oxley For Dummies,* by Jill Gilbert Welytok (Wiley), for information on this important act.

✔ **What is the accepted range of variance?** The range of variance is the +/– value associated with the budget and the schedule. For example, a project may have a budget of $450,000, +45,000 to –$25,000. This means the project could actually cost as much as $495,000 or as little as $425,000. You can actually apply the same methods to the project schedule. This nugget of info can help you plan and react to problems within the project — and you know there'll be problems.

Check out Figure 2-1. This fancy-schmancy triangle is a model of how most organizations operate. Each level of your organization has different needs, different concerns, and different goals for your project. You need to address each level of your organization to get the project moving to completion.

Figure 2-1: Organizations are comprised of executives, functional management, and operations.

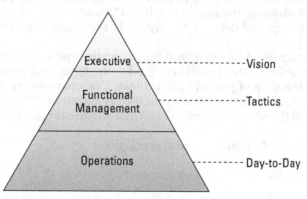

Executive ----------------- Vision

Functional Management --------------- Tactics

Operations --------- Day-to-Day

Discussing high-level stuff with the executives

At the top of the pyramid live all of the executives with their elegant high heels, expensive suits, diamond earrings, cufflinks, fancy ties, and caviar dinners. Executives are responsible for setting the vision and direction of their organization. This small group of people (or sometimes even a single person) has a vision for the organization and is interested in taking herself and her employees there. Usually.

The executives want to know why any project is occurring because they want to confirm that the project aligns with their vision. If your project doesn't align with the company's vision, kill it before someone else does.

Questions you need to ask executives, assuming you'll be interacting with this crowd:

- ✔ What are the factors for project success?
- ✔ What's your vision for the project result?
- ✔ What's more important, time or budget?
- ✔ What risks do you anticipate for this project's success?

Sometimes you experience a disconnect between a project's stated purpose and its actual purpose. The more detailed information you get from the executives the more likely you are to identify this disconnect early and straighten it out.

Playing nice with functional management

In the middle of the pyramid are all the folks who comprise functional management. You may know this layer as middle management. Their purpose is to carry out the vision of the executives. It's at this level of the organization that tactics, strategy, and delivery of purpose to the employees take place.

The functional managers must support the vision the executives have in the decisions they make. At this layer of the model, the functional managers need to understand the *what* of project management. The what centers on what the project will accomplish. What areas of the organization will the project affect? What will the project schedule be? What will the project cost?

Questions you'll need to ask functional managers:

- ✔ What are the factors for project success?
- ✔ Are there scheduling issues that will affect the project's end date?
- ✔ What resources are available for the software creation?
- ✔ What departments and customers will need to interact?

✔ How will the project team be assembled?

✔ Do you have a preset budget in mind for the project?

✔ What risks do you see for this project?

You may notice that some of these questions are the same questions you ask executives and operations (see the previous and following sections). That's right. You may ask the same question to all three groups and get three different answers. As the project manager, your job is to iron out these differences to make sure that everyone's happy (actually, you need to make the executives happy — operations is almost never happy).

Having a chat with operations

Down deep in the pyramid you'll find operations. These are the people that do the work. They answer the question, "How is this going to get done?" The people in operations focus on the day-to-day activities of getting things done.

When it comes to project management, these employees are concerned with the activities that support the layers of the triangle above them.

Questions you'll need to ask folks in operations:

✔ What are the factors for project success?

✔ How will the software be used?

✔ What other software projects are you working on now?

✔ What immediate risks do you see in the project?

✔ Who has the experience to get this done?

✔ Do we need training to create this software?

✔ What areas of the project are you dreading?

Each layer, from the bottom to the top, must support the layer above it. If a project is initiated that doesn't support the layer above, you can bet the project will be a failure — if it ever even gets momentum. And we hope you're not on that project (the guy next to you, okay, but not you).

The project manager spans all three layers in the organization, but spends the bulk of his or her time managing and leading the people working on the project. The project manager is there to supervise, lead, and manage the project to completion. As the project manager, your presence may meander through all three layers in the organization. However, more likely than not, you spend more of your time in one of the layers than the others. Which one depends on your company's specific organizational structure.

Reaching project consensus

Sometimes project initiating meetings are opportunities for stakeholders to shoehorn their own pet agendas, wish lists, and one-upmanship into your project. The trouble, besides being a real pain, is that it's tough to discern what's central to your project objectives and what's bunk. And then, depending on your power and role in the project, what you can do about any of it.

Understanding the project purpose during initiation is essential to guiding project consensus. Determining all the bits that go into the project scope comes later in the project. Right now, during the initiation processes, your goal is to get the majority of the stakeholders on the same page. To reach project consensus, your goal is to find common ground, and then to address ancillary requests that don't infringe, change, or drive out the original project purpose.

There are several approaches to accomplishing this goal:

- **Conduct interviews:** This is fundamental business. You and the key stakeholders must meet several times before the project work begins so that you can discuss the project goals and determine whether both parties are in agreement to the project deliverables.

- **Do root cause analysis:** We know this sounds like a procedure a dentist does just before saying, "Well, I've got some bad news," but *root cause analysis* is actually pretty cool. If your project is to create software that solves the problem of multiple databases and recursion issues, a root cause analysis can help you design a solution by examining potential causes to specific problems.

 One example of a tool to aid you in determining root cause analysis is the *Ishikawa diagram,* also referred to as a *cause and effect diagram* or a *fishbone diagram* (because it looks like a fish bone). The first person to document using this tool was Kaoru Ishikawa, in the 1960s. Figure 2-2 illustrates an Ishikawa diagram. The effect (or problem) is the recursion issue. The causes are the network speed, the multiple databases, poor coding, and so on. The goal is to use the diagram to find the causes that contribute to the effect. When the stakeholders are in agreement, you can move forward to planning how to solve the problems.

- **Do business analysis:** Some organizations use a business analyst to serve as the liaison between the project manager and the key stakeholders. A business analyst can lighten the burden of the project manager by gathering and prioritizing the project needs for the project manager and the key stakeholders.

- **Walk a mile in the stakeholders' shoes:** Sometimes the easiest approach to reaching consensus is to experience the pain the project customer is experiencing. If the stakeholders need an application to take orders via the Web, experience how they take orders now. If the stakeholders hate their current toolbars, macros, or forms, monkey around with the current software interface. If you can see things from their perspective, it'll help you solve the problems faster.

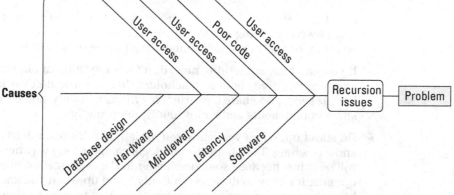

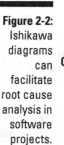

Figure 2-2: Ishikawa diagrams can facilitate root cause analysis in software projects.

Early in the project, the customer should direct what the deliverables should be. How to get there isn't an issue — yet.

The goal, what should be everyone's goal, is to determine what's key for the project's success. Which means you and the folks around the table need to get back to the central theme of initiating the project: Why is the project being considered?

Dealing with Politics

Imagine an environment where everyone works together to make the organization better. Greed, ambition, and self-serving opportunists screw that up for most entities. Politics, also know as *political capital,* can wreck a project's objectives. The sacrifice of incredible features in the software to advance self-serving interests is a shame.

Often, depending on who's making political demands, you can't do much but ride the wave and hope for the best. Other times, when you've got some leverage based on cost, time, or feasibility issues, you can create solid risk assessment of the tradeoffs and present a valid argument.

Another approach is to prioritize a project's feasibility based on all of the objectives presented. Find or create the central goal of the project's deliverables. Get everyone to agree first on the primary goals of the project's deliverables and then treat every other requirement as ancillary.

If you can treat any additional deliverables as items that either support or hinder the project goal, politics become more clear and easier to ward off.

As you know, every organization is different, but there are some rules that can help you keep the focus on the project and away from politics and personalities. Follow these do's and don'ts:

- ✔ **Don't feed the fire.** When stakeholders try to get you on their side of an issue by complaining, gossiping, or moaning about a problem, a project solution, or another team member, don't agree or contribute.

- ✔ **If you can't say something nice, don't say anything at all.** Don't say anything negative about a stakeholder that you wouldn't say in his or her presence. Do share constructive criticism openly, and certainly do share compliments and kudos loudly and proudly.

- ✔ **Do stand up.** When you know you're right, don't succumb to what you know is wrong. Tact, honesty, and logic can go a long way here, but don't roll over just because someone higher in the organization has a differing opinion. It's okay to disagree, but only stand up when you know you have the ammo to back up your position. Also be sure to stand up and admit when you're wrong. This goes a long way to increasing your credibility and integrity.

- ✔ **Do protect your reputation.** When you get down to it, your reputation is important. You have to deliver on your promises, keep out of the gossip, treat everyone fairly, and focus on project deliverables. In other words, have integrity.

- ✔ **Don't micromanage.** As a software project manager, chances are you've come up through the ranks. You've worked with different software languages, developed countless applications, and can out-code your project team members. But not anymore. Your job is to lead, manage, and provide guidance. You have to let your project team do the work.

- ✔ **Do play fair.** Some team members, stakeholders, and customers will drive you nuts, but you must treat everyone the same when it comes to discipline, time off, and kudos. If you're fair to your stakeholders they'll respect you — and respect is what you need the most to abstain from office politics.

Moving from Here to There

We like to think of projects in two states (no, not the states of confusion and disappointment). The states that all project stakeholders should envision is the current state and the desired future state. Figure 2-3 shows the processes that all software projects move through. We introduce these processes in Chapter 1. Now, we dive right in and give you some of the exciting details of the process groups.

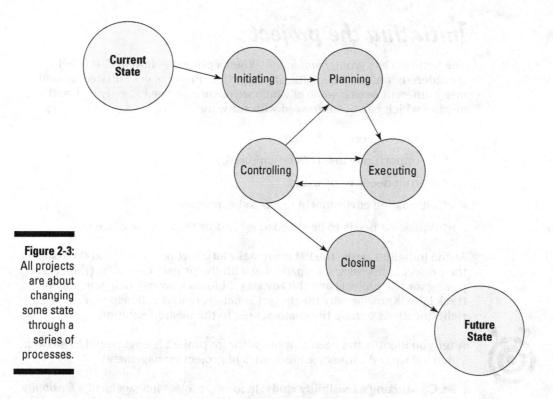

Figure 2-3:
All projects
are about
changing
some state
through a
series of
processes.

The current state is easy to see: the problems, the opportunity the project will achieve, the reasons why the project should happen, and so on.

The future state is tougher to see. You are asking your stakeholders to see the invisible. You'll help them see this vision through questions, interviews, and experiences on past projects. You'll help them begin to create a vision of that desired future state. The tough part, at least for now, is getting everyone else to share your vision of the future state as well. Communication and clarity is paramount.

Sometimes you aren't the one with vision, but your customer is, or your project team members are, or the person experiencing the problem is, or your vendor is. Before you can be an effective project manager, you must first realize the current state and then create or inherit the vision for the desired future state.

And then you can work on getting there by moving your project through the five process groups touched on in Chapter 1.

Initiating the project

The first process group is *initiation*. When a project is initiated, it is being considered; it hasn't been officially launched. Projects get initiated to fulfill many different needs, some of which we're sure you've experienced, and most of which can be addressed with software:

- A problem needs to be solved.
- An opportunity needs to be captured.
- A profit needs to be made.
- An existing environment needs to be improved.
- A process needs to be speeded up and/or made more efficient.

At the initiation stage, the PM must make an effort to understand the reasons the project is necessary. Empathizing with the project customer (the person paying for the project) and the key stakeholders now can help you stay on track later. Knowing why the project is being created will help you ask the right questions to help the customer get to the desired solution.

After you identify the need that the software project is engineered to answer, you need to deal with some mechanics of project management:

- **Conducting a feasibility study:** In formal project management a *feasibility study* examines the high-level goals of the project, the needed resources, and any other factors that could influence the project's success. The point of a feasibility study is to determine whether this project can feasibly accomplish the time, cost, and scope objectives.

    Sometimes the project isn't feasible and the idea is tanked, outsourced, sent back to the drawing board, or even broken down into multiple projects.

- **Determining the project deliverable:** If the project is deemed feasible, then a *product description* is created. The product description is an early rendition of the product scope. The product scope for most software projects consists of the design documents that detail the end result of the software project.

    In some instances, the product scope is *very* detailed — down to the color scheme, button fonts, and graphics. In other instances, the customer leaves the details to the project team, choosing instead to focus the product description on detailing the ideal functions of the software.

- **Creating the project charter:** A project charter is written by the person who has the authority within an organization to authorize the project to move forward. This individual has the positional power to authorize resources and funds.

Getting up close and personal with the product description

The product description is the first version of the product scope document. The best way to save aspirin is to make this document as detailed and exact as possible. You may be scratching your head and wondering, "Doesn't making it exact take time and restrict the project team's creativity?"

The answer, dear PM, is yes, and yes.

The product description should be as exact as possible, *especially* in software project management, because this document is like a road map that ensures that the project manager and the customer are both heading in the right direction toward the same destination. Before the project moves too far along, you need to capture as much of the following information as possible:

✔ The purpose of the project

✔ The business needs to be targeted and met

✔ The functionality of the software

✔ A description of what the project will deliver to the customer

✔ An understanding of the desired future state (what the organization will be like once the deliverable is in production)

Although ideally you have all this information before the project is officially launched, you probably won't. Some of this business will get taken care of once the project team is assembled and you're officially planning the project work. But as a rule, the earlier you know these details the better off the project will be.

The project charter may be written by the project manager, but is signed by someone with more power in the organization than you. This person typically becomes the project sponsor.

Technically, the charter should be signed by a person whose role in the organization is higher than all managers that may have employees on your project team. Imagine the trouble if Bob signs a charter authorizing you to use Susan's resources on your project team, even though Bob has no real authority over Susan.

After the charter is signed by your project sponsor, all key stakeholders need a copy of the charter. Some organizations use a boilerplate charter that is sent via e-mail, while other organizations have a formal, paper-based charter that is delivered in hard copy. Either way, all key stakeholders should receive the charter so they're aware of the official project launch, your authority as the project manager, and who's the sponsor of the project.

A project charter accomplishes the following:

- ✔ It identifies the project manager in writing.
- ✔ It identifies the project sponsor in writing.
- ✔ It authorizes the project manager to spend organizational resources on the project.
- ✔ It describes the product. That's right; the description you worked so hard to create goes in the project charter.
- ✔ It specifically identifies the business need that the project was undertaken to address. If you have a business case, you can pull information from there.

A charter can't solve all your power struggles, negotiations, and other miseries — it's not a panacea. But a charter does, more than anything else, authorize the project.

Contracts, purchase orders, statements of work, and even work orders can be considered charters of sorts. See Chapter 12 for more information about contracts, vendors, and procurement.

Planning the project

The second process group, the *planning process,* determines how the project will move forward after the project feasibility, description, and charter are complete. The planning process group gets the project rolling in a big way.

Setting up a spreadsheet of mistakes and successes

During the planning phase of your project, create a spreadsheet of mistakes and successes so that you can add information to it on an ongoing basis. The information you include in the spreadsheet can easily be translated later into a lessons learned document. After you create the template for the spreadsheet and share it with your team, be sure to make documenting lessons learned a regular agenda item for your team meetings. Always ask the question, "What did we learn from this?" Members of your team will likely take ownership of this lessons learned documentation process when they see the cumulative results of their contributions. When you close out the project, putting that lessons learned document together will be relatively easy, and you'll be sure never to forget important lessons, such as the print testing fiasco (we won't ask) or the great system the team came up with for streamlining the interface (congratulations). Chapter 17 has a sample spreadsheet template you can use.

Planning isn't a one-time deal. Planning is an *iterative* (or repeated) process that happens as many times as it must throughout the project life cycle. You instinctively plan and restructure your plan all the time, stepping back, examining the problem, and then creating and refining the solution.

The point of planning in software project management is to communicate exactly what you'll be doing in the project. It's a guide for all future project decisions. Enjoy.

You may think we're putting the cart before the horse, but trust us when we tell you that you should also be gathering information for your *lessons learned documentation* (we introduce lessons learned documentation in "Closing the project," later in this chapter, and we discuss it throughout the book; we talk about lessons learned in detail in Chapter 17). The most important thing to know is that you should always be thinking proactively about providing historical information for future project managers. No project goes perfectly; because software projects can be large in scope and scale, whatever information you can provide to help others in similar situations, as well as to aid you in your development as a software project manager, will be immeasurably beneficial. And it's such good karma.

Examining project planning approaches

You can plan in lots of ways. You and your team can sketch out a plan on the back of a napkin to create a formal detailed approach to delivery. Or you can follow one of these formal project management planning methodologies:

- ✔ **Rolling wave planning:** Waves crest before they fall. The concept of the rolling wave approach is to crest with planning and then go do the work. You have several successions of planning and executing your plan. This is a fine approach in a software project.

- ✔ **Scrum:** You may have heard of the software project management approach of *scrum,* named after the rugby term for getting a ball into play. Scrum calls for quick, daily meetings with members of the project team. The focus of these meetings is simple. You identify what each team member has done so far, what team members will be doing today, and what issues need to be solved in the next week or so.

- ✔ **Extreme programming:** This software creation approach calls for rounds of planning, testing, team involvement, and execution. Communication and teamwork are paramount in this approach, which puts a primary focus on customer satisfaction. If you're interested in learning more details about extreme programming, you may want to read *eXtreme Programming in Action: Practical Experiences from Real World Projects,* by Martin Lippert, Stephen Roock, and Henning Wolf (Wiley).

Executing the project

Execution, the third process group, is all about getting things done. You authorize the project work to begin and your project team goes about the business of designing, building, and testing the project's creation. This is the meat of the project — doing the work.

In this process group, you're also tackling some other key activities:

✔ Beginning your procurement activities, if needed

✔ Working with your organization's quality assurance programs

✔ Communicating project information to appropriate stakeholders

✔ Managing project risk assessments

✔ Developing the project team

✔ Managing conflicts among the team and among stakeholders

Controlling the project

The executing process group's twin process is *controlling,* which is the fourth process group. Controlling is all about ensuring the project is done according to plan. You control stuff — quality, scope, budgets, the schedule, risks — and you get to monitor performance. It's fun, fun, fun. Don't forget to document all these changes in performance so that you can write up a thorough lessons learned document later.

The reason we relate controlling and executing is that they (more than all the other process groups) depend on each other. As your project team executes the project plan, you control the work by ensuring the quality is present as planned. You ensure that the costs are kept in check, and that the schedule is consistent, as planned. And if there's trouble afoot, you go back to the planning process group.

Closing the project

At some point, the project, like a bad date, has to come to its merciful end. ("See ya! Bye.") The fifth process group, *closing,* for good project managers, involves lots of activities, including the following:

✔ **Tying up loose financial ends:** Doing your final math to see where the project stands financially, verifying the procurement documents, verifying the deliverables, and so on.

- ✓ **Unveiling the product to the customer for final acceptance:** When the customer is happy, he or she signs off on the project.

- ✓ **Finalizing the project documentation:** Final reports on the project team, including time spent on the project, final costs, and so on, need to be completed, as well as the lessons learned documentation. Finally, you can archive the project records, and if you've been working on gathering historical documentation all along, this part should go surprisingly smoothly (see Chapters 16 and 17).

- ✓ **Moving on:** And then the project manager and the project team go on to other projects. Well, not yet. Don't forget to celebrate with your project team for a job well done!

Living with Stakeholders

If the project is a success, it's because of everyone's great effort; if the project fails, then it's your fault, and your fault alone. That's just the way project management goes. It's not always fun, not always rewarding, and it's never easy.

A *project stakeholder* is anyone who has a vested interest in the outcome of your project. Everyone involved in the project, from the creators to its eventual users and even your organization's customers, is a stakeholder. Some of these stakeholders are more crucial than others, and you're generally only concerned with *key stakeholders.* Key stakeholders are the stakeholders who have an immediate influence over your project success:

- ✓ The project manager (that's you)
- ✓ The project sponsor
- ✓ The project team
- ✓ Functional managers
- ✓ Subject matter experts (SMEs) who help you make decisions
- ✓ Anyone who can directly influence decisions about the project
- ✓ Customers who pay for the project expenses
- ✓ End users

Loving your project team

Your project team is the collection of people you rely on to complete the project work. They have the biggest influence on your project success, so you don't want to tick them off. There must be a level of respect between the project manager and the project team.

Most often project team members are professionals just like you. They are usually interested in completing their assignments, doing a good job, and meeting goals so that they can go home. There should not be, unless you like trouble, an us-against-them relationship between the project team and the project manager.

Loving your project sponsor

The project sponsor is an individual high enough in the organization to have power over the functional managers you'll deal with on your project. In other words, you don't want Bob the VP to be the project sponsor if you'll be using resources from Susan the VP's department. Susan will, no doubt, question why she has to answer to someone at her same level in the organizational chart.

Avoid playing dirty politics, such as pretending to agree with stakeholders just because they are in a powerful position. In such situations, politics may impede progress. On the other hand, when done correctly and ethically, politics may also facilitate progress. Building positive, supportive working relationships with your stakeholders is an example of a positive aspect of politics.

The point of the project sponsor is to grant you the authority to act on his or her behalf to make sure the project gets the care and feeding it needs. This person assigns to you a level of autonomy to get the project done. If there are problems between you and the functional managers, the project team, or even stakeholders, the project sponsor should come to your defense. Really!

Balancing stakeholder expectations

One of the trickiest parts of the project manager's job is balancing stakeholder expectations. You've experienced this. Everyone wants something. Bob, the sales manager, demands connectivity to a database that lets his sales people search first by last activity of the customer.

Janice, the manager of Manufacturing, also deals with customers and wants the database to first search by the size of the order against the amount of materials she has on hand.

Or Fred wants caller ID to look up the customer first.

Or Sally Ann wants to filter out customers that aren't in her region.

Or Pi wants every sales lead sent to his inbox.

And on, and on, and on.

The bottom line is that you can take in all the input in the world, but you may not be able to build super software that will meet every user's most minute need. Nor should you. Software that purports to do everything often does everything poorly. Think of all the different wonky Web browsers that have toolbars, search engines, e-mail support, chat, and more. They brag about being feature rich, but we know they are lousy. At some point, the project team can become counterproductive because too many customizations spoil the broth. (More stuff means more tech support, and more documentation.)

You and all the stakeholders must be in agreement about the purpose of the project and then work backwards to their wish lists from there.

The goal of negotiation in project management is not to get the best deal for a particular party. The goal is to find the best solution for the project.

Through rounds of give and take, compromise, and negotiations, you must reach a consensus with the stakeholders on why the project is going to occur and what the project will accomplish. Then you have to tell people (diplomatically, of course) that they're going to have to live with their disappointment if they don't get everything they want.

Early in the project life you want the stakeholders to define, own, and control the product scope. Check out Figure 2-4. Stakeholders have the highest level of influence on your project early in the project. The product scope describes all of the attributes and features of the software you and your project team will be delivering. After the product scope has been created, however, there must be an agreed aversion to change. After the stakeholders agree on the product scope, the project manager owns the scope and controls any changes that are made to the scope. In other words, stakeholders can't go changing horses midstream.

Figure 2-4:
Stakeholder influence wanes as the project moves toward completion.

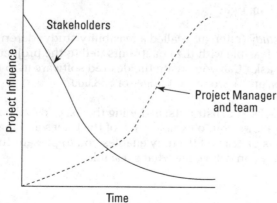

Handling questions about cost

Most business entities typically have one central question: How much will this cost? The trouble is that when you're still at the initiation stage of a project, and you don't have a real grasp on the project expectations for delivery, giving an accurate estimate is tough at best (and impossible most of the time).

For-profit companies also want to factor in the return on investment (ROI) for the project. Again, because you're initiating the project, not launching it, you may be at a loss for an answer.

Situations will vary from organization to organization, but for the most part, your project is still being considered, not launched. The reality, however, is that what you say now will become the gospel. There's a big chance the project will launch based on early calculations for cost, ROI, and likelihood of completion.

When you have a general sense of the scope of the project, you can do some initial research to see what similar endeavors have cost other companies or even your own company. This research will at least (you hope) get you into the right ball park. But be sure to season everything you say with, "This is an estimate." Your estimate should include a range of variance, a time period the estimate is valid, and any assumptions that you've based your cost figure on.

What the project can deliver may vary based on the amount of cash, the amount of available time, and the return on investment. And this is why, sometimes, you may find yourself answering executives' questions with one simple question of your own: "How much can the company afford to invest?"

Completing a Project Feasibility Study

Not all projects are feasible. News flash. But what if you know a project is not feasible before the project work begins? It'd make a huge difference to have this knowledge early on, right?

A *project feasibility study* (often just called a feasibility study) determines whether a project is feasible with the constraints tied to the project. For example, you might ask, "Can you create the desired software in four months, with two developers, and a proposed budget of $58,000?"

A feasibility study looks at constraints, including the exact details of the product scope, and allows you to explore each of the issues and make a judgment. At the very least, a feasibility study enables you to present the facts to managers so that they can determine what's feasible.

What feasibility studies do (and don't do)

You don't always have to do a feasibility study. You may not have the time or resources. However, feasibility studies can answer questions, discover scenarios, and unearth possibilities long before the project work begins.

Some reasons to consider conducting a feasibility study are that these studies

- **Can save time and money.** Some project managers consider the time and initial capital invested in a feasibility study a waste. They are wrong. When you consider the amount of time and money needed to take a project from concept to completion, and the high likelihood of project failure, spending the time and money at the front end can protect larger amounts of time and capital in the long run. Feasibility studies just make good financial sense.

- **Can give you and the stakeholders an opportunity to do a risk assessment.** Sure, you'll assess risks in more detail when you're planning the project, but an initial risk assessment at this stage can help the organization determine whether a marginal project should move forward.

A feasibility study does not

- **Serve as a research paper.** It's a factual exploration of the project's likelihood for success.

- **Cheerlead the project manager's point of view.** For that matter, it's neutral all the way around and shouldn't promote anyone's point of view.

- **Present alternate ideas.** Your focus is on the merits and pitfalls of the project as it's been articulated at this point. You shouldn't be tweaking the ideas.

- **Campaign for additional time or funds.** When the project is chartered and you and the project team move into planning, you can determine time and cost estimates in detail. And if management won't budge on the budget or schedule? You must consider the lack of time and money a risk and document the problem in a risk statement.

- **Offer advice on the project's initiation.** A feasibility study just presents the facts; it doesn't make a recommendation for the project to be launched or squelched.

Finding a feasibility consultant

So how do you go about creating a feasibility study? It's possible that you or one of your project team members can complete the study, but typically not. It is preferred that the study be accomplished by a business consultant or other *subject matter expert* (SME).

You and the project team may not be as objective as a consultant, so bringing in an outsider is often very useful. A feasibility study completed by a consultant ensures objectivity, exposes harsh realizations of the project's risks, provides an accurate estimate of the likelihood of success or failure, and even provides the motivation and validation your project team needs to complete the work.

You can find an SME to help with your project feasibility study using any of countless methods, but we prefer using personal referrals from colleagues. You can also find SMEs through user group meetings, trade associations, IT integrators, and, of course, the Web. Regardless of your approach to finding an SME, a good consultant will have the following characteristics:

- ✔ **Experience:** The consultant should be experienced, not just with creating studies for other organizations, but with the technology you're considering for your project.

- ✔ **Effective communication:** Someone who is able and willing to listen to your project team, stakeholders, management, and you, the project manager, is more likely to be listened to when the time comes to deliver the results of the study.

- ✔ **Willingness to participate:** A consultant who participates in interviews, meetings, and analysis of the problems or opportunities of the project is always better than one who keeps a distance. Your SME needs to be involved in order to understand the proposed project.

- ✔ **Willingness to adhere to a contractual agreement and timeline:** In order to complete the project on schedule and within a given budget, you need to consider these factors even at this early stage.

- ✔ **Ability to provide useful information on an ongoing basis:** The SME must continue to provide useful, accurate, information as the study progresses. (There's nothing worse than paying for a feasibility study that's fluff.)

Understanding How Executives Select Projects

Most companies, at least the ones we work with, have a limited amount of capital to invest in new projects. This means, of course, that not all proposed projects get launched. Some projects (no surprise) have a higher priority than others. For example, projects that are tied to government regulations have a funny way of earning a higher priority than other projects.

Projects may get selected in one of two ways:

- **Constrained optimization:** This is a complex approach that considers multiple variables, factors, and likelihood of project success. Selection committees use dynamic algorithms and linear and nonlinear programming to choose their projects. Doesn't that sound like fun?

- **Benefit comparison methods:** Most organizations use this approach. Benefit comparison methods use accessible formulas, comparison models, and systems to choose which projects should be launched and which should not. Because these are the most common, we focus on giving you details on several models.

Say you have a proposed project that's dear to you. You, the project manager, really want your company's project selection committee to choose your project, and you need some ammo as to why your project should be launched. Well, friend, it'd behoove you to know which approach your management team uses to select a project and then present the team with the facts to help your project get launched.

By the way, if you're wondering when, in the initiation process, all of this project selection stuff happens, well, that depends. Each organization has its own internal procedures. A bank, for example, may choose projects immediately after it conducts a feasibility study to determine whether the project can truly be profitable. On the other hand, an IT integrator may elect to select a project right after a rough order of magnitude estimate, but *before* the feasibility study. There's no hard-and-fast rule as to when it takes place, but project selection always takes place through one of the approaches in the following sections.

Using the benefit comparison selection model

The most common approach to selecting projects is the benefit comparison selection model. This basically means you use a predefined approach to selecting projects and choose the project, or projects, that have the best attributes. So, if you propose a project with lots of benefits, but your archrival, Paully, proposes a project that also boasts lots of benefits, management examines which project, yours or Paully's, has the most to offer. Managers compare projects and choose the best one for your organization.

Using a scoring model

A scoring model establishes a foundation of desired attributes such as profitability, cost, timeline, return on investment (see the section, "Finding a project's ROI"), required staffing, and so on. Each attribute is assigned a value. As each proposed project is reviewed, the attributes of the project are assigned scores. The projects with the highest scores are chosen for launch. In Table 2-1, each project (in the first column) is scored based on its attractiveness in various areas. Then the final scores are tallied (in the last column).

Table 2-1	Sample Scoring Model				
Project	**Experience**	**Schedule**	**Cost**	**Portfolio**	**Final Score**
Project ABC	10	5	3	8	26
Code and Code Project	4	9	4	6	23
Web App Project	7	2	9	7	25
Patch and Fix Project	7	6	5	2	20

Facing a murder board

Yep, *murder boards* are as much fun as the name implies. A murder board is a committee of people (well, they claim to be people) who play the devil's advocate against the project. Their job is to ask all sorts of questions to look for the project's weaknesses. This method of assessing a project attempts to get a feel for the likelihood of the project's success. In the process, it definitely weeds out project managers who kind of know what's going on and favors project managers who can think under pressure.

Before facing one of these committees, be sure to prepare by coming up with a list of questions you think will be asked. Then prepare and practice your answer to each proposed question.

Finding a project's ROI

Every organization, for-profit or otherwise, should be concerned with the *return on investment* (ROI) of a project. In particular, project managers, and sometimes project selection committees, are concerned with how valuable the project will be in dollars and cents (and sometimes that's dollars and sense).

TIP

Relying on benefit-cost ratios

Sometimes you hear the phrase *benefit-cost ratio* bandied about. There's nothing too fancy about a benefit-cost ratio; it's simply a ratio that compares the number of benefits the project will create with the costs the project will incur.

For example, a project that has a benefit-cost ratio (BCR) of 4:1 is attractive, while a project with a BCR of 1:3 isn't looking too keen. Guess which one should be selected.

The ROI concept is straightforward. If you invest $100,000 in a project, a good ROI is one that earns substantially more than $100,000. A project with a great ROI is Microsoft's investment to explore operating system technology.

Finding the present value

It's math time! The *present value* is a formula that determines how much a future amount of dollars is worth today. Imagine a project manager that boasts his project deliverables will be worth $275,000 in five years. But what's $275,000 today?

Here's what the formula looks like:

```
Future Value ÷ (1+I)ⁿ
```

I is the interest rate and n is the number of time periods for the project. If the project manager promises $275,000 in five years and our interest rate is 6 percent, the formula would be $\$275,000 \div (1.06)^5$. That'd be roughly $205,000 in today's dollars (see Figure 2-5).

Figure 2-5:
The present value of a future amount of money can be quickly calculated.

$$\text{Present Value} = \frac{\text{Future Value}}{(1+I)^n}$$

$$\text{Present Value} = \frac{\$275,000}{(1+.06)^5}$$

$$\text{Present Value} = \$205,000$$

So what? If the project costs more than $205,000, it'd be better to leave the cash in the bank where it can earn 6 percent interest instead.

Finding the future value

If you can calculate the present value of a future amount of cash you can do the inverse. Future value allows us to take a present value and see what it will be worth in the future. The formula is

```
PV x (1+I)ⁿ
```

where I is the interest rate and n is the number of time periods.

So imagine Jane's software promises to be worth $500,000 in five years, but she'll need $275,000 to make it happen. So you want to know whether the $275,000 investment for Jane's project is worth it. If the compounded interest rate is 6 percent, the formula to use is $275,000 \text{ x } (1+.06)^5$.

This works out to approximately $368,012, which means that if Jane's project can really deliver what it promises it would be a better investment — by a few thousand bucks — than leaving the money in the bank at a 6 percent interest rate (see Figure 2-6).

Figure 2-6:
The future value of a present amount of money can be found through some math magic.

$$\text{Future Value} = (\text{Present Value}) (1+I)^n$$

$$\text{Future Value} = (\$275,000) (1+.06)^5$$

$$\text{Future Value} = \$368,012$$

Finding the net present value

Software projects can be delivered in stages, or versions. Each release of the software has some value, some functionality, and some contribution to the organization. In these instances it gets trickier to find the present value for the whole project because there are planned multiple releases of the software. And with each release, we assume, there's some financial benefit to the organization as well as some costs incurred.

As a rule, a *net present value* (NPV) greater than 1 promises at least a dollar profit. If the net present value is a negative number, well, it isn't good.

The NPV finds the present value for each time period over the planned release of the software to determine the true total value of the deliverable's worth. Here's how it works:

1. **Complete the present value for each release of the software.**

2. **Find the sum of each release's present value.**

3. **Subtract the organization's original investment from the sum of present value.**

    This value is your mystical NPV. The bigger the number, the more potential the project has. If you end up with a negative number, your project won't be profitable.

Table 2-2 shows you what this might look like for a project that will be released over three years with predicted future values for each year.

Table 2-2	Finding the Net Present Value	
Year	Future Value	Present Value
1	$35,000	$33,019
2	$48,000	$42,720
3	$81,000	$68,009
Sum PV:		$143,748
Investment	$97,000	
NPV (Sum of PV – Investment)		$46,748

We know what you're thinking: What does this mean for me when you've got a score of projects, frustrations, and stakeholders pestering you for changes, updates, and new deliverables every day?

The NPV is a decision tool not only to help managers and customers select projects, but also to determine which projects get cut first. Doesn't that sound nice? The point (the honest, real-world truth) is that these formulas can help you predict which projects should demand the bulk of your time, resources, and accountability.

Writing the Product Description

One of the key activities for the project manager, the key project stakeholders, the customers, and in some instances, the project team is writing the product description. You have to write the product description during the initiation stage because it officially captures what the project will create.

Verbally everyone can agree on what the project will create, but to have it on paper makes it official.

The *product description* captures the essence of what the project will create. It describes the deliverables, the function of the deliverables, and how the product will affect the organization.

The product description is also known as the *product scope*. Figure 2-7 captures the satellite view of the project. In this figure, the project purpose feeds into the product scope. The project plan and execution support the product scope and create the project deliverable. During project closure, you and the key stakeholders must walk through the project deliverables to ensure that what you promised in the product scope is what you and the project team have delivered.

Every product scope should include the following:

- ✔ Overall function of the software
- ✔ Features of the software the project will create or revise
- ✔ Purpose of the project work (whether it's to solve a specific problem, seize a particular opportunity, or what have you)
- ✔ Any optional or desired components that may be incorporated into the product based on the project manager's discretion
- ✔ Metrics for product acceptance (speed, reliability, and consistency, for example)

Figure 2-7: The process-to-project completion must support the original project purpose.

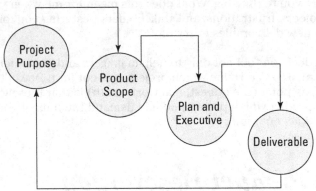

If you're working with a vendor, then the product scope is also a meaningful way to document your expectations for the vendor. Sure, all of this information will also go into the final contract between you and the vendor, but the product scope is a pre-project execution document that helps you get on the same page with the vendor.

If you're shopping for a vendor, rather than working with a preferred provider, your product description may be included in the *Statement of Work* (SOW). The SOW ensures that you and the potential vendors are all in agreement as to what the contract and project will create. You can find out more about vendors and procurement in Chapter 12.

Making Your Project Wish List

When a project is about to begin and you know that you're going to be the one in charge of it, you should start to work immediately on a mental checklist. We like to begin by running through what we're going to need, who we want on the project, and what resources we want to gather to hedge our bets and make the project a success.

In the confines of project management education you're not supposed to do that. You're supposed to follow some processes, some rules, and some guidelines that the organization, the mechanics of formal project management, and polite people call for.

Finding the ideal tools

Tools are the things you need to get the project work done. They can include anything from hardware (two monitors, faster processors) to the language you'll be using to develop the software. Technically, you shouldn't be jumping the gun by creating your dream list of the hardware and software you might need to complete the project, but, depending on your experience, organizational conditions, and the nature of the work you do, your instincts may already be telling you what general direction the project is moving.

If you're brand new to software project management, just tuck these things into the back of your mind and come back to them later. If you've got a bit more experience, check this list to see whether you've considered everything:

✔ **Development language:** You need to know which code will deliver the product the fastest, and which code will deliver the best product for the customer. Unfortunately, you may find that the fastest software development environment isn't the best quality environment. If you see an opportunity to train your team in a new language and create a better product for the customer, your decision may be easy. But if time is an issue (and when isn't it?), and time is money (as they say), allotting time for training and on-the-job education may not be practical.

- ✔ **Hardware:** Hardware is so freakin' cheap nowadays that we don't think you should worry too much about this tool. If your team says it needs a faster machine and can prove it, don't scrimp. We know one developer who boosted his productivity immensely simply because he added a second monitor to a PC. When it comes to hardware we're not stingy, and we don't think you should be.

- ✔ **Training:** In ideal circumstances, your team already knows how to accomplish their tasks. At the very least, they have some experience working in a particular development environment. Well, the world's not always ideal. If some or all members of the project team don't know how to do the work, train them or send them to training. This is part of team development, the cost of quality, and it has huge effects on team morale. We know some project managers who say, "But if I train my team, I might lose them." Our answer? But if you don't train your team you will keep them. Which is worse? Training and maybe losing your talented employees, or keeping employees who can't do the work? Just think of training as an investment.

- ✔ **Other resources:** Typically, when people think of resources they think of people, but resources are also things. And the things you want on your wish list are items that keep your developers happy. Let's face it: Developers are unique people. If they're happy, they'll deliver. So the resources you want here can range from sodas and pizzas to reference books and Internet subscriptions to relevant IT Web sites.

Building a dream team

In some organizations, the project manager works with the same team over and over. In other companies, the project manager gets to cherry-pick the talent to be on the project team. Still others get their project team based on who's available for the project.

Our dream team is based on a combination of people skills and technical competence. Although we like to be around happy, friendly people, we can accept grumps who can deliver what they promise any day. On the other hand, you may have the most skilled programmer or developer on your team, but he can't seem to hold a conversation so that anyone can understand him. Both skills are important. Your team members need to have technical expertise, but they also need to know how to play well in the sandbox with others. If you have the control over who works on your team, you need to figure out the most productive team makeup.

Most often, you'll find that your teams are a blend of assigned team members, some resource selection, and some contractors that fill in the gaps.

However your team is created, every team goes through four phases of development:

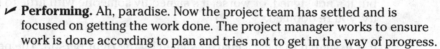

✔ **Forming:** In this stage, folks all come together, shake hands, and play nice. It's your job as the project manager to make certain everyone communicates with one another, feels comfortable, and recognizes who's in charge (you, of course) and what each person's roles are.

✔ **Storming:** In this stage, attitudes, personalities, and alliances begin to form. This process can be heated or passive (you can hope for a quiet storm), but you're guaranteed to see someone (besides you) take charge on the project team. Usually this works out based on the experience or passion of the leader of the team. Sometimes though, you may have to influence the process to make your life easier — and the project deliverables better.

✔ **Norming:** After roles have been clearly identified, politics have been accepted or bucked, and things have calmed, you can focus on how to get the work done. This is a natural process and there's not much the project manager can really do to force the team to move into *norming,* or normalizing. You can threaten and coerce the team to complete the work, but if storms are still brewing, the norming process won't take hold and you won't have calm and cohesive teamwork in the project.

If you seem to be stuck in the storming phase, be patient. Still waiting? You may have to evaluate whether some people will ever play nicely with each other, and how big a problem that's really going to be in the long run.

✔ **Performing.** Ah, paradise. Now the project team has settled and is focused on getting the work done. The project manager works to ensure work is done according to plan and tries not to get in the way of progress.

To find out more about team building and resolving team conflicts, take a look at *Managing For Dummies,* 2nd Edition, by Bob Nelson, Peter Economy, and Ken Blanchard (Wiley).

Finding a preferred vendor

Most projects require you to buy stuff or contract developers, programmers, or other experts. Every organization has its own policies and approaches to *procurement,* and the project manager must follow the correct procedures. There's no monkeying around here. Rules are rules, especially when it comes to finding and selecting a vendor. You don't want to be a part of indiscretions, conflicts of interest, or even an appearance of a lack of scruples.

But this doesn't mean you don't want some influence on which vendor you're relying on. After you know what the rules are for the vendors to bid on the project work, you need to be assertive about finding the most suitable vendor to complete project work.

Project managers have long been in the position to influence decisions for personal gain. It's best to err on the side of caution and avoid any appearance of discrepancies. In other words, don't hire your buddy, your brother, or your girlfriend just because you have a relationship with that person. Create a logical approach to vendor selection, document it, and then stick to it. No one can accuse you of taking kickbacks, bribes, or playing favorites with this approach.

Ideally, you should use vendors who are talented, experienced, and have a decent price. The lowest bidder isn't always the best bidder.

After the charter is signed by your project sponsor, all key stakeholders need a copy of the charter. Some organizations use a boilerplate charter that is sent via e-mail, while other organizations have a formal, paper-based charter that is delivered in hard copy. Either way, all key stakeholders should receive the charter so they're aware of the official project launch, your authority as the project manager, and who's the sponsor of the project.

Recognizing Doomed Projects

Charters authorize the project based on the person that signs the charter. If you don't have a charter, you may not have a project. If you have a charter, but it's not signed, or worse, it's signed by someone with little to no authority, you're doomed.

It is essential to have a charter signed by the right person. The person that signs the charter must have, well, enough clout to squelch any problems or challenges against the project's success.

The most common problem when it comes to charters is the utilization of resources. Say your boss, John Hancock, signs the charter to complete a new piece of software. You're the project manager and you need Tony, a lead salesperson, to contribute to the project. Sharon is Tony's boss and she says, "No freaking way. Tony is busy getting sales."

You whip out your charter to show that your boss signed off on the work and you need Tony. Now here's the trouble: Your boss and Sharon are at the same level in the organizational flowchart. Your boss, swell guy that he is, has no power over Sharon.

If you don't want your project to fail (and, really, who wants their project to fail?), find the right sponsor. Without the right sponsor your charter might as well be signed by your mailman. Charters are great. Charters with power are best.

Chapter 3

Creating the Software Scope

*Y*ou wouldn't build a house without a blueprint. You wouldn't start cooking dinner without some idea of what the meal was actually going to include. You wouldn't head out for vacation without an idea of how to get to your destination. So you wouldn't start creating a new piece of software without knowing what the software will actually do.

Out here in the real world, where we hang out, stakeholders present project managers with software wish lists, Picasso-like dreams, and impossible anticipations. They expect the project manager and the project team to create a stellar deliverable. You can't create a stellar software product unless you know what it is supposed to do. You must work with the stakeholders to create the *product scope*.

This chapter shows you how to identify the key elements of the product so that you can determine the best path to successfully completing the project. We also show you how to work with your project team and your stakeholders to gather requirements and how to understand and manage potential conflicts.

Understanding Product Scope and Project Scope

Before you can really get started on a project, you need to know the end product's essential ingredients — as well as its limitations. The *product scope* is the summation of the attributes and features that will comprise the product you're creating for your customer. When the stakeholders are in agreement on the product scope, then you can focus on creating the software *project scope*.

The difference between the two is that the product scope describes the end result of the project — the things the customer sees. The project scope describes the work that must be completed in order to complete the project — the things the project manager focuses on. As shown in Figure 3-1, the product scope and the project scope support one another.

The best way to determine the product scope is to analyze the concrete (and sometimes hidden) needs and expectations of the stakeholders. The following sections help you in this process.

Figure 3-1:
The product
scope and
the project
scope
support one
another.

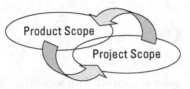

Completing stakeholder analysis

Stakeholder analysis is the process of determining who your stakeholders are and what their interests and concerns for their project are. As the project manager, you inherit their vision of the software solution.

A *stakeholder,* technically, is anyone who has a vested interest in your project's success. Obviously, you and the project team are stakeholders. Your project sponsor is also a stakeholder. But the big stakeholders, the ones who influence your project decisions, are the folks paying for the project work. These stakeholders are sometimes called customers, clients, or project champions.

In a large organization, you may not immediately know who all of the stakeholders are. The software you create for the sales department, for example, may have ripples into manufacturing, marketing, training, and even distribution. As the project manager, you have to look not only at the immediate and obvious stakeholders, but ask questions and examine the effects of your project in entities within your organization.

Interviewing stakeholders now to avoid surprises later

One of your most important responsibilities is to interview your stakeholders. This is a vital step because it ensures that you, the hub of the project, are in tune with what the project stakeholders really want.

Ninety percent of project management is knowing how to communicate. Set expectations for communications early on in the project management life cycle by asking your stakeholders lots of questions. You need to help them communicate to you as much as you must communicate with them. We discuss communications in more depth in Chapter 4.

When gathering stakeholder requirements and other information, be sure you have considered all stakeholders, not just those that are the most visible. As you communicate with your project team and other stakeholders, be sure to ask whether other stakeholders should be considered. You can check with your organization's marketing or communications department (if you have one) for help reaching out to hidden stakeholders.

Stakeholder analysis isn't just examining who the stakeholders are — but also their demands and wishes for the project deliverables. You've got to ask lots of questions, for example:

- Can you describe the conditions this deliverable will operate in?
- What's the opportunity this project will grasp?
- What's the main problem this software will solve?
- How do you see the deliverable solving your problem?
- What other software will this deliverable interact with?
- What are the primary and secondary features of the software?
- How will this software make the end-users' jobs better or easier?
- Are there other stakeholders that we should consider?
- How do you see this deliverable benefiting your customer?

Your questions should be open ended but focused. Make sure that the stakeholder has an opportunity to talk in his or her own words about the expectations and goals of the software, but lead the discussion so that the answers you receive are specific enough to help you plan the project effectively.

One of the most effective ways of completing stakeholder analysis is to put yourself in the stakeholders' shoes. Over the course of the project, you'll work side-by-side with the stakeholders to experience how they currently perform their job functions. You'll work with them through the tasks they do now and observe their use of the software later.

Managing Stakeholder Objectives

Don't expect stakeholders to play nicely with each other. Like all people, stakeholders have individual personalities, and competing stakeholder objectives can haunt a project through its duration. Some examples of competing stakeholder objectives include conflicting demands between two or more managers, or time and cost responsibilities within the organization.

Sometimes, stakeholders don't know exactly what they want and they're counting on you to show them. Proceed with caution. When you're working with these wishy-washy folks, they'll expect you and your project team to create software that they can try and then modify. And then the process starts over: Your project team creates a masterpiece, they try it out, and then your team modifies it. And again, and again. It's frustrating to you, the project team, and even the stakeholder. And it's a big, freaking waste of time and money.

Stress to the stakeholder that you both must have a clear vision of what the project will create. Without a real grasp on the deliverables, writing an effective project scope — let alone creating an effective application — is impossible.

The following sections help you manage stakeholder expectations so that the project stays on track.

Knowing the sources of common conflicts

You are a software project manager. Chances are you've come up through the ranks as an IT professional, business analyst, or junior engineer. In your position you've got some power, but you don't want to jeopardize your political capital, anger the wrong people, or make waves when you don't have to. That said, sometimes you'll have to resolve conflicts to move a project toward completion. The goal of conflict resolution is to resolve the problem, move the project along, and not make enemies.

But regardless of the patience and leadership you demonstrate, some folks won't be happy with your decisions, or the project objectives. Some people will blame you because their requests for the software features can't be added to the project. You can bet on it.

Conflicts (surprise, surprise) come in all flavors. But you may be surprised to discover which conflicts are the most common. My pals over at the Project Management Institute (PMI) rank the following conflicts in order of frequency. Sure, sure, they may be different where you are, but there's no need to bicker:

- ✔ **Schedules:** Think of all the different projects, responsibilities, and demands that carve out chunks of your day. Now think of the other people your software project involves and how their schedule is affected by your project. No wonder scheduling mayhem is at the top of the list. Egads! For information about creating effective schedules, see Chapter 8.

- ✔ **Priorities:** What's important to Jane isn't always important to Bob. Stakeholders will have pet features, ideas, and components they'll want your project team to build into the software. Some of these components, such as which database technology to use (SQL or Oracle), are mutually exclusive — you can't have it both ways. Because everyone won't get the component he or she wants, you should prepare for unhappiness.

- ✔ **Resources:** As a software project manager, you know your project team and the abilities of all its individuals. If demands spread your project team too thin they'll never get their work done and their morale will plummet, which puts the crunch on your project's success. Resources, especially good developers, are in high demand.

- ✔ **Technical beliefs:** If you've ever hung around software programmers for more than, oh, say ten minutes, then you know these IT folks can disagree over eight ways to accomplish the same task. Technical beliefs can be a real stumbling block for project team members with diverse backgrounds.

- ✔ **Policies and procedures:** Don't you just hate it when your organization's rules, procedures, and policies get in the way of progress? If you yield to temptation and cut corners, you'll pay the price later. If you try to argue your way through the red tape and procedures, you may make enemies, anger management, and waste time. Policies and procedures, both good and bad, exist for some reason — even if no one can explain what that reason is.

- ✔ **Costs:** When it comes to software project management, costs are usually tied to a timeframe for research and development, simulations, reworking kinks, learning, and productive coding. Stakeholders don't always see the value of any dollars committed to time that isn't directly attributed to creating productive code. Time is money, and software development takes time. Chapter 9 covers project costs and budgets in a lot more detail.

- ✔ **Personalities:** Some project managers find it hard to believe that personality is the least common source of problems on projects, but according to the PMI, it's true. Most people can work together toward a common goal — the successful completion of the project. Personality conflicts, as a rule, only become a problem when they prevent the project from moving forward. In other words, annoying people may give you a few headaches, but they don't usually prevent the job from getting done.

As a project manager, your focus is on one thing: getting the project success-fully completed. Conflicts and arguments are sometimes necessary because they help the stakeholders define vague priorities and resolve differences about what's *truly* best for the project. Much of the time, however, arguments are over power trips, politics, and technical preferences. You don't have time for petty arguments when it comes to software project management, so you'll have to be decisive and swift when it comes to making decisions.

Resolving common conflicts

The preceding section, "Knowing the sources of common conflicts," identi-fied several conflicts you're likely to come up against in a typical software project. This section examines how to deal with them.

To help you resolve conflicts, you've got five approaches you and other stakeholders ought to use:

- ✔ **Problem solving:** Utilizing problem-solving strategies is the pinnacle of conflict resolution. This approach requires both parties to work together for the good of the project. Both parties want the solution that works best for the project. Using problem-solving techniques means removing ego and politics from the scenario to create a win-win solution.

- ✔ **Forcing:** You've seen this approach to conflict resolution before. Forcing means the person with the power makes a decision and there is no fur-ther discussion. And you know that just because someone has power doesn't mean that this person always makes the best decision for the project. That's why forcing usually results in a win-lose solution.

- ✔ **Compromising:** This sounds nice, but really it's not. True compromising means that both parties in the disagreement have to give up something they want. Both parties get part of what they want, but neither gets everything. Compromising is different than problem solving because it's more confrontational, whereas problem solving has a spirit of coopera-tion for the best solution. Compromising is considered a lose-lose sce-nario because no one wins 100 percent.

- ✔ **Smoothing:** This solution allows the project manager or other people in power to downplay the differences between the stakeholders and mini-mize the problem. The project manager smoothes the conflict without offering a solution. This is a lose-lose scenario because neither side wins. On the other hand, the project manager (or other stakeholder) could smooth the conflict while offering a solution, making it a win-win situation (which is what you should strive for). For example, if one group of stake-holders insists on software functionality that will support a particular naming convention, whereas another stakeholder would prefer a different naming convention, you could smooth the situation by allowing both stakeholders to air their arguments. You may all discover that the differences have more to do with politics and personalities than with a real preference for naming conventions. Giving people the opportunity to talk things through enables stakeholders to minimize problems on their own.

Trial and error is the best approach to finding the right conflict resolution technique for each situation. No one method will work 100 percent of the time with 100 percent of your stakeholders on 100 percent of your projects. Arm yourself with as much knowledge about conflict resolution as possible, and then let experience help you figure out which methods you're most comfortable with in each situation.

✔ **Withdrawal:** Ever been in a disagreement where the other person talked the issue to death? What'd you do? I bet you threw your arms in the air and surrendered just to get moving. That's a *withdrawal* — where one side of the argument takes him- or herself out of the discussion. This is considered a yield-lose scenario because one side of the argument yields to the other without anyone really considering what the best solution for the project may be.

Building the Software Scope

When you and the stakeholders have a clear vision of where the project's going, you need a clearly defined set of requirements. Early on in the project, you and the key stakeholders define what *must* be in the project and what *would be nice* to have in software.

While ideally everything the project will create is defined at the beginning of the project, chances are you, the project team, and the project customer will have inspirations for other deliverables that can be folded into the software as the project moves along. Changes to the software scope can be dangerous because they can eat into time and the budget. But they also can bring other risks to the project, such as

✔ Creating conflicts among various stakeholders, especially when one group feels that the suggested changes benefit other stakeholders more than themselves.

✔ Negatively affecting the quality of the project, especially when bells and whistles are added without adding sufficient time for system testing.

✔ Affecting other areas of the project such as interfaces to other systems, especially when you change code for one system but don't allow enough time for testing or changing other interfaced systems after the change.

Managing an enthusiasm deficit

You will find an interesting balance between stakeholders who want to tell the project manager everything they think and other stakeholders who are too busy, too bored, or too afraid to get involved in this crucial step of your project.

But everyone must get involved. You and your project team can create what these stakeholders want — but only if you truly know what they are expecting as a result of your efforts. Your key stakeholders, you, and your project team must work together to capture all of the requirements of the project deliverable. Have meetings in which everyone is required to contribute, give stakeholders questionnaires, and do your best to inspire everyone to have a hand in the development of the project's scope.

Document scope changes and allot time to research their true impact; be sure you're examining their impact on the project, as well as on other projects; sometimes the code you change for one project can affect other systems as well.

Requirements are the things your software must create in order for the customer to accept the project deliverable. Creating good, clear requirements isn't easy. It takes time, patience, and input from your project team, the project customers, and other stakeholders, such as the project sponsor, the quality assurance folks . . . and don't forget the application testers.

Dealing with regulations and options

The software project scope is created based on the product scope. But not everything is really a requirement. Some facets of your software may be optional. It's a great idea to identify, or at least prioritize, the things your project will create. Getting everything straight enables you and the project team to evaluate the core functions of the application versus the optional features.

You know that stakeholders usually don't get everything they want when it comes to creating an application. Time, costs, ability, and even priority of the deliverable may affect what actually ends up in the finished project. But there's another concern that influences your project deliverables: regulations, standards, and organizational influence. The following sections look at each of these factors.

Adhering to regulations

A rule that has a punishment attached to it — like jail, fines, or both — is typically a regulation. Regulations are not optional. You must obey them.

Chances are your software project has to deal with regulations. Consider the following:

- ✔ **Sarbanes-Oxley Compliance (SOX).** If your organization, or the organization for which you're building the software, is a publicly held company, then you have to comply with the Sarbanes-Oxley Act of 2002. You can find out more about how this act may affect your business by reading *Sarbanes-Oxley For Dummies* by Jill Gilbert Welytok (Wiley).

- ✔ **The Health Insurance Portability and Accountability Act of 1996 (HIPPA).** HIPPA primarily affects health care and insurance organizations, so if you're doing business with these industries you'll have to complete research, audits, and provide proof of compliance.

- ✔ **Occupational Safety and Health Administration (OSHA).** OSHA requires all companies to provide protection for the safety and health of workers. Your software may have OSHA concerns depending on its usage in the organization.

- ✔ **Industry-specific regulations.** Consider pharmaceutical companies to construction industries and everything between. Every industry has specific laws and regulations that affect what an organization must do. As a software project manager, you must know and incorporate the requirements that affect your software into your project plan.

The difference between a standard and a regulation is significant. A *standard* is a particular set of guidelines to which you agree to adhere. For example, a naming convention, the method for documenting programming comments, and file formats are examples of standards. A *regulation,* on the other hand, is a requirement imposed by a government body. For example, you must adhere to the regulations listed in the previous bullet points or face consequences. Not even the meanest boss will throw you in jail if you name program files wrong.

Choosing options

At the beginning of a project, stakeholders may believe that nothing is optional. They'll want every feature, every button, and every concept they've dreamed up. Then you and your experts must discuss the feasibility of their wishes, the cost of the plans, and offer a realistic timetable to deliver everything stakeholders want. At that point, light bulbs will go off and the stakeholders will quickly discover what's optional and what's not.

Here's why prioritizing needs and wants is important:

- **Money.** Software design takes time and time costs money. If the project team can evaluate and focus on the core deliverables, you can alleviate budget concerns, either early in the project, or later, when (and I mean when, not if) financial woes sneak into the project.

- **Time.** If you're crunched for time, picking which components can be shoved to the side first and which components must be created if you've prioritized is much easier when you know in advanced what's desirable and what's absolutely essential.

- **Stakeholder buy-in.** Stakeholders know that you know which features you should focus on first, and which components are optional based on the project's health. They'll stand behind a slimmer, more efficient product that's done on time, especially when the alternative is a bulky, slow product that is not ready on time.

- **Project manager's sanity.** If you know what the customer expects, leading your team to meet that expectation is (relatively speaking) a no-brainer. You can always add some cool options and features that your team can quickly work into the deliverable without raising any alarms, keeping your customer happy.

Leading, creating focus, and making decisions based on assigned priorities is much easier than tacking on new components and removing them willy-nilly.

- **Negotiations.** This reason for prioritizing is just a little sneaky. If you know there are elements the customer would like in your deliverable, but they aren't defined as requirements, you have bargaining chips. You can use these extras to "win" your project the time, funds, or political capital your project may need for additional changes, budget crunches, or even resources assigned to the project team.

Dealing with project constraints

A *constraint* is anything that restricts a project manager's options. I'm sure you've encountered project constraints before. In software project management, you deal with lots of constraints:

- **Schedule.** You and the project team must create the software deliverable by such-and-such date — or else. Schedule constraints can also be crunched by the availability of project resources, vendors' ability to deliver, and even access to testing facilities, server rooms, and networks.

- **Budget.** Of course, you've got a budget, but is it enough? In software project management, the bulk of your budget is tied to labor. The longer your programmers take to create accurate code, the more expensive your project deliverable becomes. You must also consider the cost of software, hardware, user acceptance testing, and other expenses.

✔ **Resources.** You probably have your favorite programmers that you'd like to work with on every project because they're just so gosh-darn good. But they can't do everything, they're in high-demand, and chances are, because of their skill sets, they'll cost your project more. And even if you don't play favorites, which I bet you do, you may still face resource challenges. Most IT organizations don't dedicate their programmers to just one project at a time — so which project has priority for the resources you need? You'll have to bargain, beg, and plead (sometimes) to get the resources you need and want.

✔ **Technology.** When it comes to software project management, you have to deal with surprises, like programming in COBOL, Visual Basic, CodeWarrior, and more. And sometimes the technology you have to interface with is so old you'll be consulting with Moses just to be backward compatible. All programmers must know backward compatibility requirements. This can be a huge constraint.

✔ **Competence.** No one likes to admit to not knowing something — especially programmers. But if your project team doesn't know how to program, solve problems, interface with databases, stop leaks, repair loose code, and perform other day-to-day programming activities, you're in big trouble. You need to have an approach to skill assessment. You need to create an environment where programmers are encouraged to ask for help when they need it. It's better to train, offer materials, or hire experts to help the project than to let your team wallow in denial and churn out worthless code.

✔ **Management.** Ah, here's every project manager's favorite scapegoat. Have you ever said

- We don't have enough time!

- We don't have enough cash!

- We don't have enough programmers!

- Management is setting unrealistic expectations!

As project management consultants, when we witness these rants we have to determine who's really to blame. Usually the project managers are correct. Usually. But sometimes the project managers are so out of tune of the project management processes that they don't know how to plan or attack the project objectives. Other times, management has no concept of what software project management is. They have no concept of what it takes to develop a piece of software and the challenges therein. Management may throw a schedule and budget together and dump them on the project manager's desk. In these instances the project manager must communicate the problem. If the project manager does nothing other than rant in private, things won't change and the project will likely fail. The key here is to document the problem as a risk, share the risk assessment with management, and then document the results. If you're faced with unrealistic expectations from management, your job is not to fail and then tell the managers, "I told you so." (That will not earn you a promotion, I promise!) It's to say, "Here's a problem: unrealistic expectations. How will we fix it?"

Getting to the signature

After rounds of discussions with your project team, the project customer, and other stakeholders, you and the main stakeholder need a *requirements document* that identifies everything the project promises to create. You and the customer should sign off on this document so that everyone involved agrees that the project manager and the customer agree on their roles and expectations for the project deliverable.

In your organization, the person who signs off on the requirements document may vary. For some folks it's always the project sponsor, in other organizations it's the project customer or champion. As a rule, the person who signs off on the project acceptance and closure (discussed in Chapter 16) at the end of the project should also sign off on the project requirements. You need the same party at the start of the project as you do at the end.

Your requirements document may be an in-depth product description, statement of work, contract, or a formal documentation of all of the features and components your project is responsible for creating.

Out in the real world, your product scope may also serve as your requirements document with simple modifications. This document sets expectations and is the groundwork for creating the formal project scope.

Having a signed requirements document on hand accomplishes several things:

- ✔ Identifies what you and your project team will create for the stakeholders
- ✔ Identifies that the stakeholders are in agreement as to what the project requirements are for your project
- ✔ Identifies that you understand the software functionality the stakeholders are expecting as a result of your work
- ✔ Allows you and the stakeholders to fully share in the project buy-in by agreeing to the things your project will create
- ✔ Acts as a checklist to ensure that you meet all the requirements
- ✔ Serves as future historical information for other project managers in your organization

Creating the Project Scope

The project scope defines the products and services the project will create. It doesn't include the cost of the project, the schedule of the project, or even the resources the project requires. The project scope defines what will and will not be included in the project.

When your project team is assembled, you can go about creating the project scope. And it's fun, fun, fun.

Not really.

So where does the project scope come from? Glad you asked. The project scope is based on the requirements document you and the stakeholders have signed off on. The project scope stems from the requirements that the project must create. Figure 3-2 shows the evolution of the project scope — and beyond.

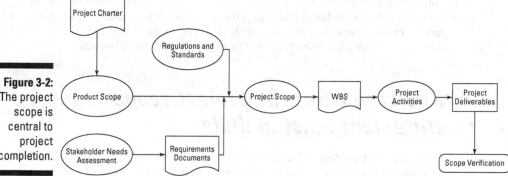

Figure 3-2: The project scope is central to project completion.

Imagine your company needs you to create a piece of software that can interface with your IP telephones. The software must

- Pull the caller ID from the inbound call
- Query a database to see whether the caller is a current customer
- Load the customer's account onto the representative's screen
- Record the time the representative took to answer the customer call
- Record the length of the conversation between the representative and the customer
- Automatically save the caller info to the database when the call is completed

These six items are all deliverables defined in the project scope. Notice that there's no mention of which coding language the software must be developed in. There's no mention of which technology the database must reside on. There's no mention of network latency, brand name IP phones, or other technical jargon. And there's no mention of money or time.

You shouldn't define every single detail of the project scope before the work gets done; that's the job of a *work breakdown structure* (WBS) (described in detail later in this chapter). What's necessary is to capture what the project will deliver.

The project scope, for most projects, won't be created in one sitting — or even one day. This is all part of planning, of determining what's needed and how much and how long it'll take to get there. There's a see-saw effect to building and agreeing on the project scope.

All successful projects have one thing in common: The project manager and stakeholders reach an agreement on the project scope. If you, the project team, and the project stakeholders, cannot come to an agreement on the project scope, your project is doomed. Think back, way back, to some of the projects you've worked on that failed. (If you don't have any failed projects, ask that weird guy down the hall.) Was the project badgered by inadequate requirements, change requests, and dissatisfied, fickle, stakeholders? Stakeholders that don't know what they want are fuses for project time bombs.

Knowing what the project scope statement must include

There are certain items that absolutely must be included in the project scope statement, which is a narrative document detailing the project scope (work to be completed) and the following information regarding your project:

- ✔ **Deliverables.** The project scope defines what the project will create for the project customer. Think of nouns: things in the software package, the screen interface, the software compatibility, and so on.

- ✔ **Assumptions.** Every project scope must list the assumptions that went into its creation. For example, you assume that the software can be developed in C++. Or you assume that you'll have access to test the software on the network. Assumptions need to be listed now so that you can test your assumptions as the project moves forward.

- ✔ **Exclusions.** These are things that won't be included in the project scope. For example, your project will create the software for the customer, but your project will not actually deploy the software to the 10,000 users on the company network.

✔ **Functions.** Your project scope must define what the software will do. Think verbs. In your scope you should document the functionality of the software.

✔ **Technical structure.** Your project scope must illustrate the flow of data, the subsystems the software may interact with, and the dependencies of the software (such as Internet, network, .asp, and operating system). With complex projects it may be necessary to illustrate the subsystems, as shown in Figure 3-3.

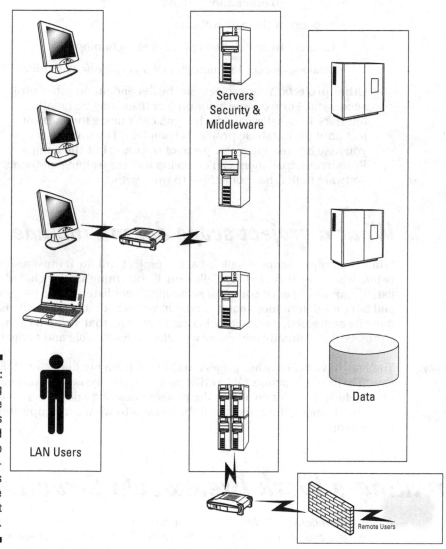

Figure 3-3:
Visualizing the subsystems affected can help stakeholders develop the project scope.

Servers Security & Middleware

Data

LAN Users

Remote Users

✔ **Influences.** Most software projects affect lines of business that may have a domino effect on other lines of business. Document the potential for any disruptions your project may cause. Consider:

- Business processes
- Organizational geographical sites
- Departments affected
- Access to data
- Changes to other applications
- Support of the new software
- Changes to or deletions of existing technology
- Dual support of technologies (if phasing one technology out)

✔ **Other projects.** Your project may be dependent on other projects to be successful. For example, your project team may be creating the Web interface for a sales catalog, but you can't move forward with your project until the database project is complete. The inverse is true, as well; you may be creating a new piece of software, but the company's Human Resources department can't develop its user training materials for your software until it has something to work with.

What a project scope doesn't include

While the project scope details what the project will do, it must also implicitly define what's *not* included. By definition, if something's not included in the list, it's not *in scope*. Of course, if something's not listed in the project scope and later it's determined that it should have been, that's a separate issue that must be addressed, particularly because anything that's added to the scope of a project that's already underway will affect the schedule and budget.

You may have heard other project managers, team members, or stakeholders say, "That's not in scope." What they're saying, really, is that whatever some chucklehead is trying to add to the project doesn't qualify. There must be a consensus among the project stakeholders as to what's in scope and what's out of scope.

Creating a Work Breakdown Structure

A *work breakdown structure* (WBS) is a visual representation of everything the project will create. Typically, a WBS includes things (deliverables, components, and so on), not activities. However, there's no hard-and-fast rule on exempting activities from your WBS. I prefer to keep work out of the WBS and focus on the things the work will create. Although we do allow some actions to sneak in, such as testing, ordering, and compiling, most of our WBSs are comprised of deliverables.

And I know you want to know why. Your WBS is also your scope baseline. As your project moves towards completion, you can compare what you've promised in the WBS against the things that your project has created. The WBS is a direct input to scope verification, which is a fancy way of saying customer acceptance.

The traditional WBS is a flowchart of objects. Another style of WBS looks more like a shopping list. While we like the traditional flowchart representation of a WBS, we're open to whichever approach works best for each project.

If you're wondering whether you have to create a WBS, well, you do. The WBS is crucial to successful projects. You'll need the WBS to do any of the following, and you'll want to do all of the following:

- ✔ **Cost estimating.** The WBS allows you to create accurate cost estimates to create the thing the project requires.

- ✔ **Cost budgeting.** The WBS allows you to track actual costs against the estimates for the things your project will create.

- ✔ **Resource planning.** The WBS components require people and things to create. By creating the WBS, you can accurately capture everything you'll need to complete the project.

- ✔ **Risk management planning.** Planning for risks when you can't see what you're creating can be tough. The WBS illustrates the things you'll create and then you'll have a clearer picture of where risks may be hiding.

- ✔ **Activity definition.** The end result of the WBS is to create an activity list. The activity list, or activity definition, lists all of the actions your project team will need to do to build the stuff in the WBS.

Creating your very own WBS

To create the WBS, you, your project team, and (in some instances) your key stakeholders convene to decompose the scope statement. The WBS decomposition is not a solo activity.

Decomposition isn't about rotting. It merely refers to breaking down something complicated into its composite parts.

Before you get to work on your WBS, you should know about the *8/80 Rule*. This is a general guideline that breaks down items into *work packages*. A work package is a unit of time allotted to a task or deliverable. The 8/80 Rule says that a work package should equate to no more than 80 hours of work and not less than 8 hours of work to create the deliverable. In other words, you don't want the WBS to be full of tiny, incremental chores and tasks (that's called *micromanagement,* which is unrealistic and kills productivity); nor do you want the work packages to be so huge that there's lots left up to the imagination (that's called *being vague,* which leads to programmers working on their blogs when they should be on the job).

The 8/80 Rule is really a *heuristic* — a broad rule. You don't have to live and die by the rule. There'll be some deliverables you want to reflect, like licensing agreements, that won't actually take 8 hours of work to create. It's perfectly fine to have exceptions to the 8/80 Rule if it helps you complete your project.

Here's what you have to do to get your WBS together:

1. **Break down the scope into major buckets of things the project will create.**

   Some project managers like to envision the phases of the project to serve as main components. I prefer to think in broad categories of deliverables. Take whichever approach works best for you and your project team. For example, you might decompose a project scope into

   - Project management deliverables

   - Database deliverables

   - Server deliverables

   - End-user deliverables

   - Education and documentation deliverables

2. **Decompose these deliverables again into smaller units or work packages.**

   If you've decomposed deliverables down and the smallest item you have still equates to 400 hours of labor, break down the WBS some more.

Using templates to create effective WBS

Don't reinvent the wheel. If you've managed similar projects in the past and you can rely on an existing WBS, go get it. In fact, we've created WBS templates for redundant projects. Templates save time and ensure that all of the deliverables are identified. A WBS template, like any other template you might use, can be modified for project specifics. Using WBS templates also ensures consistency among your projects. Sometimes you might see a WBS template identified as a WBT; don't sweat it.

Making updates to the WBS

The WBS creation is part of planning, so you have plenty of opportunities to revisit the WBS for updates and refinements. In fact, sometimes change requests will trickle (or flood) in. You should revisit the WBS to reflect the approved changes to the project. The danger of not consistently updating the WBS to reflect changes will be evident when the final deliverable doesn't match what the WBS has promised. Not modifying the WBS when you ought to can cause several problems.

The WBS is your scope baseline, so any changes to the scope must be documented here. Otherwise, the following bad things could happen:

✓ Time and cost baselines may be skewed because they don't match what's in the WBS.

✓ Your customer may be confused as to why the WBS doesn't match the deliverable you've provided.

✓ Project team members may be out of synch about what they're supposed to be creating and what the WBS calls for.

✓ If someone in management reviews the WBS and the project deliverables don't match up, you have to have *that* conversation. Nobody wants to have *that* conversation. Especially you.

✓ Future projects based on your current project will have faulty information.

When you're starting out building the WBS, use low-tech strategies to plot out how everything is going to work. Some yellow sticky notes and a blank wall can really do wonders to help you break down major deliverables into smaller components and activities (see the case study at the end of this chapter for more information). Don't rely on your project management information system (PMIS) to help create the WBS — do it by hand and then enter it into your PMIS. It'll be smarter, more concise, and easier for the whole project team to visualize.

Using a code of accounts

Want to get really organized? We thought so. A WBS can use a *code of accounts* to number and identify each element. A code of accounts is really simple to create.

You first identify a project number for your software project; let's just say, in this example, you're creating a piece of software to organize and access millions of corporate product photos. Your project is assigned the name PhotoBug 675. In your WBS, you abbreviate it to PB675. Each major component at the second level of the WBS also begins with PB675, but you append each stage or category of work with .1, .2, .3, and so on.

So, for example, say you're starting with the database component of the software (makes sense; good choice). This item is called PB675.1 in the WBS. Your SQL Server 1 and SQL Server 2, at the next level of deliverables, are identified as PB675.1.1 and PB675.1.2, respectively.

This code of accounts allows you to tie time and cost estimates to each deliverable, and provides clear communications when stakeholders ask questions about project deliverables. You can link the code of accounts back to your organization's profit and loss statements.

Finally, you can dump all the elements of the WBS into a WBS Dictionary, which you also create. The WBS Dictionary defines the code of accounts, the time and cost estimates, the characteristics of the deliverables, risk assessment, and other attributes. It's a crib sheet for anyone who needs an at-a-glance look at the WBS.

Case study: Building a WBS

Happy Yarns is a manufacturer of yarn, ribbons, and other materials. Its project manager, Sarah Montgomery, managed a software project to create a Web-based application that enables customers to place and track orders. This case study follows Sarah through the process of creating the WBS for her project.

You can assume that Sarah already has the inputs to the WBS, such as the project scope statement and scope management plan (to ensure she and her team understand the project deliverables); organizational assets such as policies, procedures, guidelines, and historical data from other projects; and approved change requests (to ensure that she and her team understand any previously approved changes to the project scope).

The first step Sarah took was to convene a WBS meeting with her project team. Her project team consisted of individuals from sales, marketing, IT, and manufacturing.

Sarah explained to her team that the purpose of the meeting was to create an initial work breakdown structure to represent all of the deliverables the project scope promised. Her goal in the meeting was to determine the major categories of deliverables within the project.

Her team determined this project had six major categories of deliverables:

- ✔ Web deliverables
- ✔ Database deliverables
- ✔ E-commerce deliverables
- ✔ Marketing deliverables
- ✔ Manufacturing deliverables
- ✔ Project management deliverables

These six categories captured all of the things that Sarah and her project team would create. Notice that one of the categories included is project management deliverables; this is important because it required Sarah to create documents, estimates, and communications to inform future project managers and enable them to do their work better. The project management deliverables were intended as future historical information.

When creating her WBS, Sarah wanted to use a numbering system called the Code of

Accounts to identify each element within the WBS. Sarah dubbed her project WEBSALES 101 and created a numbering system that followed the schema of W101.

Sarah had Brian Walker, a project team member, plot out six sticky notes across the wall. Each note reflected one of the major deliverables with the numbering schema. Next Sarah and her team began to decompose the major deliverables into smaller components. As the team formed consensus on each deliverable, Brian arranged another sticky note under the appropriate category. Here's what their WBS components looked like at this point:

```
W101.1: Web deliverables
    W101.1.1: User interface
    W101.1.2: Online product
    catalog
    W101.1.3: Java programs
    W101.1.4: Web menus
    W101.1.5: Forms
W101.2: Database deliverables
    W101.2.1: SQL Servers
    W101.2.2: Product
    databases
    W101.2.3: Manufacturing
    databases
    W101.2.4: Security
    measures
W101.3: E-commerce
    deliverables
    W101.3.1: Shopping carts
    W101.3.2: Merchant
    accounts
    W101.3.3: Security
    measures
W101.4: Marketing
    deliverables
    W101.4.1: Verbiage for Web
    content
```

```
    W101.4.2: Photos and
    graphics for online
    catalog
    W101.4.3: Promotion
    schedule
W101.5: Manufacturing
    deliverables
    W101.5.1: Schedule of
    material creation
    W101.5.2: Historical
    information of past
    production output
    W101.5.3: Profit margin
    for materials
W101.6: Project management
    deliverables
    W101.6.1: Project
    management plans
    W101.6.2: Project
    calendars
    W101.6.3: Contracts
    W101.6.4: Lessons learned
    documentation
```

With the WBS beginning to take form, Sarah and the team decomposed the deliverables again. Sarah's project team followed the 8/80 Rule: The smallest item in the WBS should equate to no less than 8 hours of labor and no more than 80 hours of labor to create. Through rounds of decomposition, the project team was able to create a robust WBS that depicted all of the project deliverables.

After the WBS was created with the project team, Sarah moved the WBS from sticky notes into her project management information system (PMIS). Sarah continued the development of the WBS to include a WBS Dictionary so she and the project team could reference details on each of the project deliverables and time and cost estimates.

Part II
Planning Your Software Project

The 5th Wave   By Rich Tennant

"This isn't a quantitative or a qualitative estimate of the job. This is a 'wish-upon-a-star' estimate of the project."

In this part . . .

Part II presents the core of software project management. You discover how to recruit key team members, who will form a hard-working, synergetic team, and how to create essential plans for communication management, risk management, and quality assurance. In this part, you get special tips that enable you to keep your project on schedule, and keep that budget from becoming a bloated mess.

Chapter 4

Planning for Communications

According to the kind-hearted folks at the Project Management Institute, project managers spend 90 percent of their time communicating. That hardly leaves time for coffee breaks.

But if you think about it, isn't that what you're doing as a project manager? No, not taking coffee breaks all day, but communicating. You constantly take calls from stakeholders, visit your project team members, participate in project status meetings, zip off e-mails, and more. We imagine even your coveted coffee breaks actually center on communications.

Communication, both verbal and nonverbal, drives what project managers do. In fact, effective communication drives just about every aspect of a project manager's activities. Likewise, ineffective communication can have disastrous effects. Ever have a misunderstanding about the requirements of a project? Ever show up for a meeting and be the only one there because you misunderstood the start time? Ever create an in-depth proposal when the stakeholder actually just wanted a short memo about whether the software could do a specific action? Poor communication costs time and money and causes headaches.

Communication skills aren't easy to cultivate. If they were, everyone would communicate brilliantly and we'd live in a world free of misunderstandings. However, there are specific strategies that you can employ if communication isn't your forte.

The Importance of Communicating Effectively

Effective communication occurs when a clear transfer of knowledge exists between you and at least one other person. You have an idea and the other person, through your conversation, gets what you're after. You get an e-mail and you understand what the stakeholder wants. You facilitate a project meeting and your project team follows your agenda, the information is presented, and everyone is in synch on what to do next.

Clear and accurate communication within your project team is vital to a project's success. Why? Software project management is labor intensive. Even though the project team is doing the actual coding, development, testing, and compiling of the software, as the project manager *you're* the one ensuring that the work is done according to the project scope and within budget, while also meeting project deadlines.

In software project management you must be able to communicate with the project team about many important things, including

- ✔ Changes in the technology
- ✔ Nuances of the software being created
- ✔ Demands being made by the customer

You and the project team must have a clear understanding about what the project is creating, the demands of the project stakeholders, and your expectations about the project deliverables. If a communication breakdown occurs, it'll compound issues, and no one, especially you, will be happy.

Ensuring accurate communication

Everyone, from members of the project team to project stakeholders, must communicate openly and accurately. Unless you facilitate each conversation with a mission to understand exactly what the person speaking is trying to convey, you're facing a potential communication meltdown. So how do you ensure accurate communication? Here are some tips:

- ✔ **Document your conversations in e-mails, memos, or meeting minutes.** If you put the conversation points in writing, the party with whom you're communicating has an opportunity to clarify various points if there are any misunderstandings.

- ✔ **Sign where the line is dotted.** Signing where the line is dotted means that you and the other party have a deal. Throughout your project you'll be faced with demands for the project customers, key stakeholders, and even your project sponsor. When you and the other party reach an agreement on any issue, you should document the issue, document the resolution, and then make sure that both parties sign off on the document. Here are some typical things you and the project sponsor or project customer both need to sign:

- **Scope statement:** This document defines all the parameters of the project work — and *only* the project work — needed to satisfy the stakeholders' objectives.

- **Scope changes:** Any changes to the scope that are approved or declined should be signed by you and the requesting party. We talk more about incorporating changes into the project in Chapter 13.

- **Budget:** You and the project sponsor both need to sign off on the budget for the project. Signing off acknowledges the budget and any range of variances that may be permitted. We talk about creating and managing a project budget in Chapter 9.

- **Schedule:** The project schedule must be signed by the project manager and the project sponsor. Agreement on the schedule is essential for acknowledging the project resources, identifying when the resources will be needed, and showing when the project work will be completed. You can find out all about scheduling in Chapter 8.

✔ **Document scope, time, or cost compromises.** As your project progresses, you'll have issues, delays, problems with vendors, problems with your project team, and more excitement. For each of these issues, you're likely to arrive at some compromise to find a solution. Document these solutions so you don't face repercussions downstream in the project.

✔ **Take minutes.** No one, at least no one we've met, likes to take minutes at meetings. But we've met plenty of project managers who wish they had taken better notes. Minutes document the business of the meeting,

- Making people accountable for what they promise.

- Prompting team members to follow through. If the participants know that their words and promises are being documented, they're more likely to follow through.

- Making it easier to recall what was discussed in meetings weeks, months, or even years later.

Hate taking minutes as much as we do? Here's a solution: Delegate this task. Better yet, rotate the task among the team. By forcing others to take minutes, you not only save yourself from the task, but you also build team ownership.

✔ **Set an agenda.** You should create an agenda before every meeting that you're facilitating. An agenda sets the direction of the meeting and prevents other nonrelevant issues from creeping into the discussion. An agenda also helps you and the project team prepare for the meeting by bringing the appropriate files, status reports, and other pertinent information. Agendas are a must.

How not to communicate

You can do more damage by communicating ineffectively than by not communicating at all. If a project team member misunderstands your solution to a problem on the project, he or she may go happily off to work on a task that you had no intention of completing at this point in the project — or even at all.

The key to successful communication is to be clear. Face-to-face communication gives you a distinct advantage over e-mails and phone calls: nonverbal communications. That's right. Sometimes what you *don't* say is important too. Phone calls and e-mails can save tons of time when it comes to project management, but they also have their drawbacks.

I'm sure you've heard of people making a little wise crack in an e-mail message only to have the joke taken seriously. Or the folks that fade in and out of phone conversations (putting you on hold while they perform other tasks) that promise to deliver such-and-such but they miss out on what it is they're supposed to be delivering.

And then there's grammar. You don't have to be John Steinbeck to be a good project manager, but you should know that errors in your writing can amplify problems beyond your imagination. Consider the following e-mail that a project manager sent to his project team member:

> Linda,
>
> I need a project team member who knows what Java is all about. You are smart, talented, on time, and savvy. Team members who are not like you admit to knowing nothing about Java. Our project is horrible when you're away. This project is going great.
>
> Best,
>
> Your favorite Project Manager

Linda sounds pretty good, eh? But what if the project manager's writing was so awful that he actually meant to tell Linda this instead:

> Linda,
>
> I need a project team member who knows what Java is. All about you are smart, talented, on time, and savvy team members who are not like you. Admit to knowing nothing about Java! Our project is horrible. When you're away, this project is going great.
>
> Best,
>
> Your favorite Project Manager

Uh, Linda doesn't seem quite as great now, does she? But imagine Linda's response when she reads the first e-mail versus the second. While we admit that this is an exaggerated example, you can't deny that poor communication includes poor writing.

Here's what you can do:

✔ Take time to proofread and edit your e-mails before sending them out to the world.

✔ If you're not much of a writer, try to keep your missives short and simple.

✔ Only send e-mail when you absolutely have to or if no other form of communication will work.

✔ Never put into an e-mail what you wouldn't say to someone's face. Performance evaluations — even compliments — should always be communicated verbally.

If you're interested in more information about face-to-face communication, especially when discussing bad news, check out Chapter 15.

Care and Feeding of Nerds

We have a theory when it comes to programmers: They're not nerds, so don't treat them that way. Programmers are a different breed, but they're not the stereotypical mutant pocket protector geeks that project managers may imagine them to be. Here's what you need to realize when it comes to programmers:

✔ **They are smart people.** They take the vision of what the software should be and then string lines of code together to achieve that vision. Don't treat them as imbeciles, and they'll reciprocate.

✔ **They are creative.** If you've ever peeked over the shoulder of a programmer to see what he or she was doing, you probably saw lines of text that didn't make much sense. (You probably also drove the programmer nuts by shoulder surfing.) Programmers take nothing and make something — that's creativity. Respect what they do and they'll do the same for you.

✔ **They can understand intangible things.** It's software. You can't touch, smell, taste, or feel it. Software is, after all, a tool for talking to a computer to get the computer to do what you want it to do. Programmers understand this concept and they may assume that you do, too. Understand that they think logically and use deductive reasoning to get to a solution, even though they understand concepts you can't conceive.

✔ **They often communicate in absolutes.** Programmers, at least the ones we've worked with, look at issues as easy-to-solve bugs or impossible-to-beat eight-headed monsters. Programmers have a tendency to go to a solution immediately or not at all. They may need your careful, humble guidance to get to a solution.

✔ **They are proud of their work.** If you've ever been critical of a programmer's work, you may have noticed his or her immediate defense of the work, an explanation of why you're wrong, or even teary eyes. No joke. Programmers, skilled or not, are proud of their creations, and some consider every line of code a work of genius. First, be certain that you and the programmers are clear on the objectives of the project work. Second, use kid gloves if you have to constructively criticize their work.

✔ **They're often in demand.** It's a good feeling to have lots of folks wanting your attention, your time, even your employment. But this is a dangerous spot for a software project manager to be in. Usually, you want to keep your project team members from bailing in the middle of a project. Stress to the programmers how much you need them, and how you're proud of the progress they're making. But don't go overboard — you won't come across as genuine.

TIP

Taking charge with programmers

If you want to communicate with a programmer, you have to take charge. Programmers are a tricky bunch sometimes. But you, not the programmer, are in charge of the project. Although the programmer is in charge of a large portion of the project *work,* you're the one responsible if the project fails.

You must establish dominance without being too aggressive. Establish five things through your early communications:

✔ **Leadership:** Leadership is focused on motivating, aligning objectives, and moving your project team to a destination. Assume that you're leading the project and that your project team will follow.

✔ **Management:** Management is focused on getting results. As a project manager, your core focus is on getting the project successfully completed. Management of a group of programmers means you must see results.

✔ **Discipline:** When your programmers aren't getting their work done as promised, don't hesitate to discipline according to your human resources guidelines.

Be careful about making snap judgments, thought. First, find out why they aren't completing the work. Were your instructions unclear? Was there a miscommunication on your end? The problem could be yours and not the programmers'.

✔ **Organization:** Your ability to communicate, lead, manage, and discipline your project team centers on your organizational skills. Be organized and your project team will respect you for having everything on the ball.

✔ **Balance:** In all your decisions you must be fair. Your team of programmers will respect you even more if you show balance and fairness in all of your work assignments and disciplinary actions. Don't play favorites.

Avoiding Communication Breakdowns

Larger projects require more detail than smaller projects. Larger projects, of course, have more stakeholders because of the size and scope of the project.

We know, we know. That's like saying it'll take a long time to swim to Hawaii. The point we're making is that the larger the project, the larger the opportunity for failure. The larger the project, the more demands you have on your time for planning, controlling, and ensuring that the project is executed as planned. And the larger the project, the tougher it is to communicate effectively, and the more critical it is to communicate effectively.

We know because we've been there. One of the largest projects Joe ever managed was the development of an e-mail interface for nearly 40,000 users worldwide. The project involved directors twice Joe's age and income, programmers from around the world, and stakeholders that Joe had never met face to face. In addition to the development, testing, and rollout of the new application, Joe had to coordinate all the training materials, training classes, dual support, and interoperability of two systems over six months. Joe also had to handle all the logistics of testing, versioning, and making hot fixes. It was the most fun Joe ever had on a project — really! Communication was a crucial element that held everything together, and so was a good attitude. But he also discovered that he would have done a few things differently, especially in the area of communication.

Facing the risks of communication meltdowns

The risk of a communication breakdown is that problems that could have been easily solved haunt your project. Here are some risks of miscommunication, in order of severity, along with possible solutions:

✔ **Problem: Wasted time.** You kill hours every day answering the same question over and over and over. It'll drive you mad. At least, it drives us crazy, and because we're writing the book, we've listed it here at the top of the list.

   Solution: Take the time to communicate your plans with the stakeholders and then make those plans available through a Web site. You can save so much time if you use the technological tools available to you. We recommend creating an FAQ *(frequently asked questions)* for your project and posting it on a project Web site. Include the Web address of the FAQ as part of every e-mail you send. When folks ask the same old question, answer the e-mail by directing them to the FAQ for a whole list of project questions and answers. Add new questions and answers to the FAQ as they arise.

✔ **Problem: Wasted money.** Of course when you waste time you're going to be wasting dollars, but this fact also translates to your programmers. Software creation is time intensive; if the programmers on the project team are creating the wrong stuff based on miscommunications, you're not going to be happy. You might as well throw money in the gutter — it's essentially what you do when programmers waste time on useless code and have to start over.

Solution: Require the programmers to e-mail you weekly status reports that include "accomplishments for the week." Hold regularly scheduled team meetings with a standing agenda item of progress and issues.

Over time, lost time and money have a negative impact on programmers' morale, confidence in you as a project manager, and desire for accuracy. When people race to meet deadlines, they make mistakes.

✔ **Problem: Frustration.** Communication breakdowns, whether they're your fault or not, frustrate you, your project team, stakeholders, and the end users. When these people get frustrated, they're going to vent, steam, and grumble about the project. This, of course, leads to more complaints, gripes, and general unrest.

Solution: You can never completely stamp out frustration, but you can manage it. Be proactive by being aware of morale problems and frustrations before they get out of hand. Never assume that people will just get over whatever issue they may have. If you see a problem, address it immediately so that mole hills don't become mountains.

✔ **Problem: Lack of confidence.** When a stakeholder sees that you've directed your team to do something that's not included in the project, or you've directed the team to leave something out of the software that should be included, the stakeholder won't be pleased. But, perhaps more importantly, he or she will begin to wonder whether you're capable of completing the project according to specs. Clients wonder whether you've made this mistake because you can't stand up and tell team members what they're doing wrong or whether you're afraid of hard work. Maybe they wonder whether a miscommunication is the source. We don't know all the things they worry about, but we do know this — they always wonder what other mistakes are lurking in the software.

✔ **Solution:** Demonstrate your leadership skills by taking accountability for your miscommunication. Swiftly step in to perform damage control and rectify the situation. The specific steps you take will depend on the severity of the problem.

Managing communications across the enterprise

In the massive project we discuss in "Avoiding Communication Breakdowns," the communication between key stakeholders was planned in depth for months. Where the project broke down was when the project team began to roll out the software to pilot groups around the world. The end users of the software had gotten swept into an undercurrent of rumors and speculation.

The failure in communication was that, as the project manager, Joe had neglected to consider the impact of the software on the end users. Everyday users knew the change was coming, but they didn't understand what the change meant for them. As a result, they gossiped, spread rumors, and were generally filled with anxiety. Additionally, the sheer size of the project left Joe with a daily flood of e-mail and voicemail that slowed progress. Joe had never planned how he was going to squelch the cultural achievability issues of the software among members of the organization.

Communication can break down anywhere in the process and with any segment of people involved in the project. Never underestimate the importance of communication, even with those people you don't have direct contact with. Ensure that you have strong communication throughout the project to *all* the stakeholders that are affected.

Here's what you can do to avoid the problems we've dealt with:

- ✔ **Educate end users about the changing software and take steps to ensure that they understand what's coming to them.** End users always need to know how the software is going to change their day-to-day job functions.

  Sure, your project team may do a fantastic job creating, distributing, and training the organization on your software creation, but you have to get buy-in if you want to avoid headaches.

- ✔ **Maintain proper communication levels.** In a large project you can easily fall victim to a common phenomenon of focusing all your attention on the key stakeholders. But you must take extra measure to communicate to all of the appropriate stakeholders as the project moves towards completion. Figure 4-1 shows the typical curve of communication in an average project.

  The traditional curve represents all the communication that happens at the beginning of the project: the project charter, the kickoff meeting, the scope management plan, and the stakeholder analysis. And then you and the team disappear to plan, control, and execute. And what happens? The focus is on doing the work and not communications — until the project nears completion as represented at the end of the curve. Oh, the end is near, so excitement (or panic) drives the communication.

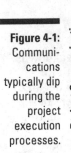

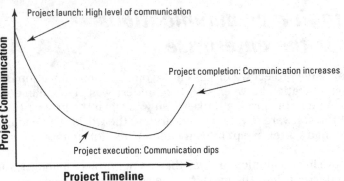

Figure 4-1:
Communications typically dip during the project execution processes.

The ideal communication curve is depicted in Figure 4-2. Communication is high at the beginning of the project, dips slightly as the project team does the work, peaks at evenly timed increments for status reports, and then begins to increase as the project nears completion. Of course, this pattern looks logical on paper, but without a dedicated effort, it's difficult to implement out there in the real world.

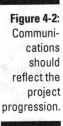

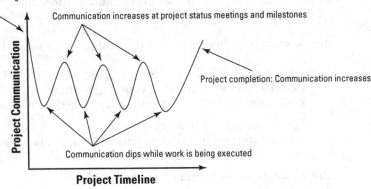

Figure 4-2:
Communications should reflect the project progression.

Calculating the Communication Channels

You can get a precise (and often scary) picture of the communication difficulties you face by applying a simple equation to your next software project. This equation gives you the number of communication channels for your project. The equation is

```
N(N-1) ÷ 2
```

with N representing the number of stakeholders working on the project. It represents a vast network of communications that can quickly sprout up between stakeholders, even working on a relatively small project. It's *huge*.

You might wonder why you're supposed to divide by two. Good question. We wish we could give you an answer, but no one's ever told us. This is a generally accepted calculation to determine the number of communication channels.

Pretend that you're the project manager of a new Web design project. Your project team is hired to create a Web site for another company to help the company sell more of its specialty product: camera filters. Here are the major things that the client would like the Web site to do:

✔ Present a professional image of the organization

✔ Enable photographers to search for filters for their cameras

✔ Enable customers to place and pay for orders

✔ Enable customers to upload digital images and to test the effects of the various filters your client sells

✔ Enable photographers to create a free photo album displaying their work

✔ Offer a database of sample photographs for customers to search and explore based on different conditions such as lighting, subject, and camera type

✔ Provide an ongoing series of articles about photography, which users can search by topic

✔ Keep a database of users for repeat business

This is a big software project. Your internal project team includes eight programmers and three Oracle database administrators. Your client brings in several outside stakeholders that you have to work with. Here's a quick list of the key stakeholders involved in the project:

✔ Nancy Martin, VP of Sales.

✔ Mika Walton, VP of Operations.

✔ Jerry Dehority, Director of Order Fulfillment.

✔ Ken Bell, Director of Sales.

✔ Joan Bell, Director of Manufacturing.

✔ Eight people from Creativity Plus — an advertising agency that will provide the design for the front end of the Web site.

✔ Four freelance photographers who will provide sample photos for Web design purposes.

✔ 24 freelance photography writers (each contracted to write five initial articles on different photography topics).

✔ 120 test users from around the world who will test the Web site and your software at staged releases over the next six months. You only have to communicate with these folks through surveys and follow-up communications based on their testing.

Guess how many stakeholders are in this project. Okay, don't guess; you have, including you, your boss, the project sponsor, and the 11 programmers and database administrators on your team, 174 stakeholders. You'll have lots of communication with 54 of those 174 stakeholders because you won't be communicating directly to the 120 test users (174 – 120 = 54 stakeholders). Using the formula to determine the number of communication channels, you end up with

```
N(N-1) ÷ 2

54(54-1) ÷ 2

54 (53) ÷ 2 = 1,431 communication channels
```

This project will take lots of coordination among all these stakeholders.

Now for something scary: There are 1,431 communication channels in this project. That's right, 1,431 opportunities for miscommunication, lack of communication, and general breakdown because of poor communication. Figure 4-3 shows the magic formula used to determine how many communication channels a project has.

Figure 4-3: Use this formula to calculate the communication channels.

$$N = \text{number of stakeholders} \quad \frac{N(N)-1}{2}$$

$$52 \text{ stakeholders} \quad \frac{54(54)-1}{2}$$

$$1,431 \text{ communication channels} \quad \frac{2,862}{2} = 1,431$$

This formula shows N as the number of key stakeholders. In this case, N = 54. At any given time, each and every member of this group can chat with 53 other people involved in the project, get off track on the project, submit change requests, gossip, put words in your mouth, and all the other nasty things that happen when a project manager doesn't plan appropriately for communication.

Large projects mean more demands on your time for communication. If you ignore your responsibility to communicate, others will do it for you. And most likely, it won't be the kind of communication you call productive. Because you're the one developing the communication management plans for your software project, you need to outline the specific plans for stakeholders to communicate.

If you fail to communicate, someone else will do it for you. Honest.

Building an Effective Communication Management Plan

In order to communicate effectively you have to plan. Every organization that wants to take project management seriously should create a *communication management plan.* This plan documents all of the communication demands within the project. Sure, the bulk of this plan may consist of boilerplate information, but it should define the specifics of each project and the communication expectations of the key stakeholders.

If you don't have a communication management plan, you're setting yourself and the project up for failure. The key to communication is to communicate effectively, so you need to create a plan that defines how and when communication should occur. We've consulted with some organizations and seen managers initially roll their eyes at the concept of using a communication plan. And then, after their projects continue to nose dive, we've seen the change in their attitudes. Inevitably, someone says, "A-ha! We need a communication management plan." We're not saying that this plan is the silver bullet for project success, but it's better than a kick in the knee.

Knowing the six things every communication plan needs

If you want to take the concept of the communication management plan and run with it, which we urge you to do, it can be an overwhelming task — especially if you've never created one before. Don't worry; the communication management plan can evolve just as your project management approach evolves. For starters, you want to create a plan that accomplishes some basic goals for effective communication.

Here are six demands that your communication management plan makes:

- **Communication explanation:** The communication documents are reports, e-mails, or scheduled meetings that you need. They may not be documents only, however; communication at meetings (such as status meetings) counts, too.

- **Purpose:** For each communication document you list in your plan, you need a brief explanation of the document's or meeting's purpose. You want to answer why the communication is needed and under what conditions.

- **Frequency:** By writing down the expectations, you ensure that all stakeholders understand how often communication is needed.

  Defining when milestones are due is essential to the process because you can measure the accuracy of the cost and time baselines to date, and the overall project status.

- You may also want to set up *conditional reporting* to establish that when specified conditions are met, individuals should report accordingly. Some examples of conditional reporting include cost and schedule variance reports, team member performance reports, risk activities, and change requests.

- **Modality:** The modality is the format for the communication pieces. Some stakeholders may expect a paper status report, while other information, such as schedule updates, may be preferred via e-mail. There's no right or wrong way to present information, but the preferences and reasons for the modality have to be documented in your plan.

  For example, you may request that your project team members complete a weekly status report of their assignments in a Microsoft Word form and e-mail it to you. But (and here's the rub), at each project status meeting the team members should bring the Word document in hard copy so they can use it to verbally review their progress. To save your sanity, you have each team member submit status reports prior to the meeting so you have all the reports at the status meeting. And it's all documented in your plan. Ingenious!

- **Duration:** Not all stakeholders need project information throughout the entire project — you don't want to bog people down with information that's not relevant to them. The duration defines how long, and when, the stakeholders will need to participate in project communications. For example, a contracted network engineer may be involved in your project for three months at the end of the project. This engineer doesn't need or want tons of information before his or her involvement begins.

- **Responsibility:** One common misunderstanding is that the project manager is responsible for every piece of communication. That's just not true. The project manager is responsible to ensure that communication takes place, but you can't be responsible for the actual communicating.

For example, if you contract a network engineer, chances are good that that person needs to communicate with your senior programmers. Those people need to communicate with one another — not to you. Sure, sure, you'll introduce them and facilitate the initial meeting, but it's their responsibility to communicate to each other. This portion of the project plan helps define that responsibility.

A good plan also establishes the escalation of authority. When issues can't get resolved by the project team, even with your intervention, everyone should know who is next in line to tackle the issue. By establishing this methodology up front, you ensure that everyone knows who to talk to next without circumventing anyone's authority.

You also need to set up some directions for updating the plan. No plan is perfect, so you must build in an opportunity to fine-tune the communication management plan as the project progresses or as the organization matures in its project model.

The communication responsibility matrix: Determining who communicates to whom

Establishing responsibility in communication is crucial. Of course, it sounds great on paper, but everyone knows how difficult this aspect of group dynamics can be. How do you know who needs to communicate to whom? How can you possibly know that Jan, the Java guru, needs to speak with Nat the Network Engineer? You ask.

Creating a communication management plan is not a solo activity. You cannot — *must not* — plan this part alone. Your project team is involved in the process. In Chapter 3 we talk about creating the WBS, or work breakdown structure. When you create the WBS, you have an ideal opportunity to also document which stakeholders need to talk to whom.

You do this by creating a communication responsibility matrix. This is just a fancy table with all the stakeholders and a marker to represent if they need to talk with one another. This matrix can then help you follow through on what information needs to be communicated and by whom in your communication management plan.

The first step in creating a communication responsibility matrix is to list all of the stakeholders in a table. Whenever two stakeholders need to communicate with each other, simply mark the intersection of the two stakeholders with an X in the table. Table 4-1 shows you a sample.

Table 4-1	Sample Communication Responsibility Matrix				
Stakeholders	Java Jan	Network Ned	Contractor Chuck	C# Chaz	PM Gayle
Java Jan		X	X	X	X
Network Ned	X			X	X
Contractor Chuck	X				X
C# Chaz	X	X			X
PM Gayle	X	X	X	X	

Setting up ten-minute meetings

Because software projects are labor intensive, it's not to anyone's advantage to talk issues to death. Still, there must be a steady stream of communication between you and the project team. Without an open and trusting channel of communication, you and your project team may develop an us-against-them relationship. Make yourself available and encourage your project team to come to you with problems or issues that they can't solve on their own.

If you want to be successful in software project management, and we know you do, then you must create a plan on how you will communicate on a regular basis with your project team.

One approach that works well in software project management is the daily task meeting. The agenda of this meeting is simple and requires participants to answer just three questions:

✔ What did you get done yesterday?

✔ What must you get done today?

✔ What issues or problems are preventing the project from moving forward?

Ideally, this meeting lasts only 10 to 15 minutes, happens every morning, and involves only the project team. There's no real need for other stakeholders to be in this initial get-up-and-go meeting. The point is to communicate with one another what's been done and what's remaining to do in small increments. It also gives you an opportunity to learn of any issues or red flags.

Fascinating facts about communication

Whenever people communicate, whether in speech or in writing, the flow of communication follows a model:

1. The sender sends the message.

2. The encoder encodes the message, either with spoken and nonverbal cues or in a written form.

   The medium (telephone, e-mail, at the head of the conference table) is the means of transport.

3. The decoder decodes the message back into useable format, either by reading your e-mail or interpreting your verbal and nonverbal cues.

   At the end of this process, the receiver receives the message.

If, at any point, a breakdown in communication occurs, the receiver won't get the message that was actually sent. Perfecting communication is a lifelong practice, and we're not just talking about writing skills and grammar.

When you were a kid, did your mom ever tell you that it's not what you say, but how you say it, that matters? She was right, you know. *Paralinguistics* is the study of the pitch and tone of voice — all the features besides the words — that affect the message's effectiveness. For example, if you say something that's meant to be encouraging but your tone of voice is staccato, you may not have the same impact that you would if your tone was even and low.

Another idea that your mom may have pointed out to you is *body language.* Your posture, facial expression, eye contact, and hand gestures reveal what you're thinking when you're speaking or when you're listening to someone else's message. In fact, 55 percent of all communication is nonverbal, which, if you think about it, makes sense. You don't speak all the time in a

conversation. You nod your head yes or no, smile, frown, cross your arms, and use expressions and gestures to drive your point home — or to tell the person speaking how you really feel about what they're conveying. In a sense, what you don't say (but what you reveal with your body language) is just as meaningful as what you say and how you say it.

Nonverbal communication is so important, but you often lose out on opportunities to practice effective listening and visual cues when you communicate by phone, instant messaging, *texting* (text messaging), or e-mail. You can't see the other person to determine if they understand your message during the conversation. Any conversation that is not face to face suffers from a lack of nonverbal information.

When you speak up during a conversation and ask questions, you're being an *active listener.* It's important for you and your project team to be active listeners — otherwise you may make assumptions. Making a bad assumption because of miscommunication is bad, bad news.

As a speaker, you have to ask for *feedback,* especially if people aren't actively asking for clarification. Asking for feedback encourages active listening because it requires your audience to confirm that your message has been received and understood. To be effective, you should do more than just ask, "Okay, anyone have a question?" You need to ask the participants specific questions about what you've just told them so that you can confirm that they understand your message. For example, you might ask, "Susan, how will you interface the Oracle server with the existing AS/400 servers?"

This specific question makes Susan think about what you've been discussing and it confirms that she's with you on the conversation. If she's not, your question will give her the opportunity to clarify the problem.

Defining Who Needs What Information

Every organization is broken down into three distinct layers, as Figure 4-4 demonstrates. Each layer has its own project objectives with various communication needs:

- ✔ **Executive:** Executives set the vision for the organization.

- ✔ **Functional management:** Managers determine the functions, tactics, and strategies for the entities within the organization.

- ✔ **Operations:** The workers perform activities to support the endeavors of the organization, satisfying the tactics set up by functional management, and supporting the vision of the organization, set up by the executives.

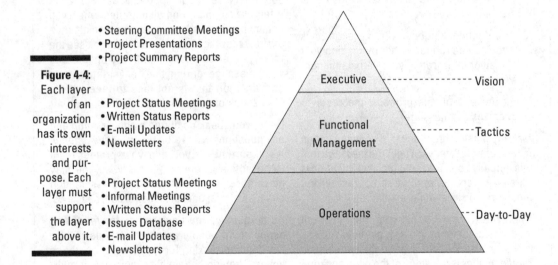

- Steering Committee Meetings
- Project Presentations
- Project Summary Reports

Figure 4-4:
Each layer
of an
organization
has its own
interests
and pur-
pose. Each
layer must
support
the layer
above it.

- Project Status Meetings
- Written Status Reports
- E-mail Updates
- Newsletters

- Project Status Meetings
- Informal Meetings
- Written Status Reports
- Issues Database
- E-mail Updates
- Newsletters

As a project manager, you have to communicate with each layer of an organization, as well as with individuals and groups outside of the organization. As a software project manager, you have to translate technical info from the operational level so that managers and executives can track the project's progress. At every level of this pyramid, the terminology you use must be clear and relevant.

What executives want to hear

Two attributes affect your interaction with executives: the size of the company and the scope of the project. In a smaller organization you may communicate daily with the executives. Heck, you may even be an executive in the company.

In a larger company, you probably won't rub shoulders often with the president or CEO very often. Your interactions may be limited to an occasional briefing; the CEO may attend a kickoff meeting. If the project is large enough, you may do periodic status reports for executives.

Large projects in larger companies have a direct impact on a company's operating expenses, cash flow, and predicted profitability, so the success of a project may be closer to a CEO's heart than you imagine.

Here are some general guidelines for talking with executives:

- ✔ **Keep it simple and quick.** Executives want to hear what's happening with a project, but they don't want all the details, and they don't want to spend a lot of time. Don't belabor anything; say what you need to say and move on. These are busy people and they want summations. If they want or need more detail they'll let you know.

- ✔ **Follow your plan.** Your communication to executives may also be controlled by the flow of communications as described in your communication management plan. It may not be your place at all to discuss the project with the executives unless they ask you for information directly. Always follow the flow of communication just as you'd expect your project team to do.

- ✔ **Be direct.** When you speak with executives about your project, you want to be, as with everyone you communicate with, direct. If the project's going great, tell 'em. If the project is bleeding cash, let 'em know. Don't sugarcoat anything. Chances are executives will have heard bad news already from the functional layer of the company.

- ✔ **Set up project summary reports as needed.** Your communication management plan should define what types of reports executives receive, if any. Some organizations require project managers to complete *project summary* reports or dashboards, one-page snapshots of a project's health. These reports summarize

  - A project's scope

  - The impact of the project

  - The cost variance of the project

  - The schedule variance of the project

  - Milestones achieved and pending

What functional managers need to hear

In the middle of the organizational pyramid you find functional management. Functional management, also known as good ol' middle management, focuses on directing operations. This layer of your company contains the managers, vice presidents, and directors that schedule, manage people, and make decisions that affect a project manager's sanity.

Basically, managers want to know how your project affects them. Managers often have their employees on your project team. They want to know

- ✔ When you'll need their resources to work on your project
- ✔ How their resources will contribute to your project
- ✔ How their employees are performing on the project
- ✔ Whether your project is performing to expectations

You may often complete projects for functional management. In these instances, managers are stakeholders and want to focus on project performance. Your communication in these instances centers on

- ✔ Overall project performance
- ✔ Milestone reporting
- ✔ Cost variances
- ✔ Schedule variances
- ✔ Scope verification

Depending on their role in your project, their power over you in the organization, and whether they have team members participating in your project, individual managers affect how and what you communicate with them.

The overall theme for communicating with functional managers is performance. Focus on communicating the performance of the project (if you're completing the project for them), or the performance of the project team if their employees are working on your project.

What your project team needs to hear

Your software project team is comprised of programmers, of course. Programmers need to hear the information that relates to them. They don't need fancy statistics and reports that you'll give to management and executives. They need relevant, applicable communication to help them do their job better.

Here's what programmers must hear from you:

- ✔ **What activities are pending:** You need to let them know what work is pending and where the project should be at this point in time.
- ✔ **What activities are lagging:** You must address issues with your project team when they are late. We all get behind from time to time, and without

someone (namely you) urging programmers back to duty, activities will continue to slide, and your project won't be completed on time.

✔ **What risks are looming:** You need to track risks that are in play or pending in the project and keep the project team informed. Risks are any events or conditions that can threaten a project's ability to succeed. Chapter 5 covers risks in detail.

✔ **What issues are being resolved:** Throughout your project, issues may pop up to wreak havoc. Some issues include the quality of the project work and complaints from customers. You must address these problems by communicating them to the people who have the power to fix them. You can't hide under your desk and hope that the problems will just go away. They won't. Besides, under you desk isn't really that comfy.

✔ **Recognition:** When your project team members are doing a good job, give them kudos. Sometimes it's appropriate to mention a job well done to a team member in private, but usually public recognition of a significant accomplishment is the best action.

What you need to hear

Every project is different — especially when it comes to developing software, but there are some common themes you need to hear from your stakeholders. Here's the stuff you need to hear:

✔ **Progress:** Your staff needs to trust you enough to report honest assessments on their work so you can get a heartbeat on the project progress. You'll be able to inspect the progress of the project and get an actual assessment of progress, but you simply won't have time to double-check your project team's progress every day.

✔ **Issues:** Your project team sees the issues and problems in the project work before you do. You must establish confidence in the project team to report these issues so that you can document them, help them address the problems, and keep the project moving forward.

✔ **Risks:** Risk identification is an iterative process. Your project team is closest to the work, so your programmers will identify risks that affect the project before you.

Some project team members may feel as if they're letting you down if they tell you about pending or new risks they've identified. Encourage them to share discovered risks so you and the team can deal with them.

✔ **Change orders:** Instruct your team and the stakeholders on the proper method to ask for changes to the project scope. Your project team should not be doing changes on the fly, and all change requests should flow through you so can determine their validity and then catalog your decisions. Read Chapter 13 for more detailed information on change management.

✔ **Encouragement and recognition:** You need some encouragement. Your stakeholders, project team, and project sponsor, may not realize this. It's hard to ask for encouragement and recognition, but you can ask stakeholders whether they're satisfied with the project. If they say yes, thank them and count that as your encouragement.

Defining When Communication Is Needed

Perhaps the most effective communication in a project is ad-hoc communication. You know, when Bob the Oracle expert pops into your office to ask a quick question. Or your project sponsor catches you in the elevator and asks for a quick rap on how the project's going. Or your project team is situated close together so they can solve problems and discuss project issues.

But not all communications can happen unannounced. There must be an element of planning, as defined in the communication management plan.

Creating a communication schedule

Although communicating through ad-hoc meetings is important, scheduling time to communicate is just as crucial. A communication schedule defines when you, your project team, project sponsor, and key stakeholders will need to communicate with each other.

The first thing you'll want to schedule is how often you and the project team meet. If you choose to go with the daily morning meeting to discuss project status and the day's work, then you'll want to schedule this on your calendar for the duration of the project. If you're more apt to meet weekly, go ahead and make a weekly appointment for the status meeting. The point we want you to get is that if you don't schedule your status meetings well in advance, other activities, meetings, and events will crowd your calendar, and your meetings will slip.

Your organization may also require you to complete weekly or monthly status reports to track the project progress. Go ahead and schedule this business as well. You know you won't forget to complete your obligations by keeping tabs on when the information is needed.

You will also want to schedule a few other odds and ends in your calendar:

- ✔ **Team member performance reviews:** On a short-term project, you may save the reviews for the project closeout only. On a project with a longer duration, schedule performance reviews throughout the project. Set up quarterly reviews or do one every six months. Be sure to follow your organization's HR policies as they may specify how often a performance review is to occur. If the project team recognizes that you'll be reviewing their work, and knows when the review is slated to take place, as well as who will receive a copy of the review, you will see a more concentrated effort to do work correctly the first time.

- ✔ **Milestone reports:** Software builds, testing, or other achievements within the project should be tied to a communication activity so that pending milestones are on your radar and you can communicate these achievements to management.

- ✔ **Meetings:** Because so much of project management centers on communication, you must schedule lots of meetings:

    - **Planning sessions:** This includes work breakdown schedule (WBS) creation, scope change assessments, quality assurance meetings, work reviews, risk management meetings, vendor management meetings, and any meetings about issues that affect the project outcome, particularly such issues that require more planning to find the best answer.

    - **Risk management meetings:** Risk identification is an iterative process. You and the project team must revisit risk management as the project is in motion, not just pre-project execution.

    - **Procurement management meetings:** You need to choose vendors, which means that you need to work with your project team, experts, and even other vendors, to determine the *statement of work* (SOW). After you solicit vendors you also need to host a bidders' conference so that bidders come together to meet you and ask questions about the SOW. We discuss procurement in Chapter 12.

- ✔ **Cash flow forecasting.** Many organizations require the project manager to complete cash flow forecasting reports. This report informs management and the finance department when you expect to spend money for your project. If your project is large and you expect to receive incoming cash flow while the project is still active, you should report this information, as well. For example, a project to create software to track baseball stats may be available in both English and Spanish. The English portion may be completed in June and sales may be coming in. But because the Spanish version won't be unveiled until December, the project has incoming and outgoing cash flow. Excellent! See Chapter 9 for more information on creating your project budget.

Hosting team and stakeholder meetings

All meetings have one thing in common: Someone needs to communicate information to at least one other person. Before you schedule a meeting as a facilitator or as a participant, determine the meeting's purpose and then prepare accordingly. We assume that you're the facilitator for your meetings, which is usually the case for project managers.

Here's the first rule of a successful meeting: Set an agenda. All participants in the scheduled meeting should receive a meeting agenda before the meeting begins. Ideally, the agenda is distributed via e-mail with enough time to enable meeting participants to add items to the agenda.

Meeting agendas should include the following:

- ✔ Purpose of the meeting
- ✔ Scheduled start and finish time, as well as the location of the meeting
- ✔ Participants of the meeting
- ✔ Items to be discussed in the meeting
- ✔ Review of action items

A meeting agenda helps you and the participants avoid *WOT,* or *Waste of Time* meetings. Avoid the temptation to allow others to meander in their conversation or war stories. You create an agenda to save time and accomplish communications in the meeting. If people get off track, tell them you will put that topic on the *parking lot,* a list of items to be addressed later but that are parked for now.

Hosting a team meeting

Even though you will meet with your team a bunch, we still recommend creating an agenda for every meeting with your project team. This lets everyone prepare for the meeting's purpose, streamlines the conversation, and creates an expectation between you and the team members that they should not just attend the meeting but actively participate by being prepared to provide meaningful updates.

If you're meeting with your team daily or weekly and the topic is just project status, create a template that you could disperse each week, or just write the topic headings on a whiteboard and save a tree. This agenda acknowledges the daily meetings and introduces the primary topics for your weekly meetings.

You may be wondering about special meetings with your project team. Good. Special meetings between you and the project team are necessary and so is the agenda to go with them. You won't waste time if you create an agenda for these meetings as well. Always create an agenda for each meeting and your time will be used more efficiently.

Hosting a key stakeholder meeting

You'll meet with your key stakeholders (sponsors or customers) often. This is nothing to worry about — other than the fact that key stakeholders control how your project moves forward, usually pay for the software creation, and can bug the heck out of you. Talk about a love-hate relationship.

When you meet with key stakeholders, you must maintain a professional image. You want the stakeholders to have confidence in your ability as project manager, right? Well if they don't have confidence in your ability to organize and facilitate a project meeting, their confidence in your ability as a project manager will slip.

Just as with your project team, you'll need to create an agenda for your stakeholder meetings. Stakeholder meetings usually come in one of five of the following flavors:

- **Stakeholder analysis meetings.** In this type of meeting, you need to figure out what the goal of the project is, get to the root of a problem, and so on.

- **Scope management meetings.** Scope management meetings start from the beginning of the project, and enable the key stakeholders to sign off on your requirements or to add things to the project scope statement before the project execution begins. Scope management also enables you to prevent *scope creep,* or unnecessary changes. Stakeholders may see a first build and want to tweak it, or they may want to add a button here or there. In worst-case scenarios, they may get a groovy idea for something to add on to the project after it's in full swing. Scope management meetings help you determine whether a proposed change is worth pursuing despite the extra effort, schedule changes, and cost increases. A formal change management process is presented in Chapter 13. You're likely to link it with a scope management meeting.

- **Training sessions.** If you create a swell piece of software, but no one understands how to use it, frustration begins. Training is an essential part of software development. It's your responsibility to communicate with the training manager to make sure that there is an effective training plan.

- **Status reporting.** Your stakeholders want to know about the overall health of the project, what issues have arisen, whether certain risks have come to fruition, and so on. Don't avoid telling your stakeholders bad news — just be prepared to present the bad news with a proposed solution.

- **Scope verification meetings.** After the project has completed some work, typically at the end of a phase or milestone, you should present the work to the stakeholders for approval. You also verify the scope at the end of the project.

Defining Communication Modalities

Modality is just a fancy way of clarifying the form communication takes. Some communication should be paper-based, while other communication should be electronic. On other occasions, a formal, face-to-face presentation is the necessary modality.

You really need to determine and document in your communication management plan the modality of the communication before the project execution begins. By documenting the modality, you've set the expectations for what type of communication is needed, when it's needed, and in what format. No assumptions are made between you and the stakeholders as to what information is being exchanged and how it'll be received.

Sometimes you have to wear suits and sometimes you get to wear jeans. The occasion dictates what you should wear just as the occasion in your project communication dictates whether the communication should be formal or informal. As a rule, you always present your communications professionally and clearly — regardless of the formal and informal boundaries.

Modalities for formal communication

If you're communicating to stakeholders in a formal setting, here are the types of communication modes you should employ:

- **Presentations:** Throughout your software project management career you'll likely have to get up in front of your stakeholders and present the project plan, the status of the project, or serious issues that creep into the project. Sometimes a PowerPoint presentation can help you to make your point, and at other times PowerPoint can be a distraction. The secret to a good presentation is to be prepared, speak with authority, and put your audience at ease.

- **Reports:** We once heard a project manager say, "If it's in writing, then it's formal communication." We agree with the statement, for the most part. Your reports, from status to quality control, are formal. Take time to ensure the accuracy of the data you present, not to mention your grammar.

- **Conference/phone calls:** Some of your stakeholders and team members may be dispersed all over the world, so the most efficient way to communicate with them is via conference calls. When you communicate using the telephone, remember that others cannot see your facial expressions to help determine your emotions. Keep the communication clear and thorough so as to not leave a lot of room for interpretation.

- **E-mail:** E-mail can be a form of formal communication in some environments. In software project management you're dealing primarily with folks that are IT-savvy and will rely heavily on e-mail. If you're presenting formal communications through e-mail, write it just as you'd put it in a letter. Leave out the emoticons, jokes, and asides. And then save your e-mail, attachments, and any responses.

Modalities for informal communication

If you're communicating to stakeholders in an informal setting, here are the types of communication modes you should employ:

- ✔ **E-mail.** Yep. E-mail can be either formal or informal, depending on the context. You have quick questions for project team members so you zip off an e-mail and they reply. Done. No need for fancy reports, faxes, or detailed discussions. It's always a good idea to keep all project communications, though, even if it's just a quick e-mail.

- ✔ **Ad-hoc meetings.** Quick hallway meetings, stop-and-chats, quick phone calls, and lunch discussions can be some of the most effective communications you have. The trouble with these meetings is that they can pop up unexpectedly and suck your time away. The other problem with ad-hoc meetings is that the folks you're communicating with may not follow through with the promises made during the discussion. Take care to document the discussion and then follow up with everyone involved if promises were made during ad-hoc meetings.

- ✔ **Instant messaging and text messaging:** If you have a dispersed team, this mode of communication can be especially useful. It's quick and efficient to communicate through IM or by sending text messages. The only thing you have to be concerned with is the many time zones your stakeholders may reside in. You may not want to text message someone when it's the middle of the night in his or her time zone. Some popular instant messaging programs include AIM (AOL Instant Messenger), Yahoo! Messenger, and Windows Messenger.

- ✔ **Coffee talk.** Sometimes you need to get your team together for some camaraderie. It doesn't have to be over coffee, of course, but coffee and donuts, pizza, whatever, can help ease the tension of a software project, let the team vent a little about the project if they want, or just let everyone know how much you appreciate their hard work. This is about motivation and team development.

Automating communications

So much of project management is redundant work. Your project team fills out a form and e-mails it to you. You review the form and plug results into your *project management information system* (PMIS). From there, you may need to generate more reports, more e-mails, and more communication. And don't forget all the repetition from stakeholders: questions on the project status, budget, schedule, change requests, and more.

All of this monotonous, repetitive communication is needed and you're typically at the hub of the communication. Good news! Several programs are available that can help you and your project team automate the communication of the project:

- **Microsoft's Project Server** (visit www.office.microsoft.com and click the <u>Project</u> hyperlink) is a server-based system that ties into Microsoft Project, Microsoft Internet Information Server, Microsoft Exchange, and SQL Server, allowing add-on components from third-party vendors. This tool is certainly at the top of the heap; it enables you to publish Web forms that your project team members, key stakeholders, and even vendors can use to report progress, issues, change requests, and just about anything else project related. This information can then be piped into your SQL database to generate reports, statistics, and automate communications by publishing and allowing querying of data to a secured Web site.

- **Pacific Edge** (www.pacificedge.com) and **Primavera** (www.primavera.com) offer many similar features as the ubiquitous Project Server.

The goal of any PMIS is to help project managers do their job better, not replace the project manager.

Chapter 5

Planning for Software Project Risks

*R*isk is an uncertain event that could have a positive or negative outcome. Risk is everywhere: whether you're driving, sky diving, crossing the street, trading stocks, or swimming with sharks. When you do something risky, you must calculate whether the potential reward is worth the potential risk. Some things are easy — the reward of driving from Point A to Point B is usually considered worth the risk of a traffic accident. For every risk there is some reward. If you're lucky, the reward works in your favor, like buying low and selling high in the stock market. The risk is that you buy a stock and it tanks — you took a risk and you lost your investment.

One of the toughest jobs for any project manager is managing project risks. In addition to risks that affect your ability to complete your assignments, project risks include the following:

✔ Inadequate time for completing the project

✔ Inadequate budget for completing the project

✔ Unrealistic scope expectations

✔ A project team that needs additional time to ramp up development language

✔ Stakeholders that do not or cannot provide clear project requirements

In software project management, the risks are rampant: time, cost, scope, quality, project team, and so on. We examine each of these risks, and more, in this chapter. The goal of risk management is to identify, quantify, plan for, and then react to the risk potential to keep the risks from affecting the project's success.

Identifying Pure and Business Risks

When most people think of risks, they have an immediate negative connotation about risk. The risk, however, isn't what makes folks frown; it's the impact of the risk. Risk itself is not really a bad thing.

Taking risks can even have a positive impact. Consider a risk that you may get a discount from a vendor because of past orders. Or consider the risk that a change request from the customer allows your project six more weeks of development time. Or consider the risk of a new technology superseding your existing development processes. Positive risks are called *risk opportunities.*

You can't possibly consider every single risk in a project. All projects deal with risks that are usually so far off the risk radar that they aren't even a concern:

- ✔ The company might go out of business
- ✔ An asteroid could crash into the office building
- ✔ Big Foot could appear and take all the back-up tapes
- ✔ The senior developer might move to Hawaii

See? These risks are unusual, highly improbable, and are way, way, out there in left field. But all of these are risks — you just have to accept them. As a project manager, you must consider the risk result, and you also have to categorize risks. In life and project management there are two types of risks to be concerned with:

- ✔ **Pure risks:** These risks have no upside, only a downside. Pure risks include things like loss of life or limb, fire, flood, and other bad stuff that nobody likes.

- ✔ **Business risks:** These risks are the calculated risks you are concerned with in project management. A perfect example of a business risk is using a worker with less experience in order to save money on the project's budget. The risk is that the worker will screw up and your project will be doomed. The reward is that the worker will cost less than the more experienced worker and save the project some cash. An additional reward is that by challenging this employee you will encourage his or her growth and buy in on the project. This worker is more likely to be of greater value to you in future projects.

Dealing with pure risks in software projects

All right, we admit that you won't have too many pure risks in software projects. Although some programmers might whine that they're typing their fingers off, aside of the danger of carpal tunnel syndrome, there's really not any risk of loss of life or limb.

Some MBA types may argue that you still have pure risks in software projects because folks could steal software, steal hardware, or get electrocuted when they spill their coffee on their PC. Sure. And we may win the lottery if we ever play. For the most part, however, you won't have to worry too much about pure risks — unless you're just the worrying type.

Just because you likely won't have pure risks in your software project doesn't mean you shouldn't look for pure risks. When you conduct a risk assessment, you should consider the project deliverable. For example, will your software be used in environments where life and limb depend on your software? Consider health care, fire and police stations, and even manufacturing.

Assessing business risks

Business risks are a big concern for any project manager with an eye towards reality. Business risks are the more common risks you encounter in your project management activities:

- ✔ Employees quit
- ✔ Mistakes are made in the requirements gathering process
- ✔ The software is full of bugs, errors, and failures
- ✔ The scope of the project grows, but the budget (or the timeline) doesn't
- ✔ The expectations of the project time, cost, and scope are not realistic to begin with
- ✔ The project is larger than the capacity of the project team
- ✔ The project manager, sponsor, or other stakeholders are not as knowledgeable as you would hope

These are all real-life risks that you have to deal with — or they'll deal with you. Just because you choose to ignore a risk doesn't mean it'll go away.

Contrary to what your mom said, ignoring pests doesn't mean that they'll all go away. This plan just doesn't work in project management.

Business risks, however, also have some upsides. Sometimes it's worthwhile to accept a risk to save time, reduce costs, or to make people nervous. (Just kidding on the nervous thing; you want to instill confidence in your stakeholders.) A good example of a risk that you may deem acceptable is to move forward with a software implementation even though the application doesn't have a key feature that stakeholders want. You may decide to move forward with the implementation in order to save some project time. The risk is that the stakeholders won't get everything they want exactly when they want it, but the reward, assuming the feature will be available in the next upgrade, is that your project just saved some time in the schedule.

Business risks are not bad; it's their impact that has the potential to hurt you or the project.

Accepting everyday technology risks with your software project

Every software project has risks. Don't think so? Look in the mirror — you're a risk to your software project. Your leadership, ability to communicate, ability to get your project team to perform, and more could fill a bucket of risks that's just waiting to spill all over your project. But we know you won't let that happen, right?

The real risks we're talking about are built into the nature of the work: technology. Technology changes extremely fast and with that fast change there's opportunity for risk to creep in. Consider these risks in every software project:

- ✔ Speed of technology surpasses demand for your creation.
- ✔ Delays in your schedule shorten the window for the demand of your software.
- ✔ Your programmers' ability to learn new programming languages and adapt to new development environments may threaten the project schedule.
- ✔ Your stakeholders may have a tough time explaining what they want the project deliverable to be.
- ✔ Because programmers are in demand, a programmer could leave your project team, putting your project at risk from loss of talent, time

> away from progress, and time devoted to getting a new developer up
> to speed.
>
> ✔ If your project has never been attempted before, you risk suffering from
> the first-time, first-use penalty. This penalty basically means that
> because it's never been done before there is a higher risk of facing prob-
> lems you couldn't possibly anticipate.

Determining Stakeholder Risk Tolerance

A person's willingness to accept risks is called his or her *utility function.* You
don't need to know the details, but the idea of utility function is tied to investment theory. Would you rather invest your hard-earned millions into an initial
public offering that is just as likely to earn you billions as it is to lose all of
your cash? Or would you prefer to stick with an old, faithful stock that might
earn just 6 percent a year?

Your willingness to invest in a riskier venture, and the amount you're comfortable investing, describe your utility function. The same theory applies to
your stakeholders. You, your project team, and the key stakeholders will be
happy to accept some risks and will refuse to accept others.

Generally, stakeholders of smaller, lower-priority projects are more willing to
accept risks than those involved in high-profile projects. Consider a project
in your organization to replace all of the monitors throughout the company.
Although the project may be deemed important, it's not likely to affect the
success of the day-to-day operations of your organization, so it's not a huge
risk on productivity within the organization.

Figure 5-1 shows an S-curve. As you can see, the higher the project priority is
the lower the utility function is. In other words, the higher the project priority, the more likely you are to reduce risks. The amount of acceptable risks
will diminish.

Now consider a software project that will create a program to track the workflow from sales, to order fulfillment, to accounting, to billing, and to customer
follow-up. This project has a higher impact, if it fails, than a simple project to
swap monitors.

It's obvious which project your organization would be more risk adverse
towards: the software implementation.

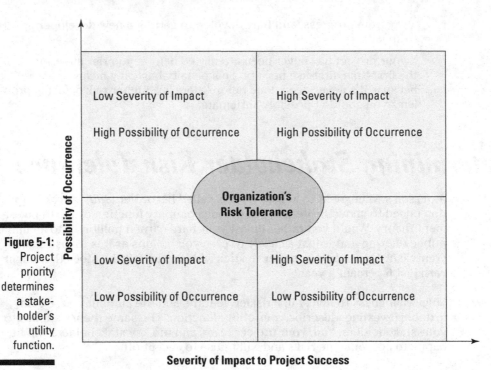

Mitigating Risks Early On

Here's a rule for you to remember for the rest of your life — well, for the rest of your life as a project manager: Projects are more likely to fail at the beginning and more likely to succeed at the end. In other words, when a project is first starting out, it faces lots of unknowns that can affect its ability to even get moving. Although a project is more likely to fail at the beginning, the fact that you haven't invested as much in the project at the beginning means that the impact of the failure isn't as great as it would be if you'd spent months working on the project before it died its untimely death. Although your project is less likely to fail at the end, the fact that you have already invested so much time and money in the project means that the impact of the failure can be significant. Figure 5-2 shows that as the project moves closer to the end of development, it's more likely to succeed.

This rule underscores why software projects (and, really, all projects) usually fail at the beginning, not the end. A failure to capture requirements, develop concepts, and plan, plan, plan are a poor foundation for project success. The project manager with a poor foundation that is hoping for a successful project is kidding himself. Good luck is always for the ill-prepared.

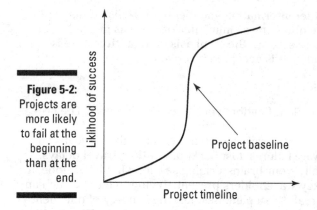

Figure 5-2:
Projects are more likely to fail at the beginning than at the end.

(Chart labels: Likelihood of success — vertical axis; Project timeline — horizontal axis; Project baseline)

Managing Risks in Your Organization

Every organization has its own approach to risk management. Even yours. We can hear some of you now, "But we don't have an approach. We just do whatever."

Groovy. That's your approach. Not a really good one, but it *is* an approach. A no-approach risk management strategy leads to project failures, frustration, surprises, and "I-told-you-so's" throughout the project. Not to mention all the extra cash and time the risks eat up.

Tighter organizations (which, coincidentally, usually aren't tottering on the edge of bankruptcy) have a step-by-step strategy to handling risks. These organizations have procedures, templates, and processes to identify, capture, and asses the risks that threaten the project's success.

Identifying risks

Regardless of your company's official risk management strategy, you can rely on *qualitative risk analysis* to get things moving. Qualitative analysis is the process of creating a risk ranking based on all the identified risks within the project.

The best way to conduct qualitative risk analysis is for you to invite the project team and all the other key stakeholders to get together for a risk identification party. Alright, it's hardly a party, but it needs to be done on every project.

The method you use to gather information and identify risks is not as important as the fact that you are obtaining as much information as possible. For these risk identification exercises, put the emphasis on quantity. More is better. If a risk is not identified, it is accepted by default.

Brainstorming

During the first stage of risk identification, you should brainstorm. The crucial element of a brainstorm is spontaneity. Anything goes; no risk is too far out there. Include any conceivable risk that could threaten the project's success: server crashes, software failures, lost backup, weather, travel delays, meteorites, and so on. Ideally, your brainstorming session should be done in a big meeting with all the key stakeholders present. Trying to handle such an assessment via e-mail can really be a pain. Besides, the synergy of one identified risk can spur another team member to think of another risk. The qualitative risk party is a blast, especially if you have a whiteboard and lots of colorful dry erase markers.

Following the Delphi method

Another method of identifying project risks is to use the *Delphi method*. This allows stakeholders to anonymously offer their input into identifying risks. They can send their suggestions via e-mail to one person who will then consolidate the information into one document — without naming the source of the information.

Ranking risks

After you and the key stakeholders identify all the risks you can think of, you need to rank them. We suggest ranking project risks by using a *risk impact matrix*. You can use two different approaches to risk ranking:

✔ **Ordinal:** This assessment simply ranks risks as high, medium, or low.

Most folks use ordinal for the first round of risk analysis.

✔ **Cardinal:** When you use this ranking system, you assign scores with hard numbers, like .67 or .99.

With each risk, you and your project team, and sometimes the key stakeholders, need to follow these steps:

1. **Evaluate the probability of the risk actually happening and assign that risk a score.**

2. **Score the impact of each risk.**

3. **Multiply the probability and the impact to get a risk score.**

   Table 5-1 gives you a quick example of a risk rating matrix. In this example, we used an ordinal scoring method because it's a bit more tangible.

Eight risks every software project has

Every project has risks, but software projects are special. You face several risks in every software project endeavor you manage. Here are the biggies:

✔ **Time.** You need to be realistic about time estimates. Making an overly eager time estimate is a risk that could haunt you throughout the project. As the project team struggles to meet the deadlines, quality could suffer, which means work may need to be redone and more delays. We discuss time management in Chapter 8.

✔ **Costs.** In software development your largest expense is usually tied to the developers' time. If the time estimates are invalid, so then will be the cost estimates. As costs begin to pile up, stakeholders, primarily management, begin to lose faith in you, putting pressure on you to push the project team harder to complete the project. The result can be more errors, lost time, and lost dollars. We discuss cost management in Chapter 9.

✔ **Scope.** Scope is the agreed body of work that the project will capture. *Scope creep,* often also called *mission creep,* is project poison. When stakeholders begin to sneak in little change requests that circumvent the identified change request system, both time and cost are affected. Scope changes can also stem from the project team not having a clear understanding of what's considered *in scope* and what's *out of scope.* As a rule, you should decline any changes to scope unless they are absolutely necessary. Changes to scope must be reflected in the time and cost estimates. We discuss scope changes in Chapter 13.

✔ **Feasibility.** Some projects are unrealistic. Expectations for the project scope, schedule, and budget may be completely flawed. It's the project manager's job to identify the unfeasible aspects of a project or face the consequences.

✔ **Quality.** What good is a project if it's completed on time and on budget but the software is full of bugs, errors, and crashes all the time? Quality is the successful completion of the project scope, not just the consumption of the project budget and schedule. We discuss quality in Chapter 6.

✔ **Stakeholder expectations.** Managing stakeholder expectations is an ongoing process — you'll do this through your communication (see Chapter 4). From the moment of the project launch, you must work alongside the stakeholders to capture their vision for the project deliverable and then document that vision into requirements, architecture, and execution. Throughout the project, constant communication ensures that the project is moving in alignment with the expectations of the stakeholders.

✔ **Human Resources.** Knowledgeable technical resources are in great demand. You run the risk of your top developers being recruited by other firms. What steps are you taking toward employee retention?

✔ **Technical accuracy.** If your project team doesn't know how to create the deliverable that the stakeholder is expecting, this is a risk. The project team must be trained and developed in order to reach the project conclusion that you and the stakeholder are expecting. Team development is discussed in Chapter 7.

Table 5-1	Sample Qualitative Risk Impact Matrix		
Risk	*Probability*	*Impact*	*Risk Score*
Server crashes	Low	Medium	Low
Lack of developers	High	Medium	High
Firmware changes	Low	Medium	Low
Requirement to install service packs	High	Medium	Medium
Meteorites strike company headquarters	Low	Low	Low

As you can probably guess, rating impact can be a subjective process, but as long as you're not doing your risk assessment in a vacuum, the subjectivity isn't likely to bring your project down. Calm down; you're probably safe. With the help of your team members to assign the probability and impact, you can apply multiple perspectives in your rankings. There's not a ton of proof that any of these risks are more or less likely to occur, but don't underestimate the experience of project team members and stakeholders.

Prepare for some heated discussions on why a risk is rated Medium instead of High. Remind the participants that this is only the first round of risk analysis and that scores can change.

When everyone agrees on the ranking of each of the risks, you must determine which risks are small enough to accept and which risks need more analysis.

Usually risks with a medium or greater ranking qualify for quantitative analysis.

Relying on Quantitative Analysis

Quantitative analysis is the process of measuring your risk exposure. Quantification requires more than going with your gut feeling; you need to conduct interviews, set up prototypes, do expert analysis, and set up simulations.

As you can guess, quantitative analysis takes time — and usually some investment. Someone has to interview the stakeholders. Someone has to create the prototype, the simulations, and complete the analysis. Some stakeholders, customers, and project managers are likely to argue against completing a quantitative analysis because of the time and cost involved to do it correctly. It's up to you to convince them that it's worth the extra effort.

The investment in completing the interviews, prototypes, and simulations is generally much smaller than responding to the crushing effects on a project's time and cost baselines if a risk is realized.

Here's a trick to remember the difference between qualitative and quantitative analyses: Qualitative analysis means that you're describing the qualities of the risks; quantitative analysis gives a quantity, usually a number, and often with a dollar sign next to it, of the impacts of those risks. Qualitative analysis is better for smaller projects (under $100,000 and shorter than three months). Larger projects, with more money at stake and longer durations, require more quantitative analysis.

Creating a Contingency Reserve

Quantitative analysis also uses a risk impact matrix, like qualitative analysis, though a *cardinal scale* is mostly used here (see "Ranking risks," earlier in this chapter). This risk impact matrix also quantifies the dollars or time the project stands to lose, or gain, because of the risk.

What the project needs is a contingency reserve that will alleviate the expenses of the risks should they come into fruition. You know how much to set aside for this contingency reserve by using the quantitative risk impact matrix. Table 5-2 gives you an idea of what a matrix might reveal.

Table 5-2	Sample Quantitative Risk Impact Matrix		
Risk	**Probability**	**Impact**	**Risk Score**
Server crashes	.10	($5,000)	($500)
Lack of developers	.90	($80,000)	($72,000)
Firmware changes	.20	(10 days)	(2 days)
Requirement to install service packs	.70	($2,000)	($1,400)
Rebate from Manufacturer (risk opportunity)	.80	$1,000	$800
Contingency reserve needed			$73,100

The impact of each risk is quantified by a negative dollar amount or by an assessment of time lost, though some organizations turn time into dollars. This negative dollar amount represents the cost the project will incur if the risk event occurs. Notice that the rebate from the manufacturer risk will actually save the project $1,000 if it comes to fruition.

The sum of the risk event values, both positive and negative, is the amount of contingency funds that should be reserved for this project. Don't get too excited that the amount of the contingency reserve is less than the sum of all the risks. The probability for all of the risks occurring is not 100 percent, so you won't get 100 percent of the dollar amount associated with each risk. You're banking that some of the risk events will occur and some of the events won't.

Using Software Models for Risk Management

Within software project management, there are models that help the project manager alleviate the biggest risk of them all — failure. Models are adapted from grandfather programs, serious thought and planning, or they evolve based on past experience. Whatever approach you or your organization takes, the model needs to be documented, and the rules need to be defined and then followed.

Avoiding the code-and-fix model

The *code-and-fix model* of risk management is hardly a model at all, but we remain amazed at how often we discover its use when we consult with various companies. The code-and-fix model is reactionary — and it's rubbish. Basically, you start out with a dreamy set of requirements and willing programmers. The project manager and the project team meet, yak about the software, and then coding begins.

Everyone holds their breath like they're in the waiting room of the hospital. The programmers are the surgeons, but they really don't understand the operation, so they hack away until the cash and time dribbles away or lightning strikes and they declare, "It's alive!"

The code part comes first, and it's followed by rounds (and rounds) of fixing. This model, if you really want to call it that, is weak, weak, weak. It might be ideal for an afternoon of prototyping or playing what-ifs, but it's a *risk-enriched* approach (that is an approach that is chock-full of risks); in fact, it's the highest-risk model you can use in software development. Avoid it like, well, just avoid it.

You can find dozens of software development models. Each of them has pros and cons, but one thing is always true: Whichever model you use must be accepted and followed by everyone, from the management team to the project team and the stakeholders. It doesn't do anyone much good to have a model and not follow it. The following sections describe the most popular software models on a continuum from *risk-enriched models* (high-risk approaches) to *risk-averse models* (relatively risk-free approaches).

There's no such thing as an organization that doesn't have a software development model. Even if it's patched together and made up as the project moves along, it's a model. The point of any model is to reduce the risk of failure.

Using the waterfall model

If you've ever taken a programming class, you've encountered the classic waterfall approach to programming. In case you were lucky, and never had to take a programming class, here's the deal: The *waterfall model* uses a series of phases to move the project along. Each phase creates a deliverable, usually a document that captures what the phase has accomplished. Figure 5-3 shows the progression of the model.

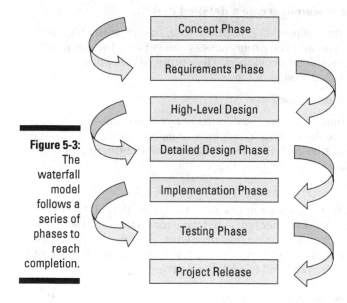

Figure 5-3:
The waterfall model follows a series of phases to reach completion.

Concept Phase

Requirements Phase

High-Level Design

Detailed Design Phase

Implementation Phase

Testing Phase

Project Release

With the completion of each phase comes a new stage, with the product of the phase transitioning (just like a waterfall) into the next phase. Here's the progression:

1. **Come up with a concept.**

   In phase one, you and the stakeholders build the concept document, which explains the goals and constraints (such as time and cost) of the project, and a *rough order of magnitude estimate* (ROM) is created. We discuss ROM in more detail in Chapter 9.

2. **Determine the requirements.**

   In phase two, using the concept document, the project team completes the document that details the requirements of the project deliverables. This document includes all of the systems, technologies, and technical interfaces for the deliverables. The requirements document is really the *progressively elaborated* version of the concept document. (How's that for jargon?)

3. **Create a high-level design.**

   You may hear the high-level design phase (phase three) referred to as the *satellite point of view* or the *view from 20,000 feet*. Whatever. The high-level phase consists of the big architectural building blocks of the software you're creating. The high-level design document defines how programmers will implement the requirements document. See an evolution here?

4. **Narrow down the design to create a detailed design.**

   Ah, now we're getting somewhere. In phase four, based on the high-level design document, you and the programmers can get into the details of how the application will be developed. The output of this phase? You guessed it: the detailed design document.

5. **Code implementation phase.**

   In phase five, it's time to follow the documents you've created with your project team by actually coding. This phase usually includes unit testing to ensure that what's being built actually follows all the documents created up until now.

6. **Testing phase.**

   At this stage, you test the entire application to ensure that all the units are coded and working as expected — before your customers see it. This is the quality control phase. If you find problems, then you've got more work to do. The goal of this phase, of course, is to keep mistakes out of the customers' hands. When all is well, the deliverable is released.

At first glance this looks like a rock-solid model, and it can be. However, the risk with this model is that if changes trickle, or flood, into the project, you basically have to start over. This is because the project is founded on the original capture of the project vision, the requirements, and so on. Changes to the fundamentals can (and will) affect how the application is built. And then troubles ensue.

Using the spiral model

The spiral model is the safest, or most risk adverse, model available. An organization that uses the spiral model examines the project as a whole and then breaks down the project into subprojects, each of which are categorized by risks. The subprojects are then organized from risk heavy to risk lean.

With the spiral model, you tackle the areas of the project where most of the toughest risks are first. This approach, which is frankly our favorite, hits the project risks head-on and then moves on to the next risk-laden subproject.

We like this approach so much because there's nothing more frustrating than investing months in a project only to have it roadblocked by giant risks in month seven. With this approach, everyone knows whether the project can succeed right away based on the team's ability to plow through the hardest risks first. This model builds confidence and gains momentum. The logic is simple: If these are the toughest risks, then the project will only get easier from here. And it usually does.

So why's it called a spiral model? Take a look at Figure 5-4; see how the project starts at the center and spirals out like a cinnamon roll? The completion of each subproject enables the project to move on to the next subproject until the project spirals all the way out to the release.

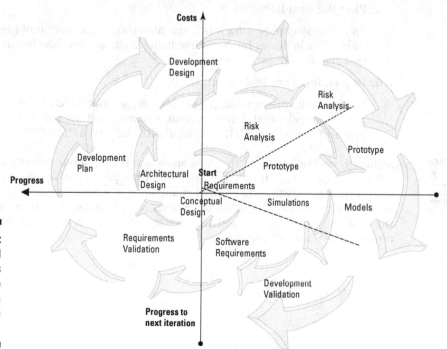

Figure 5-4: The spiral model uses iterations to move the project to completion.

Here's the general approach:

1. **Set a goal.**

   In the goal-setting phase, all the stakeholders work together to determine the goals, constraints, and alternatives for the project completion.

2. **Conduct alternative investigations.**

   The purpose here is to investigate all of the possibilities to best achieve the project goals. In some organizations, you may create a feasibility study at this stage.

3. **Conduct risk management.**

   Remember all that business earlier in this chapter about qualitative and quantitative risk analysis? This is it. You and the stakeholders have to examine, rank, and score all the project risks. Examining and ranking risks is a key activity for the spiral model because this process helps you and the project team to arrange the subprojects.

4. **Create the deliverables.**

   Based on the goals, alternative identification, and risk management, the project team creates a deliverable for this subproject. Each subproject delivers something that enables the project to move to the next iteration of the process. When you're starting out, the first deliverable may just be the verification of the goals, feasibility, and risk assessment.

5. **Plan the next iteration.**

   As the project moves forward, you plan the next iteration of the software. This includes business like fixing bugs, adding new features, and making other improvements.

6. **Determine what to do next.**

   Based on the previous step, you determine what needs to happen next. After you make that determination, you move all the way back to step one and move through these steps with the next subproject.

Although we readily admit that this approach is one of our favorites, we also acknowledge that it's tough to implement. Change- and process-averse project managers may find this model challenging. It's time consuming to implement, but it creates good software. Some companies use this approach for the first few iterations of a software release and then all future iterations move in the waterfall approach.

Using the V model

This model is called the V model because, well, because the progression of the project forms a V. Look at Figure 5-5; see the V? This is a risk-averse development model because the completion of each phase prompts a corresponding test phase. Before the project moves forward, the test must be passed. This model is technically an expansion of the waterfall model, with added verification and testing. Like the waterfall model, each phase creates documentation of what's been completed in the project.

Here's a breakdown of the V model progression:

1. **Set the project requirements.**

   The project requirements are identified and agreed upon by the project manager, the project sponsor, and other key stakeholders.

2. **Design the architecture.**

   The requirements are decomposed into functions and system components, and the project estimates for time and costs are updated. The refined estimates must be approved by the customer or the project's management team before the project moves forward.

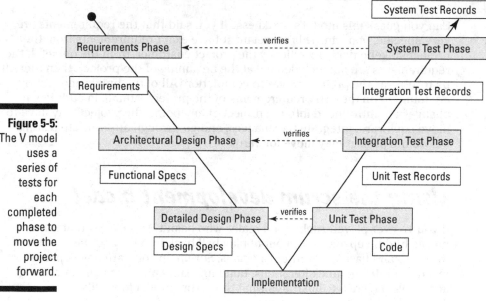

Figure 5-5:
The V model uses a series of tests for each completed phase to move the project forward.

3. **Elaborate on the architecture with a detailed design.**

   In the detailed design phase, the software's design phase is broken down further and designed, and a detailed design document is created. The detailed design document maps to the project requirements and specifies how the software will be created.

4. **Implement the code.**

   In the implementation phase, the code is implemented according to the detailed design document.

5. **Test individual units.**

   In order for the project to move forward, units are tested to confirm that the software works as described in the detailed design document. This is called the unit test phase. If the project passes the tests, the project moves forward. If not, the problems must be corrected and passed through the tests again.

6. **Test how everything works together.**

   In the integration test phase, you confirm that the software operates as the project stakeholders defined it (see Step 1).

7. **Test the whole system.**

   In the system test phase, compile the software and test the system as a whole. Successful testing of this phase allows the system to be released.

Can you guess this model's weakness? If you said that the requirements are very specific, you win. This model must have exact requirements from the project stakeholders, specifically the project customer, from the outset. If the requirements are not well defined at the beginning of the project, then there'll be trouble as the project moves to completion. All of the builds and testing are founded on the early requirements of the project launch. In addition, if changes are introduced into the project at any point, the project may have to move backward, integrate the changes, and go through appropriate testing before the project may move forward.

Using the scrum development model

If you've ever played rugby (and really, who hasn't?) you know that *scrum* means huddle up and get an out-of-play ball back into play so the teams can hurry up and bash each others' noggins. Scrum, in software development, means working in quick iterations, building team empowerment, and being adaptable. Figure 5-6 illustrates what the scrum model looks like.

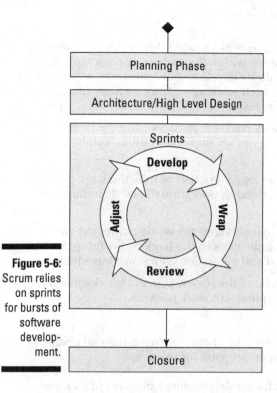

Figure 5-6:
Scrum relies on sprints for bursts of software development.

As in rugby, the scrum development model has lots of rules that the project team and the project manager must live by. The first key rule in scrum is to *never* interrupt the programmers while they're working. The second crucial rule is that everyone must follow the same process for work prioritization. In addition, scrum depends on solid communication, collocated teams, and quick, accurate team meetings. Here's how it works:

1. **Set up a plan.**

   In the planning phase, the project team plans how to reach the project objectives. This phase includes prioritizing and making time and cost estimates, and focuses on detailing the software's functions.

2. **Design the architecture.**

   In the architecture design phase, the team designs the software functions, breaks down the functions into units, and defines any additional features or components.

3. **Start sprinting.**

Sprints are short, iterative bursts of software development. The result of a sprint is to reach a milestone within the project. Sprints typically last from one to four weeks. Multiple development teams may work simultaneously within the project, each working on their own sprints. Each sprint includes the following features:

- **Development.** The work packet is initiated. The development team completes the analysis, design, implementation, testing, and documentation.

- **Wrap.** The packet is *wrapped.* In other words, the work packet is closed. The code is verified as operational, and documentation of the work is created.

- **Review.** The project team reviews the work, points out and resolves issues, and adds items to the backlog for future resolutions. Risk is reviewed and mitigation efforts are introduced.

- **Adjustment.** The results of the review process are documented and, if necessary, compiled into work packets.

4. **Close out the project.**

During the closure phase, the project results are tested and deemed accurate. The software is then prepped for release.

The scrum model is ideal for software development because of its rapid acceptance of changes and adaptability to issues within the development process. However, scrum requires managers and project stakeholders to respect all of the rules of scrum for it to be successful.

Preparing a Risk Response Plan

Every project, regardless of the software development model you use, has project risks. As the expert project manager, you (along with your project team) surely have identified the project risks, used quantitative and qualitative risk analyses, and scored and ranked your risks. But is this enough? Of course not.

Typically you, the project team, and the project stakeholders do an initial qualitative risk analysis. That's the listing and ranking of your project risks. Figure 5-7 shows the scale of the risks you can usually live with, the risks with impacts you want to reduce, and the risks you want to work to eliminate. The *risk response plan* helps you come to these decisions.

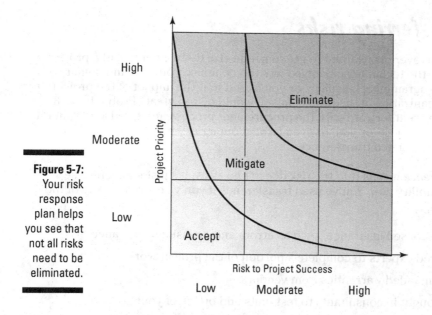

The risk response plan is a document that details the identified risks within a project, their impact, and their associated costs, and then identifies how the project team will respond to the risks. In addition, the risk response plan nods to the process of risk management. Risk identification, the first step of risk management, is an iterative process that happens throughout the project — not just at the beginning.

Avoiding risks

Often the most desirable risk response is to just avoid the risk. This means getting creative in the project scheduling, assigning senior developers to key activities, or creating other workarounds so that the risk doesn't come into play. You've done risk avoidance if you've done any of the following:

- ✔ Changed a project plan to avoid risk interruption
- ✔ Used an established approach to software development rather than a newfangled model
- ✔ Hired experts to consult the project team during the development process
- ✔ Spent additional time with the project stakeholders to clarify all project objectives and requirements

Transferring risks

Have you ever just wanted to get someone else to do a portion of a project because the technology involved was too complex, you were unfamiliar with a new programming language, or you feared that the impact of the project on your organization, if the project failed, would be too great? Probably so. If you ever went forward with the procurement process and hired a consultant to do the project for you, or even farmed out a risky portion of a project, you've completed transference.

Transference means that the risk doesn't go away. It's just someone else's responsibility now. You've used transference if you've ever done any of the following:

- Purchased insurance, such as errors and omissions insurance
- Hired experts to complete a portion of the project work
- Demanded warranties from vendors
- Brought in consultants to test units and builds of your software

Be aware that the risk has not disappeared; you have just transferred it. In fact, if the vendor doesn't deliver on time, you still absorb the impact. Transferring risks introduces a whole new set of risks that you and your team must identify, analyze, and respond to.

Mitigating risks

Risk mitigation is about reducing the impact and/or the probability of risk. Remember qualitative and quantitative risk analyses? (If not, read some of the earlier sections in this chapter.) When you implement risk mitigation strategies, you typically examine the risks with medium to high scores for risk mitigation opportunities. In other words, you attempt to answer questions like, "How can the impact, the probability, or both be reduced to a level that we can live with?"

Ideally, you'd like to reduce both the impact and the likelihood of a risk occurring, but often when you're mitigating risk you choose to mitigate either one or the other — usually you suck it up and accept the lesser of two evils. You've used mitigation if you've ever done the following:

- Added extra testing, verification, or customer approval activities to ensure that the software conforms to requirements
- Reduced the number of processes, activities, or interactions within a smaller project to streamline and focus project management activities on accomplishing specific project tasks

✔ Developed and tested prototypes, used user acceptability testing processes, or launched pilot groups within your organization before releasing the software

Accepting the risks

When you accept certain risks, either the risks are so low that the project can live with them, or the risks are inevitable but the project must move forward anyway. Sometimes you just know that you can't prevent an identified risk, you just suck it up, work towards a solution, and deal with it.

Here's an example of risk acceptance. Say you're working with a non-collocated team and you'll be doing lots of traveling between sites to manage and lead the project team. A risk that you have to accept, like it or not, is weather. Weather delays could affect the project and you have very little response to weather delays other than communicating electronically.

Usually, risk acceptance is for the smaller, puny risks that have a very low probability, a very low impact, or both. However, any risk you do not identify, you automatically accept!

Examining Risk Responses and Impacts

Have you ever made one small change to your software development plan and watched, aghast, as the change mushroomed into a huge issue that delayed your project for weeks? The same thing can happen with your risk response plan. Before a risk response is implemented, the project manager and the project team need to examine the full effect of the response.

The project team and the project manager should determine when the risk response should be implemented. Two terms here to recognize are

✔ **Risk threshold:** The line of demarcation that signals that a risk is about to come into play and that some response should happen. The risk threshold can be a date for completion, a percentage of the work that is not complete, a failed test, or any other event that signals a pending risk.

✔ **Risk trigger:** A trigger is an event within the project that triggers a preplanned response to the identified risk.

Thresholds and triggers often work together. For example, you may decide that if the project is not 50 percent complete by March 1 then you risk missing the final deadline. To reduce this risk, you plan to hire consultants to help finish the project if that March 1 deadline isn't met. The *threshold* is the requirement for March 1, and the *trigger* is whether or not the project is 50 percent complete.

If the team passes through the threshold without meeting the requirements, the trigger is squeezed and consultants come aboard to help finish the project.

Handling the ripple effect of risk response

Any response to a risk can create other problems: schedule delays, a dip in team morale, an increase in cost, and more. Acknowledging the domino effect that risk responses can have on a project is important if you want to be realistic in your project management role. There are two key risks that come from risk responses that should be examined with every risk response:

- **Residual risks:** Residual risks are usually tiny risks that linger after a risk response. These are generally accepted and the project moves forward. For example, if you switch gears and bring in consultants to help meet your final deadline, responsibilities within your project team might shift. You may lose a day as your programmers adjust to their new roles. This residual risk is not as big a deal as possibly missing your final deadline, so it's one you can accept and live with.

- **Secondary risks:** Secondary risks are more serious. They occur when a risk response creates significant new project risks. For example, say you hire a company to help complete the project work. A secondary risk could be that the company you've hired doesn't complete the project on time. Each secondary risk should be analyzed and a risk response should be planned for the risk event. You can begin to see why risk management is an iterative and ongoing process!

Getting to say, "I told you so!"

Your best friend when it comes to risk identification is documentation. If you fail to document a risk, then the risk never existed — at least as far as your management team is concerned. Risk documentation is vital for project success. Each risk should be documented as part of qualitative risk analysis and then periodically revisited to see whether the initial risk analysis was flawed.

Some organizations create a risk management database to enter all of the identified risks along with their risk scores, impacts, and probability ratings. As the project moves forward, you can use the risk database to view risks that are pending, have passed, or that may have come to fruition.

Risk management is an important phase of your project planning and deserves the time and analysis of you and your project team. To find out more about this ever growing field, read *Project Manager's Spotlight on Risk Management* by Kim Heldman (Wiley).

Chapter 6

Planning for Software Quality

· ·

In This Chapter

▶ Defining quality in software projects

▶ Working with your organization's quality policy

▶ Creating a quality management plan

▶ Identifying how changes in time and cost will affect project quality

· ·

When it comes to quality, you've probably heard some great clichés:

> ✔ Quality is planned into a project, not added through inspection (you should spend your time in planning quality instead of inspecting after you have errors).
>
> ✔ It's always cheaper (and more efficient) to do a job right the first time around.
>
> ✔ Why is there always time to do work right the second time?
>
> ✔ Always underpromise and overdeliver.

These sure are some catchy slogans, and clichés become clichés because they're usually accurate. In this chapter we explore what quality is, how to plan it into your project, and how to create a quality management plan.

Defining Quality

Before you can plan for quality, you must first define what quality is. Ask your customers, your project team, your management team, and even yourself what quality is and you get a variety of answers:

> ✔ **What customers say:** The software you create lives up to expectations, is reliable, and does some incredible things the customer doesn't expect (or even think of).
>
> ✔ **What your project team says:** The work is completed as planned and as expected, with few errors — and fewer surprises.

- ✔ **What managers say:** The customer is happy and the project delivers on time and on budget.

- ✔ **What you may say:** The project team completes its work according to its estimates, the customer is happy, and management is happy with the final costs and schedule.

Quality, for everyone concerned, is the ability of the project and the project's deliverable to satisfy the stated and implied requirements. Quality is all of the items we mention here, but it's more than just the deliverable; it's following a process, meeting specified requirements, and performing to create the best possible deliverable. Everything, from the project kickoff meeting to the final testing, affects the project quality.

Referring to the product scope

As the project manager, your primary concern is satisfying the *product scope*. The product scope is the description of the software the customer expects from your project.

If you work primarily to satisfy the product scope, then you'll be in good shape with satisfying the customer's expectations for quality. But, in order to satisfy the product scope you must first have several documents:

- ✔ **Product scope description document.** This document defines what the customer expects from the project. What are the characteristics of the software? This description becomes more complete as you progress through the project and gather more knowledge.

- ✔ **Project requirements document.** This document defines exactly what the project must create without being deemed a failure. What types of functionality should stakeholders be able to perform with the software? This document prioritizes the stakeholders' requirements.

- ✔ **Detailed design document.** This document specifies how the project team will create units that meet the project requirements, which in turn will satisfy the product scope.

- ✔ **Metrics for acceptability.** Many software projects need *metrics for acceptability*. These metrics include speeds, data accuracy, and metrics from user acceptability tests. You'll need to avoid vague metrics, such as *good* and *fast*. Instead, aim to define accurate numbers and determine how the values will be captured.

Satisfying the product scope will assure that the customer is happy with you and with deliverables the project team has created. You will only satisfy the product scope if you plan how to do it. Quality is no accident.

Referring to the project scope

The *project scope* defines all of the work (and only the required work) to create the project deliverable. The project scope defines what will and won't be included in the project deliverable. Project scope is different than the product scope, because the product scope describes only the finished deliverable, whereas the project scope describes the work and activities needed to reach the deliverable.

You really have to put the project scope in writing, and have it signed by the project manager and the project sponsor. For some projects, such as internal projects, other stakeholders may also need to sign off on the project scope. For projects that are completed for customers outside of the organization, the project scope is written in a *statement of work* (SOW), and included in the contract details.

You must define the project scope so that you can use it as an appropriate quality tool. The project scope draws a line in the sand when it comes to project changes. Changes, as we're sure you've experienced, can trickle into the project and cause problems with quality. Even the most innocent changes can bloom into monsters that wreck your project.

Figure 6-1 shows the project manager's approach to project changes and quality. Early in the project, during the initiation and planning stages, you can safely entertain changes to the project. After you create the project scope, however, your rule when it comes to changes should be "Just say no!"

Figure 6-1:
Stakeholder
influence
wanes as
the project
moves
towards
completion.

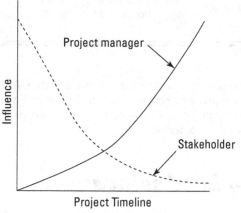

Changes to the project may affect the quality of the product. This isn't to say that changes should come into a project at all — far from it. But changes to the project must be examined, weighed, and considered for the affect on time, cost, and impact on project quality.

Going the extra mile?

One cliché that rings true is that it's always better to underpromise and overdeliver. We've heard project managers tell us this is their approach to keep people happy. It sounds good, right? A customer asks for a piece of software that can communicate with a database through a Web form. Your project team, however, creates a piece of software that can communicate through a Web form to the customer's database, and you add lots of query combinations for each table in the database. Fantastic!

A valid argument can be made that you should *never* underpromise, but promise what you can deliver and live up to those promises. Technically, in project management, quality is achieved by meeting the customer's expectations — not more than they expect, and certainly not less than they expect.

Surprising the customer with more than the project scope outlines can actually backfire, for the following reasons:

✔ The customer may believe the project deliverable could have been completed faster without all the extras you've included.

✔ The customer may believe the project deliverable could have been completed for fewer dollars without all the extras you've included.

✔ If the customer discovers bugs in the software, the blame may lie with the extras.

✔ The customer may not want the extras, regardless of how ingenious you believe they are.

✔ Overdelivering is not meeting expectations; you're not giving the customer what he or she asked for.

Now, having put the wet blanket on the fire of creativity, let us say this: communicate. We can't emphasize enough how important it is to tell the customer what you can do, even if it's more than what the customer has originally asked for. In software development, customers may need guidance on what each deliverable can do, and they look to you as the expert to help them make those decisions. But notice this process is done before the project execution begins, not during the implementation phase.

The product scope and the project scope support one another. If the customer changes details in the product scope, your project scope will also change. If not, then your project team will be completing a project scope that won't create what the customer expects.

Avoiding gold-plated software

You create *gold-plated software* when you complete a project, and the software is ready to go to the customer, but suddenly realize that you have money to burn. If you find yourself with a hefty sum of cash remaining in the project budget, you may feel tempted to fix the situation with a lot of bling. After all, if you give the project deliverable to the customer exactly as planned, several things may happen:

- ✔ Your customer may be initially happy that you've delivered underbudget. Then they'll wonder whether you cut corners or just didn't have a clue as to the actual cost of the project.

- ✔ The customer may wonder why your estimate and the actual cost of the project deliverable are not in sync.

- ✔ The remaining budget will be returned to the customer unless your contract stipulates otherwise.

- ✔ Other project managers may not be happy that you've created a massive, unused project budget when their projects have been strapped for cash.

- ✔ Key stakeholders may lose confidence in your future estimates and believe them to be bloated, padded, or fudged.

This is, in case you haven't guessed, a bad thing. The best thing to do is to deliver an accurate estimate to begin with and avoid this scenario altogether. We discuss time estimates in Chapter 8 and cost estimates in Chapter 9. For now, know that your customer's confidence in future estimates is always measured on your ability to provide accurate estimates at the beginning of the process.

If you find yourself in the scenario where you have a considerable amount of cash left in the project budget, the best thing to do is to give an accurate assessment to the customer of what you've accomplished in the project and what's left in the kitty. Don't eat up the budget with extras, and don't beat yourself up over it. Mistakes happen, especially to beginners, and it's still more forgivable to be underbudget than it is to be overbudget.

So should you also present extras to the customer when you present the project's status and the remaining budget? If the extras are value-added scope changes, we say yes. If the extras are truly gold-plated extras to earn more dollars, then we say no. Software quality is based on whether the product delivers on its promises. If the proposed changes don't make the software better, no one needs them.

What you do on your current project may influence what you get to do on future projects. Honesty now pays dividends later.

Examining quality versus grade

Quality and *grade* are not the same thing. Low quality is always a problem, but low grade may not be. Quality, as you know, is the ability of software to deliver on its promises. Grade is the ranking or classification we assign to things.

Consider your next flight. You expect the airplane to safely launch, fly, and land. And you expect to be reasonably comfortable during the flight. You expect the behavior of the crew and fellow passengers to be relatively considerate, even if they're a little cramped and annoyed. (You have to factor in that crying baby three rows back. It's not the baby's fault, after all.)

Now consider where you're seated on the airplane. Are you in first class or coach? That's the grade!

Within software developments we also have grades and quality issues. A quick, cheap software fix may be considered low grade, but it can still be a high-quality software solution because it satisfies the scope of the simple project. On the other hand, the rinky-dink approach won't work during the development of a program to track financial data through e-commerce solutions for an international company.

During the planning process, one goal of stakeholder analysis is to determine the requirements for quality and grade.

Working with a Quality Policy

A *quality policy* isn't a policy that's "real good." A quality policy is an organization-wide policy that dictates how your organization will plan, manage, and then control quality in all projects. This policy sets the expectations for your projects, and everyone else's, for metrics of acceptability.

Quality policies fall under the big umbrella of *quality assurance* (QA). QA is an organization-wide program, the goal of which is to improve quality and to prevent mistakes.

So who decides what quality is and what's bunk? You might guess and say the customer, which to some extent is true, but generally the quality policy is set by management. The quality policy can be written by the geniuses within your organization, or your organization may follow a quality system and the proven quality approaches within these systems. For example, your company might participate in any number of proprietary and nonproprietary organizations, thereby pledging to adhere to their quality policies. The following sections discuss a few of them.

Working ISO programs

The *International Organization for Standardization* (ISO) is a worldwide body with 153 members that convenes in Geneva, Switzerland. The goal of the ISO is to set compatibility standards for all industries, to establish common ground, and to maintain interoperability between businesses, countries, and devices.

In case you're wondering, the abbreviation for the International Organization for Standardization is ISO, not IOS. This is because of all the different countries represented and the varying languages; they decided to use the abbreviation of ISO taken from the Greek *isos,* which means equal.

There are many different ISO programs, but the most popular is *ISO 9000.* An ISO 9000-certified organization focuses on business-to-business dealing and striving to ensure customer satisfaction. An ISO 9000-certified organization must ensure that it

- ✔ Establishes and meets the customer's quality requirements
- ✔ Adheres to applicable regulatory requirements
- ✔ Achieves customer satisfaction throughout the project
- ✔ Takes internal measures to continually improve performance, not just once

You can learn more about ISO programs and how your organization can participate by visiting their Web site: www.iso.org.

Visit these Web sites for more assistance with quality management:

- ✔ www.managementhelp.org
- ✔ www.cqm.org
- ✔ www.asq.org

Getting a Total Quality Management workout

The U.S. Naval Air Systems Command originated the term Total Quality Management (TQM) as a means of describing the Japanese-style management approach to quality improvement.

TQM requires that all members of an organization contribute to quality improvements in products, services, and the work culture. The idea is that if everyone is involved in quality and works to make the total environment better, then the services and products of the organization will continue to improve.

In software development, TQM means that the entire team works to make the development of the software better, the process from start to completion better, and the deliverable better as well. TQM is largely based on W. Edwards Deming's 14 Points for Quality. Here's how Deming's 14 points and TQM are specifically applicable to software development (you can find out more about W. Edwards Deming in the nearby sidebar, "W. Edwards Deming and the software project manager"):

1. **Create constancy of purpose for improving products and services.** Every developer must agree and actively pursue quality in all of his or her software creation, testing, and development.

2. **Adopt the new philosophy.** This philosophy can't be a fad. The software project manager has to constantly motivate the project team to work towards quality.

3. **Cease dependence on inspection to achieve quality.** Software development has a tradition of coding and inspection, and then reacting to errors. This model is dangerous because developers begin to lean on the testing phase to catch errors, rather than striving to incorporate quality into the development phase. As a rule, quality should be planned into software design, never inspected in.

4. **End the practice of awarding business on price alone; instead, minimize total cost by working with a single supplier.** The idea here is that a relationship will foster a commitment to quality between you and the supplier that's a bit more substantial than an invoice and a check.

5. **Constantly strive to improve every process for planning, production, and service.** Quality planning and delivery is an iterative process.

6. **Institute training on the job.** If your software developers don't know how to develop, they'll certainly create some lousy software. If your team doesn't know how to do something, you must train them.

7. **Adopt and institute leadership.** The project manager must identify how to lead and motivate the project team, or the team may lead itself, remaining stagnant.

8. **Drive out fear.** Are your software developers afraid of you? If so, how can they approach you with ideas for quality improvements, news on development, and flaws they've identified within the software? Fear does nothing to improve quality.

9. **Break down barriers between staff areas.** If your office looks more like the set of *West Side Story,* with your developers (the Sharks) out to get the database administrators and the database administrators (the Jets)

out to get the network engineers, you need to stop the hate. Okay, hate may be too strong of a word, but gulfs between related areas are actually giant pitfalls that trap your quality. You've got to establish relationships, trust, and open communication between the staff areas that interoperate.

10. **Eliminate slogans, exhortations, and targets for the workforce.** Slogans don't improve quality; they frustrate workers. When you constantly remind people that "Quality is Everyone's Job!" you underscore the fact that simply talking about quality doesn't actually improve it. See Points 3 and 5.

TIP

W. Edwards Deming and the software project manager

William Edwards Deming was born on October 14, 1900, long before software development. So what do his philosophies on quality have to do with software project management? Plenty.

Deming is most known for his influence on the manufacturing success Japan experienced after World War II. It was Deming's demand for statistical quality control and his management principles that allowed Japan to recover from the financial impact of WWII and then become a leader in the world economy. Deming's greatest influence on software development, in our opinion, is what's called the Deming Cycle, as the following figure demonstrates.

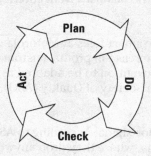

Here's how this cycle applies to software project management:

1. **Plan.** You and your project team plan the project work, anticipate changes by analyzing strengths, weaknesses, opportunities, and threats (SWOT), and then predict the results for the different facets of your project. Projects fail at the beginning, not the end.

2. **Do.** With your plan established, you can execute the work. The work, however, should be completed in small steps in a controlled environment.

3. **Study.** This is the quality control portion of the circle. You, the project team, and the subject matter experts must check the work for accuracy.

4. **Act.** Act to improve the process or standardize your approach in project development. When you're done, the process starts over.

This approach is ideal in software project management because it's logical regardless of the software development model to which you subscribe. The goal is always the same — to reduce the number of errors and improve the results. Deming's approach is iterative and enables projects to constantly improve from launch to completion.

11. **Eliminate numerical quotas for the workforce and numerical goals for management.** You can tell your developers to churn out 2,000 lines of code a day, and they'll probably do it. But they won't guarantee that the code will be any good. A quota is not the same as a demand for quality code.

12. **Remove barriers that rob people of pride of workmanship, and eliminate the annual rating or merit system.** Developers should be able to take pride in their work and their accomplishments, and be rewarded accordingly.

13. **Institute a vigorous program of education and self-improvement for everyone.** Training, especially in IT, is paramount. Without proper education, how can you expect your team to deliver?

14. **Put everybody in the company to work accomplishing the transformation.** For Deming's approach to work, everyone must participate. A few folks here and there won't make much of an impact in most organizations.

Slipping into the sixth sigma

Unless you've been living in a cave or coding COBOL for the past few years, you've no doubt heard of Six Sigma. *Six Sigma* is a procedure that strives to reduce waste, errors, and constantly improve quality through the services and deliverables an organization produces. Six Sigma was developed by some really smart people at Motorola who received the Malcolm National Quality Award in 1988 for their Six Sigma methodology.

Most software is created and tested, then the errors are fixed, patched, or ignored, and then the entire process starts over. Software development, for the most part, focuses on inspection to ensure quality; this is *quality control*. Six Sigma, however, focuses on preventing the mistakes from entering the process at all; this is *quality assurance*.

The Six Sigma program was invented by the smart folks at Motorola during the 1980s. Their creation paid off with an increase in profits, customer satisfaction, and quality awards. Their program went on to be adapted as a standard for quality assurance by the American Society of Quality (ASQ). Visit ASQ at www.asq.org.

Figure 6-2 shows the range of possibilities for sigma. According to ASQ, most organizations perform at three to four sigma, where they drop anywhere between 20 and 30 percent of their revenue due to a lack of quality. If a company can perform at Six Sigma, it only allows 3.4 defects per million opportunities.

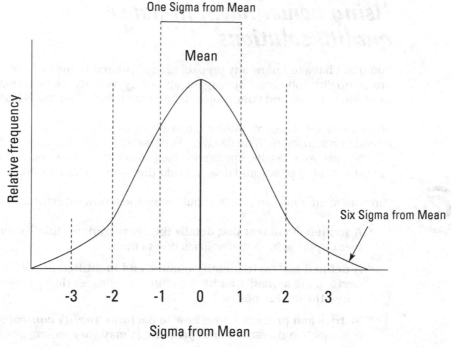

Figure 6-2:
Organizations operating at the Sixth Sigma allow only 3.4 defects per million.

The primary points of Six Sigma are

✓ **We don't know what we don't know.** Makes sense, right? A lack of knowledge keeps organizations trapped in their current environment, losing revenue, and preventing progress.

✓ **We don't do what we don't know.** If you don't know what you should be doing you cannot do it.

✓ **We won't know until we measure.** Aha! The real action in Six Sigma is to measure in order to improve.

✓ **We don't measure what we don't value.** Six Sigma looks at what does and does not need to be measured, and then prompts the developer or project manager to act accordingly. If you value your programmers' time, your software's errors, and your customer satisfaction, you'll measure them all.

✓ **We don't value what we don't measure.** This is a call to action! What should you be measuring that you're not?

Using homegrown, in-house quality solutions

You don't have to follow any prepackaged approach to quality in order to create quality software. Your organization may have its own internal quality program that you and your project team must follow. And that's just fine.

Sometimes in-house programs are more fluid than the rigid programs from outside organizations. The danger, of course, is that a fluid approach may also be seen as a passive approach. The project manager must commit to the in-house quality policy and demand that the project team do the same.

Any and all in-house solutions should have the following attributes:

- ✔ **A written document that details the organization's quality management approach.** Verbal policies don't count.

- ✔ **A defined system to identify quality, and identified procedures for performing a quality audit.** A *quality audit* proves that a project has followed the quality policy.

- ✔ **Metrics and procedures on how to perform *quality control* (QC).** QC is inspection driven, and the procedures may vary among disciplines within an organization.

- ✔ **A boilerplate quality management plan that all projects use to guide project planning, execution, and completion.** The quality management plan sets the rules of how a project should perform and defines the expectations of the project manager to achieve the expected quality.

- ✔ **Procedures on how to update, change, or challenge the quality management plan.** This is an important component because there will likely be circumstances that require the quality plan to flex, change, or evolve. If the quality management plan doesn't define this procedure, then you may fall victim to the old adage: The reason we're doing it this way is because we've *always* done it this way.

Balancing Time, Cost, and Quality

The *Iron Triangle* of project management, as shown in Figure 6-3, requires that all three constraints of a project remain balanced in order for a project to be successful. Right smack in the middle of the Iron Triangle is quality. This is because if the sides of the triangle are not kept in balance, quality is most likely to suffer. So, if your scope increases, then your time, cost, or both will also need to increase or quality will suffer.

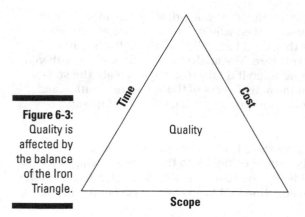

Figure 6-3:
Quality is
affected by
the balance
of the Iron
Triangle.

So how much quality is enough? When it comes to software development, you may create a scale of errors, bugs, and gremlins that sneak into the code. For example, you rank the bugs you've identified from 1 to100, with 100 being the most severe. Any bugs below a score of 20 may be accepted for now, while everything over 20 needs to be fixed. Some organizations, however, would like to aim for a zero-tolerance policy on bugs. Sounds great, but is it possible or profitable?

First, consider the possibilities. How do you know an error exists until someone finds it? You can test, complete peer reviews, and hire third parties to examine your code for months or years on end and not find errors. Does this mean there are no errors within the software? No, it just means that none have been found — yet.

Now, consider the profit. If your organization spends months or years examining, inspecting, and testing code, the market window can easily open and shut for your software before you even get the program packaged. And who pays for all of the inspection? It isn't feasible to demand perfection on most software projects because of the time and expense to prove the existence of perfection (or more accurately, the absence of *known* errors).

Examining optimal quality

Optimal quality describes how much quality is expected in return for the cost to achieve that level of quality. For example, you could create a flawless piece of software that allows users to track all of their online purchases, shipping expenses, and even the interest for each item purchased with their credit cards. But, would anyone buy the software if you charged $600? This is what you might end up charging per copy because your project team spent months perfecting and testing the code.

Probably not. We can pretend that the ideal sale price for this piece of software is $25 per copy. A business analyst would determine the market size, the percentage of the market that would actually buy the software, and predict the gross profit on your software. The analyst would then work with you to determine how long and how much it'd take to actually create the software. The difference between the actual costs of the software creation and the actual sales is the net profit. Now you're getting to optimal quality.

The gross profit would have to be greater than the costs to create the software or there's no *return on investment* (ROI). The optimal quality, in this instance, is how much quality should be built into the software while still allowing for a profit margin. Ideally, the cost of quality is much lower than the final profit margin. That's the equation that keeps businesses in the black.

Optimal quality, fun as it is, has two related costs for you to consider:

✔ **Cost of quality:** This is the amount that you have to spend to achieve optimal quality. Chalk up expenses like time for planning, development, and testing, but don't forget the cost of training or direct project expenses like hardware and software. Of course, you can't forget to pay third parties, such as quality assurance testers and consultants like your business analyst.

✔ **Cost of nonconformance to quality:** This is the cost assigned to wasted labor, wasted materials, and rework when your project team delivers poor and faulty code. This cost also ripples out to a loss of sales because of errors, returns, and unhappy customers who bought and relied on your lousy software.

When it comes to quality, your goal as a project manager is to first determine the project scope in relation to the cost and required schedule. Then you'll have to consider the costs required to achieve the expected level of quality. In some instances, you'll have to examine the profit margin expected in order to realize what the optimal quality for your project should be.

Some project managers worry that if they train their staff they'll leave the company to work for the competition. Motivational speaker Zig Ziglar said, "Which is worse: training your staff and potentially losing them or not training your staff and keeping them?"

Considering quality when making changes

One of the biggest influences on quality is changes to the project scope. We discuss change control at length in Chapter 13, but this section explains why you should consider project quality when approving changes. Don't get the idea that we believe changes should be discouraged in project management. Sometimes changes are absolutely necessary in order to make your stakeholders happy. The two points to consider regarding change control are

- ✔ Consider how changes may affect quality, and address this in your change control plan and your quality management plan.

- ✔ Changes are not evil beings to be avoided. They are a necessary part of any project, and your process for dealing with them should be addressed in your change control plan.

What you need is integrated change control. *Integrated change control* is a method to examine change and its influence on the project as a whole. When changes are proposed, answer all of the following questions:

- ✔ **What affect does this change have on the project scope?** If your scope grows, then you'll need to reflect additional time and cost considerations to incorporate the change. The inverse is true as well; the customer may want to remove deliverables from the scope, but this doesn't always mean that the cost or quality baselines should be adjusted. Sometimes you've already invested time and monies into the deliverables they now want removed from the project.

- ✔ **What affect does this change have on cost and time?** Obviously this question is considered in light of the scope growing or shrinking, but the consumption of time or funds to satisfy a change request may spread your schedule and budget too thin to maintain quality.

One of the biggest mistakes software project managers make is trying to please everyone by accepting changes without reflecting time and cost changes. Then they'll overwork their project team to achieve the project objectives, and quality suffers. Don't be *that* kind of boss.

Chapter 7

Building the Project Team

*P*rojects are not solo activities. Projects are performed by people, and these people are the folks on your project team. You need your project team to help you plan, estimate, execute, and complete the project. And your project team needs you to help them complete their work, lead the project to completion, and act as a shield against the stakeholders that may badger them for changes, gossip, and updates. The goal is to build a symbiotic relationship.

As a software project manager, you really must have two personalities: a leader and a manager. The leader in you must motivate, align, and direct your project team. You want to help your project team members reach their goals and aspire to new challenges. The manager in you, however, is concerned with just one thing: getting the project successfully completed.

When you recruit, build, and shape your project team, there must be a balance between leadership and management. On one hand you just want your project team members to get their work done. On the other hand, you'd like to inspire them to achieve great results, grow as individuals, and contribute to the project's success.

This chapter shows you how to build your project team. In Chapter 11, we address strategies for leading your project team.

Determining Your Project Needs

The first step in finding all of the resources needed for your project is to determine what resources are needed in your project. Take advantage of the people in your organization who have expertise about the software product, the programming environment, and so on. These people can help you determine the resources you need. Web application designers, analysts, developers, and database administrators, in particular, are the experts to whom you turn.

Revisiting the work breakdown structure

To accurately predict resources, you need to know exactly what the project scope entails. Remember the *work breakdown schedule* (WBS) we mention in Chapter 3? The WBS is a deliverables-oriented decomposition of the project scope. It includes everything the project will create in order to complete the project scope. The WBS is your scope baseline.

Figure 7-1 demonstrates a portion of a WBS. In this part of the WBS, you identify products and activities so that you know what roles you need to fill. If your WBS calls for CBT (computer-based training), you will require someone who knows how to create computer-based training materials.

Resources are not just people, but materials, facilities, and equipment that you need to buy, rent, or create. For example, the CBT may require new development software, new application licenses, and even hiring a training expert to help with that portion of the project.

Creating a roles and responsibilities matrix

One of the best tools you can use to identify resources is a *roles and responsibilities matrix*. The purpose of this matrix is to identify all the individuals, groups, and departments that are affected by the project and to show what project components require these different entities to interact.

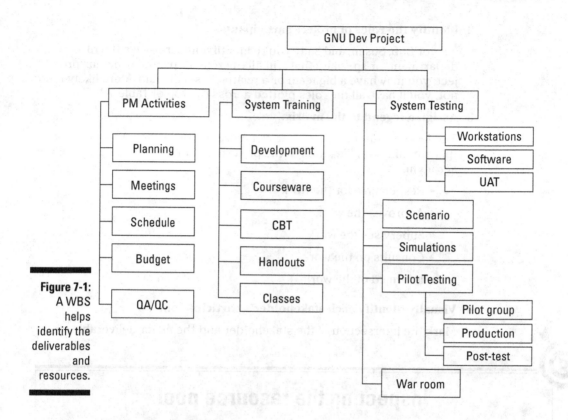

Figure 7-1:
A WBS
helps
identify the
deliverables
and
resources.

You won't identify individuals in this matrix, but departments, such as sales and marketing. You may also identify roles, such as the Visual Studio developer, the Oracle database administrator (DBA), and the project sponsor. The idea is to identify the roles of each project participant. You can fill in the names of the individuals who will fill these roles later. Here's what you need to do to create your own roles and responsibilities matrix:

1. **Identify the major deliverables of the project.**

   Use the WBS (discussed in Chapter 3) to identify the major deliverables.

   If your project is still in its infancy, you can use this time to create your WBS. The first column in Table 7-1 identifies the major deliverables.

2. **Identify the roles of project participants.**

   It's not Bob, Susan, and Sally you're identifying here — it's the title, department, or specialty that will fill the role. Depending on your project, you may have a big team or a relatively small team. More likely than not, you'll have all the roles plotted across the top of Table 7-1.

3. **Assign a legend to the matrix.**

   The *legend* identifies the coding structure the table uses. You can make this anything you like, though the preferred standard is to use the *RASCI* acronym:

   - Responsible for the work
   - Approves the work
   - Supervises the work
   - Consults on the work
   - Informed of the work

4. **Visually identify each stakeholder's participation.**

   Mark the intersection of the stakeholder and the major deliverable.

Inspecting the resource pool

In some organizations, the project manager inherits the project team. In other organizations, the project manager or the functional managers must recruit project team members. In any instance, as the project manager, you must ensure that the project team you're working with has the correct skill sets to complete the work to create the project scope.

Think about any software project you've managed in the past. When the project's business needs were identified, did you instantly begin to think of some experts in your organization that you'd like to have on the project? Or did you think of the folks that you didn't want on your project? Or, finally, did you draw a blank and think of no one that would qualify to help you complete the project work?

Examining the resource pool is more than just rifling through your mental inventory of the talent in your organization. Ideally, your organization has a database that catalogs employees' abilities, past projects, and interests in expanding their skills in various applications. This database can be built in conjunction with human resources and the historical information from past projects that your organization has completed.

If your organization doesn't have the luxury of a resource pool database, you should consider building one or having someone on your team build one. In the meantime, you have to network within your company to find the folks you need to complete the project work. Sometimes, the project team will find you instead of you finding them. When word gets out that you're starting an exciting new project, some potential team members will jump at the chance to be involved.

5. Integrate the matrix into the change control system.

After you complete the matrix and the stakeholders are in agreement about the roles and responsibilities, any proposed changes should be referred to the role that approves the work. You're setting up a clear chain of command here, so you must make sure that all the stakeholders know which roles have the authority over the identified components. This pre-execution process eliminates arguments later in the project when changes to the project scope will inevitably be proposed. Making changes to the scope is discussed in Chapter 13.

Table 7-1		Sample Roles and Responsibilities Matrix				
Major Deliverable	*Project Manager*	*Project Sponsor*	*Developer*	*DBA*	*Network Engineer*	*Key Stakeholders*
Application requirements	S/A	C	R	I	I	C/A
Database requirements	S/A	C	C	R	I	C/A
Network requirements	S/A	C	C	C	R	C/A
Application build(s)	S/A	I	R	R	I	C/A
Database design	S/A	I	C	S/A	I	C/A
Database build	S/A	I	C	R		C/A
Server and network creation	S/A	I	I	C	R	C/A
System testing	S/A	I	R	C	C	C/A
Application analysis	S/A	I	R	I	C	C/A
System engineering	S/A	I	I	I	R	C/A
System test and evaluation	S/A	C	R	I	R	C/A
Evaluation analysis	S/A	I	R	I	C	C/A
System documentation	S/A	C	R	C	C	C/A

Table 7-1 *(continued)*

Major Deliverable	Project Manager	Project Sponsor	Developer	DBA	Network Engineer	Key Stakeholders
Training	S/A	C	R	C	C	C/A
Dual support processes	S/A	C	R	C	C	C/A

Finding the Talent

If you're lucky, your organization has a database of the resources in your company, and you can quickly determine who has what talents. You can simply scan the resources, examine people's skill sets, compare their current and pending workload to your project demands, and begin building your project team.

If you read that above paragraph and thought, "Gee, that'd be nice," you're in for a tougher assignment. You have to find, investigate, survey, and hunt for the resources you need on your project. Then you have to cross your fingers, and hope they're available.

If you find yourself in the camp of project managers without the resource pool database, you can rely on historical information to see who has talent in specific areas. Historical information, the collection of past project records, can help you identify the skills in your resource pool.

What's that? You don't have historical information? Here are three sources to find the talent you need:

- Ask other project managers in your organization to point you towards the talent you need.

- Ask Human Resources staff, functional managers, and your colleagues to point you to the talent you need on your project team.

- Be a pioneer by creating and making your project's historical information to help you and other project managers in the future.

Asking the Right Questions (In the Right Way)

You want to get the right people on your project — the people that can get the work done. But project management isn't just about getting the work done, that's just plain old management. Project management also includes leadership — aligning, directing, and motivating people to act independently for the greater good of the project.

By asking the right questions of your team members, and then listening to their answers, you can come one step closer to leading an organized, unified, and loyal team while also managing the day-to-day aspects of the project.

Get used to asking open-ended questions. If you ask a team member, "You want to advance your career, right?" you're only going to get one answer. But if you ask, "In what direction would you like your career to head?" you enable the individual to answer your question honestly. See "Finding a star," later in this chapter, for more tips on getting honest answers from team members.

Asking questions that facilitate resource management

If you have team members stretched thin by several other labor-intensive projects, you need to know that — yesterday!

You need to ask questions of your project team members to determine what their schedules are like and whether they have vacations or other events looming, and to identify which areas of the project they're most interested in. You're not looking to make promises or demands here; you're only finding out what the team members' requirements and interests are.

This process allows you to make the best decisions when it comes to resource assignments. Ideally, you want to assign people to the activities they are most interested in, because they're likely to perform at their potential for these activities; however, that's not always feasible, so don't make any promises during this phase of questions. Their calendar constraints, skill sets, and your confidence in them may all discourage you from assigning them to the work they want to do.

You may discover that some of your team members love to do the boring, tedious work that software development is full of. Some individuals actually enjoy pouring over code and completing rounds and rounds of application testing. Not everyone wants to be front and center with the project development, and not everyone wants to be in the middle of lots of inefficient meetings and conferences. These folks just want to come in, write their code, and be left alone. That's fine; there's always a place for that. It's your mission, if you choose to accept it, to find out who those people are and let them code without the need to have a lot of interaction with stakeholders. Determine the interests and skills of your project team members and provide the appropriate environment for them to flourish.

Here are some questions you should ask your project team members:

- What other projects are you working on?
- What time commitments do you have on these projects?
- What areas of this project excite you the most?
- What areas of this project do you dread?
- What areas of this type of project work have you done before?
- Have you ever worked with technology such-and-such (whichever new technology you might be using for your project)?

Asking questions that facilitate leadership potential

By asking questions that help you discover what motivates people, you can put your leadership skills to their best use. We discuss project leadership in more depth in Chapter 11, but as a general rule, you must have a real desire to know your team, and empathy for the people you're trying to lead.

Project leadership requires a genuine interest in your project team members. You want to know what their interests are and what their goals are beyond your project, even your organization. Your desire is to help them reach their goals even if means that they may one day leave your project, your organization, and you, their favorite project manager, far behind.

If you don't know how to lead, emulate a leader you admire. This could be someone from your own organization — or a public figure — whose leadership skills you respect.

Here are questions you should ask your project team members in order to strengthen your leadership opportunities:

- What are your career goals?
- Are there any areas within this project that can bring you closer to achieving your career goals?
- What excites you about this project?
- What would you like to contribute to the project?
- What would you like to learn from this project?
- How can this project help you move forward?
- What opportunities do you see to make this project better?

Finding a star

When you're having a conversation with prospective project team members, your goal is to find out how they can help you complete the project and how you can help them achieve their goals so that you can create a win/win situation. The *STAR* interview method is an approach that you can use to help the prospect identify experiences, and cut through some bunk that may slip into their recollections.

STAR stands for *s*ituation, *t*ask, *a*ction, and *r*esult. The idea is that you ask questions that require the prospective team member to discuss a specific task or situation he faced and what actions he took to resolve the issue. The belief behind this concept is that a person's past behavior is an indicator of his future behavior.

Here's how it works:

1. **You present the project team member with a situation.**

   For example, you could say, "Tell me about a development project where you went above and beyond the call of duty to ensure quality in the deliverable?"

2. **The team member then responds with a situation, followed by the task of going above and beyond the call of duty.**

3. **You may have to prompt the individual for the actions that he or she took and ask the person to explain the results of his or her actions on the project.**

   The STAR approach is often used in job interviews, and gives you insight into a person's experience, accomplishments, and strengths.

 Follow your organization's rules and procedures when asking questions of your team. This process is not a job interview, but a fact-finding mission. You're trying to discover important information about the team member — not run an interrogation. Don't go overboard or intimidate your team members.

Working with organizational structures

Before you can get to the project team involvement, you need to have a project team. In some organizations, the project manager works with the same project team over and over. In other organizations, the project team is cherry-picked based on the demands of each project and the individual skills required.

Your project team will be assembled based on your organizational structure, and you have to abide by the policies implemented by your company's Human Resources team. You need to understand what you're allowed to do when it comes to recruiting team members. As a general rule, if you don't know, ask.

Determining Who Is Really in Charge

It's imperative to know who the real project manager is. If you have ever been on a project where the project team looked to you for a decision and then was shocked to see the project sponsor step in and make the decision for you, you know what we're talking about.

Here's a scenario: Your project team members bypass you and go to functional managers, stakeholders, or even the project sponsor with issues that need to be resolved.

Did you say, "Grrr . . ."?

Within your organization there needs to be a clear picture of who's in charge. That person is the only one who should be making crucial decisions, serving as the hub of communications, and approving project work. Ideally, um, that person is you.

The level of power you have as a project manager is tied to the structure of your organization. Organizational structure is just a fancy way of determining where the power is within your company. It's more than just the power at the top of the flow chart, but rather who has the project power when it comes to making decisions for your project team. Have a slurp of coffee. This stuff is theory on paper — but powerful in action.

Organizational structures come in five flavors. Each organizational structure has pros and cons, and each structure identifies the level of power the project manager should have (notice the cautionary phrase "should have"). Your organizational structure will also influence how your team is gathered. Figure 7-2 does its thing to show you five of these structures in action.

Here is an overview of the six organizational structures:

- **Projectized:** Assigns the power to the project manager

- **Strong Matrix:** Assigns more power to the project manager than the functional (department) manager

- **Balanced Matrix:** Assigns equal power to the project manager and the functional manager

- **Weak Matrix:** Assigns more power to the functional manager than the project manager

- **Functional:** Assigns the power to the functional manager

- **Composite:** Intermingles parts of the other organizational structures

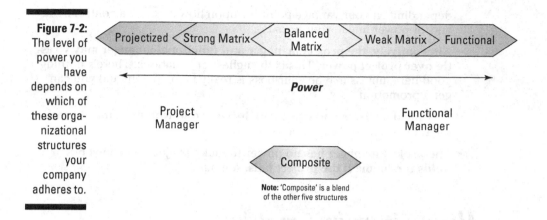

Figure 7-2:
The level of power you have depends on which of these organizational structures your company adheres to.

Functioning in a functional organization

At the bottom of the pile is the *functional structure*. The functional structure is an organization that treats each department like its own little organization; each department — Sales, Finance, IT, Manufacturing, and so on — is an independent fiefdom. Each department acts as its own entity within the organization and they purchase services from one another.

In a functional structure, the *functional manager* has all the power over all the projects in his or her realm. The members of a PM's team come from within the same department, and the project manager may also be known as a *project coordinator* or *expeditor* because he or she is just carrying out the instructions of the functional manager. The project manager has little to no authority in this structure.

Usually projects do not cross functional boundaries. The project team will work on the project on a part-time basis while the remainder of their time is assigned to their normal day-to-day activities. There are some pros and cons to this structure:

✔ **Communication is shallow, because only the team, the project manager, and the functional manager need to communicate with each other.** This feature can be either a major pain or a major benefit. With less power comes less responsibility for communicating across departments. That frees up the PM to do the more detailed aspects of his or her job well. Of course, the down side of having less power to communicate is that when you have something important to say, no one may be listening.

✔ **There is no confusion about who's in charge. The functional manager is the one with all the real power.** This can be a pro and a con, as well, depending on your vantage point (or upon how much of a control freak and/or power junkie your boss is).

✔ **Alternatively, the project manager and functional manager may wrestle over project power.** This is the ugliest of situations. There's nothing good here, unless maybe your boss is really incompetent and you can get a promotion.

✔ **Technical decisions may be made by someone with little (or no) technical experience.** Again, not too many bonuses here.

✔ **The project manager has no power to make project decisions but holds the blame if the project fails.** Ah, bliss.

Mixing it up in a matrix

A *matrix structure,* unlike the functional structure, uses resources from all over the organization, not just a single department. A matrix structure allows project team members to participate in projects and in operations. The idea is that by blending resources with a common eye towards organizational success, rather than just department success, everyone wins.

Sounds good on paper.

There are three types of matrix structures with each depicting the amount of power assigned to the project manager:

✔ **Weak matrix:** The functional manager has more power than the project manager does over the project

✔ **Balanced matrix:** The functional manager and the project manager have equal power over the project

✔ **Strong matrix:** The project manager has more power than the functional manager does over the project

The matrix structure also allows project team members to be on multiple projects at the same time, rather than one project at a time. The project manager may also be managing multiple projects or serve as a resource in one project while managing a different project. Matrix structured organizations often have projects that interact, such as the software development project and the software training project.

Pros of a matrix structure include the following:

✔ Resources can be used from all over the organization.

✔ The project manager may work as project manager on a full-time basis.

✔ The project may shift resources based on other projects or team members' roles in the project.

✔ Project team members are not on the project full-time, but only when their discipline is needed.

There are lots of problems with matrix structures:

✔ **Power struggles abound.** Welcome to the world.

✔ **The project team is often confused about who's in charge.** ("My sister, my mother, my sister, my mother . . .")

✔ **Because there's no single functional manager, the PM faces huge communications demands.** The PM must communicate with all of the functional managers of the project team members. It's a nightmare. Take our word for it.

✔ **The project team members are probably on multiple projects with different project managers.** Let's get ready to rumble — there may be competition for resources.

✔ Team members may feel overutilized as they are involved in multiple projects.

On a higher level, the project managers may compete for resources, time, and priority among all the projects in the organization.

Prospering in the projectized structure

At the top of the heap is the *projectized structure*. This model assigns the project manager all the power, and the project team is on this one project full-time for the duration of the project's life.

This is ideal for organizations that have high-profile projects or they complete projects for other organizations — such as an IT integrator. The project team focuses all of the effort and concentration on one project, completes it, and then, usually, moves on to the next project. In this type of structure, the project manager may take on functional manager responsibilities, such as salary responsibilities, hiring and firing, and other personnel management functions.

This structure is great because

✔ The project team contributes to projects full-time.

✔ Communication demands are greatly reduced.

✔ The project manager has autonomy over project decisions.

✔ Usually a project office or program office will support the project manager.

The downside of a projectized organization is that the project team may have anxiety when the project wraps up. The anxiety centers on what the project team will do after the project is completed. Some team members are folded into new projects, while other project team members may be dismissed. The project team may also feel internal power struggles for project leadership. The projectized model may use contract employees on a short-term basis, so when the project's done, these individuals may become inessential.

Five personality types you don't want on your team

There are five types of project team members that we don't ever want on our projects — and that you don't want on yours. If you notice some characteristics from the following lists in people you work with, you have to take action to mold these folks into the exciting, project-delivering team members that all project managers envy.

✔ **The Cowboy:** This person is wild and loony. Cowboys are high-strung, willing to experiment on the fly, and can't remember what they've done to the code — or why. Cowboys don't think twice about adding inappropriate comments to the code, hiding Easter eggs in the application, and tinkering with the project scope. Cowboys are often smart and fast workers and like to be creative. Rustle these folks in by establishing rules and procedures, quality control, such as peer review, and direct conversations on what's permissible and what activities should be put out to pasture.

✔ **The Mouse:** The Mouse is a shy, timid person who needs your direction, approval, and strong hand on every action he or she takes. Mice can be easily influenced by team members, stakeholders, and their own fear to move forward with their work. Your job is to teach mice to roar by building their confidence and forcing them to make decisions on their own.

✔ **The Rock:** Tough, stubborn, and hard to move, that's the Rock. Rocks are the folks who usually have years of experience and want to do things their way because it's the right way. These are the types of folks who say, "There are two ways to develop an application: my way and the right way — and they are both the same." Deal with the Rock by establishing a firm chain of command and sticking to it.

✔ **The Linguist:** Linguists love language, and they don't know when to stop talking. Their endless conversations eat up project time, meeting time, and steal time from other developers, who are working on their assignments (or trying to). You'll have to deal with these folks directly by steering them back in the right direction — toward the point of the discussion. If the linguist starts rambling during a meeting, you might say something such as "Amanda, let's get back to the topic of system testing." If a linguist disrupts the project team, you have to step in occasionally.

✔ **The Uncle:** Remember your favorite uncle? He's the guy with all the jokes, funny stories, and magic tricks. You like your uncle, but you don't need him on your project. Uncles (or aunts) are often quick workers, and they assume that the rest of the project team works as fast as they do. Assign more challenging work to these people to make sure they don't get bored and start pulling quarters from their teammates' ears.

Cooling in a composite structure

We said there were six structures, but if you were counting, and we know that you were (you're so detail oriented), we only mentioned five. The last structure is a *composite*. A composite is a structure that uses a blend of any of the five structures. For example, Wacky-Wicky, Inc., follows a traditional functional structure.

This business has a high-profile, important project in the offing, so it breaks out one project team and assigns a full-time project manager to the project. This relatively conservatively structured organization has emulated a projectized structure for one project; meanwhile, the rest of the employees at Wacky-Wicky are jealous because they still have to follow the functional structure.

Hosting Your First Project Team Meeting

The first time the project team meets, it's just to get to know one another, if they don't already, and to establish the ground rules and procedures of how the project will operate. The first meeting is your opportunity to establish several key things:

- ✔ You're in charge
- ✔ The scope of the project and what the customer is expecting
- ✔ Introductions if the project team members don't know one another
- ✔ Identification of the roles of the project team members
- ✔ High-level objectives for time, cost, and quality
- ✔ Your expectations regarding communication and issue escalation
- ✔ Any caveats, issues, or pending decisions with the project work

For your first project team meeting, and for every project team meeting hereafter, you should provide an agenda prior to the meeting and invite project team members to comment on the accuracy of the agenda. By getting an agenda together in advance, you enable the project team to take responsibility for airing important issues and other business. An agenda also enables you to set the tone ("this is official — we even have an agenda") and to stick to the agenda rather than rambling from topic to topic.

The longer your project team is in a meeting, the longer they're away from their project work, so make the effort to make your team meetings efficient and effective.

Your first project meeting should also introduce your approach to project management, especially if some (or all) members of the project team haven't worked with you in the past. You set the stage and set expectations, and you allow the project team to identify what they can expect from you in return. Your first project team meeting should also accomplish the following:

- ✔ You establish the flow of communication between you, the project team, and stakeholders

- ✔ You provide an overview of the change control system, including versioning and configuration management (find out more about change control in Chapter 13)

- ✔ You establish immediate activities for the project team

- ✔ You open the floor to discuss issues and pending decisions

- ✔ You distribute the project charter and scope statement

- ✔ You distribute a team directory (or refer to its online location) so team members can easily contact one another

If there are electronic procedures, such as how to check the software's current build, how to use the risk database access, or how to view the project plan files, this information should be printed and distributed to the project team.

Finally, your first project team meeting should identify the process of recording the team meeting minutes. Yes, someone should record the minutes of every meeting you have with your project team. This may be a project management assistant if you're operating in a projectized or strong matrix, or members of the project team can take turns documenting the meeting minutes. The minutes document promises, discussions, timelines, due dates, and the conversation of the project meeting.

Working with Organizational Policies

Every organization has rules about managing project teams. Your level of power is determined by the organizational structure, but levels of power associated with the human resources may override any power you assume you have. For example, you may be operating in a strong matrix, but that doesn't mean you can fire project team members at will, regardless of how much they bother you.

You need to work with your manager, Human Resources department, and the managers of the project team members to determine what actions you can take before there's a need to take any actions at all. Know the rules and procedures before the project work begins so that you know what you're allowed to do.

Relying on the Project Human Resources Management plan

You should have a plan for managing your project team. In each organizational structure, from functional to projectized, you need an HR Management plan that establishes several things:

✔ Who has the authority over the project team

✔ The process for team member discipline

✔ How team members are brought into and released from the project team

✔ The expectation for the roles within the project team

✔ Rules and policies specific to the project you're managing

You can create the Project Human Resources Management plan for each project from a boilerplate document. Just to be clear, you can't arbitrarily create an HR Management plan without a sign-off from someone in HR. Your plan should be in alignment with already established policies and procedures, and fit your organization's culture.

The point of the HR Management plan is to ensure that everyone on the project team knows how the project will operate, who's in charge, and what's expected. It also outlines consequences if team members don't perform as expected.

For example, if you're responsible for completing reviews of the project team members, compiling reports to send to their functional managers, or reporting each team member's performance to an HR manager, you've got some influence over team members' willingness to complete the project work.

Never go to management with just a problem. Always goes to management when you've got a problem and a suggested solution, whether it's concerning HR issues or any issues.

Chapter 8

Creating Project Time Estimates

. . . .

In This Chapter

▶ Getting organized before you start

▶ Getting a PND in order

▶ Letting history be your guide

▶ Finding the critical path

▶ Making an estimate

. . . .

*I*t's Monday morning and you're hard at work on one of the many projects you manage for your company, a large manufacturer. Susanna, the Chief Operating Officer, pops into your office because she wants to chat with you about a new project. She explains that the purpose of the project is to create a piece of software that will measure the productivity of each piece of equipment on the shop floor.

She envisions that the software will somehow connect to the machinery on the shop floor and measure the speed and efficiency of each piece of equipment. The measurements taken by the software will allow the organization to make changes to improve productivity. Susanna says that she'll leave all the tech stuff up to you and your experts, but she does have some ideas on what the software interface should look like and what components it should measure.

And then she asks, "So, how long will this take to create?"

Isn't that a great question? You don't have enough information, most likely, to give a reasonable answer. You don't know the project scope or the required resources to interface with the manufacturing equipment. You also have several other projects in the mix. But Susanna needs an answer now. You could give a guesstimate, but she'll hold you to it. What's your best move?

First, stall. In fact, whenever possible, you should avoid specifics, especially if you're just starting out as a project manager. Wait until you've had a chance to evaluate all the details. Coincidentally, the point of this chapter is to help you evaluate and plan a timeline. We explain how to create time estimates, how to schedule project work, how to create a project calendar, and how to avoid scenarios in which you give a bad estimate because you're being pressed.

Organizing Information Before You Build a Timeline

Here's a rough order of the things you need to do if you want to provide a truly useful and accurate time estimate:

1. Gather requirements (see Chapter 6).

2. Create a WBS (see Chapter 3).

3. Determine skill sets and resources (see Chapter 7).

4. Create a *project network diagram* PND (we discuss the PND in the following section).

5. Develop a *rough order of magnitude* (ROM) estimate (we discuss this topic later in this chapter).

6. Develop an approximate time estimate.

7. Create a schedule.

8. Optimize the schedule (we explain these topics later in this chapter).

9. Finalize the estimate with a schedule baseline.

Every project manager's goal is to create the most accurate estimate possible. Unfortunately, finding the best technique to accomplish this task takes time. But with the right tools, you can do it. Make sure you have a work breakdown structure (WBS). The WBS is needed because it reflects everything that the project manager and the project team must create to complete the job. The more details you have, the better prepared you'll be to factor in delays, risks, and small, time-consuming jobs when you work out the project network diagram and the project timeline.

Understanding the Importance of a Project Network Diagram

A *project network diagram* (PND) is a roadmap of the sequence of activities needed to complete the project work. In Figure 8-1, you see a PND in which each node represents an activity and the arrows indicate the dependencies. We discuss how to create your very own PND in this chapter.

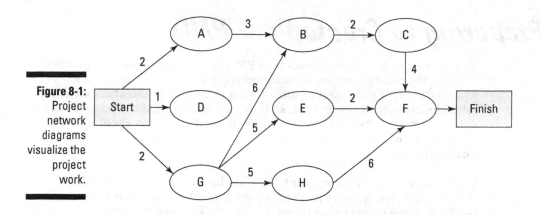

Figure 8-1:
Project
network
diagrams
visualize the
project
work.

The PND focuses on the sequence of the activities needed to complete the project scope as well as the precedent activities (represented by the arrows) and the activity durations. When you create the PND, you can examine how long the project might take to complete.

PNDs are great because they enable you to visually sequence the work. That way, you have a better chance of estimating more accurate durations. Here are some other reasons to enjoy PNDs:

✔ You won't be able to assess how long the project might actually take until you see the order in which the work should, or can, happen.

✔ You can make educated decisions about the order of the activities that may influence project timings, forecasting, and labor assignments.

The PND can help you assign tandem tasks together, streamlining your timeline. Your team can do some activities in tandem with other activities, while others must happen in a particular order.

✔ If, after putting together the PND, you discover that some tasks are more complicated than others, you can assign these activities to more experienced team members. For example, if time is tight, consider assigning a senior developer to a task instead of training a new developer to do the work. When you have a bit more time, you can provide some professional development to a less experienced developer, but not when the software is due, like, *yesterday.*

✔ Some activities are effort-driven, which means that you can add more labor to complete the work faster.

✔ Some activities are of fixed duration, which means they'll take the same amount of time regardless of how many people you put on them.

Preparing to Create Your PND

Before you can hop in and create your PND, you need to gather several items. Perhaps the most important information you must possess are the names or assigned roles of your team members. Your project team members are the folks closest to the project work, so they understand what the project work entails. You need them to help you make the best decisions about which activities should happen in which order — and how long these activities might take.

You need your favorite document, the work breakdown structure (WBS). Well, you don't need just the WBS, but also the activity list that comes from the WBS. If you haven't read Chapter 3 yet, the WBS is a deliverables-oriented decomposition of the project scope. The information in the WBS tells you what activities have to happen. At the end of your project you use the WBS to prove that your project team has completed all of the work listed in the PND according to the product scope and project scope. In other words, the WBS is a pretty important document.

You use *progressive elaboration* when you're developing a project schedule. At the start of the project, you create the schedule based on the requirements that you've gathered, but as you gain more detailed knowledge of the project specifications, you fine-tune the schedule and make it more comprehensive. The concept of progressive elaboration builds on the fundamental principle that project management is an iterative process; it just keeps getting better with age.

Determining What May Happen — and When

With your team and tools gathered, you're almost ready to begin plotting out the network diagram. Projects rarely fit together like a string of pearls — activities don't tend to happen in a sequential and orderly fashion. Most projects are more like a web, where chains of activities branch out and then come back together as the project draws to a close.

In the real world, your project will have different branches, representing relationships between activities. Activities are categorized in the following ways, depending on their placement in the project network diagram:

- **Predecessor:** Activities that precede the downstream activities
- **Successor:** Activities that come after predecessor activities

Fudging and wiggling with leads and lags

In addition to successor and predecessor relationships, which we discuss elsewhere in this chapter, lead time and lag time can help you make a more accurate PND. *Lag time* is waiting time. *Lead time* is time you spend waiting — hurry up!

Here's how you can put lead and lag time to use:

✔ Add lag time to separate activities. For example, you might add five days of lag time between compiling the software and the successor activity of operational transfer. *Operational transfer* occurs when you leave the implementation phase of your project and enter the support phase. There is usually a separate team or department that supports the software after it is implemented.

✔ Subtract lead time between activities when you know that the schedule is a bit padded. For example, you may have a finish-to-start relationship between the online help system and the training documentation. By adding three days of lead time to the training documentation activity, the start of the training activity can overlap with the online help system.

Any activity, other than the first and last activity in the network diagram, can be a predecessor and successor. The relationship between predecessors and successors describes when activities begin and end. The following describes the four relationships you can use in a network diagram:

✔ **Finish-to-start:** The predecessor activity must finish before the successor activity can start. This is the most common relationship type. *Example:* The Web server must be running before the SQL database can connect.

✔ **Finish-to-finish:** Two activities must finish at the same time. The two activities don't have to begin at once, but they must end at the same time. *Example:* The user acceptability testing and the third-party reviews of the build must complete at the same time.

✔ **Start-to-start:** Two activities must begin at the same time. The two activities may be of varying duration, so they don't have to end at the same time, but they have to start at the same time. *Example:* The final build of the software and the creation of the online help system should start at the same time.

✔ **Start-to-finish:** The predecessor activity must start in order for the successor activity to finish. This is the most unusual of all the relationship types and is rarely used. You might run across it if you do *just-in-time* scheduling or manufacturing. *Example:* The software testing can't be completed until the quality control department reviews the testing results.

Factoring in external dependencies

Many projects depend on vendors or other projects to move forward. These are referred to generally as *external dependencies,* and are typically out of the project manager's control. You need to identify as many external dependencies as possible early on so that you can plot their timing in your network diagram. For example, if you know that a consultant will be involved in the project at a specific point, you can plan all of the work that needs to be completed before the consultant is scheduled to arrive.

Putting together all the pieces

After you assemble your project team and outline all of its future activities, you need to begin snapping together the PND. Over time, you will develop your own signature method for creating a project network diagram, but try this method first:

1. **Transfer each identified activity to its own designated sticky note.**

2. **Arrange all the sticky notes on a whiteboard in the order that the activities should take place.**

   If activities can occur in tandem, place those corresponding sticky notes in a column.

3. **Draw relationships between each activity.**

   You simply draw a line with an arrow going from the predecessor to the successor activity.

4. **Let the PND creation cool for a day or two.**

5. **Revisit the PND with the project team to examine the network for errors, risks, or mistakes.**

6. **Document any risks, issues, or pending decisions.**

7. **Transfer the PND creation from the whiteboard to your favorite project management information system.**

If you have a very large software project with over 100 activities (or however many activities your organization deems a large project), you won't find using sticky notes for each activity useful as much as you will find it cumbersome and difficult to follow, if not downright sticky. For a very large project, it may be more efficient to use sticky notes for those items at the deliverable level instead of the activity level. Another option would be to break your large software project down into subprojects and use the sticky notes for the subprojects.

Using hard logic

As you and the project team begin to plot out the sequence of activities, you'll rely first on hard logic. *Hard logic* describes the work that must be done in a particular order. For example, consider that you must install an operating system before you can install the application. The application has to be installed before you can collect the data. And so on.

Hard logic is also known as evaluating *mandatory dependencies.* You and the project team need to identify the hard logic within your project so that you can map out the activities in the correct order. You can always revisit your PND and change the relationships between activities as the project moves forward; however, wouldn't you rather make sure that the relationships are correct the first time?

Relying on soft logic

You use *soft logic,* sometimes called evaluating *discretionary dependencies,* when you make choices to arrange activities in a particular order not because you have to, but because you and the project team feel it's the best order of the work. For example, you could have several developers working on different portions of the same application all at the same time, but by using soft logic you might arrange the activities to have the developers work on the different portions of the application in a sequential order.

Relying on network templates

Creating a PND sounds like a bunch of work because it *is* a bunch of work. Planning the sequence of activities takes time and effort. In addition, heated debates, conflicts, and open issues can hinder how the work progresses.

Now for some good news: If you do the same type of work over and over, you don't have to start from scratch every time. Instead, you can create a project network diagram template. A template, as you know, is a standardized document that has basic information and common activities already filled in. A good template just requires you to fill in the correct dates for the major activities your team performs.

You can easily create a template by using a past project of similar work. The catch, however, is that you'll also want to review the lessons learned from the past project to ensure that the work on your next project goes as expected. Great templates are made, not born. The network template should be accurate, yet fluid, so that you can adapt it to each future project.

Identifying subnets and fragnets

Within your PND, you may also find it useful to identify subprojects or out-sourced portions of your project. These other projects are identified as *sub-nets* and *fragnets* and are often visualized in the network diagram as a cloud that shows the predecessor activities and successor activities of the subnet.

For example, you may outsource the creation of the application's online help system. You probably won't want to map out all of the steps your vendor will follow to complete the help system, but you will want to make sure that this portion of the project work is visualized in the network diagram. Make sure that the predecessors reach the outsourced work, and that the successors are dependent on the outsourced work.

Using Historical Information to Complete Inexact Activity Time Estimates

To create an accurate time estimate of how long the project will last, you need your PND. The network diagram shows the sequence of events, which, when combined with the duration estimates and resource availability, tell you the total duration for the project.

But what if you have someone breathing down your neck right now? In the real world, you can't do all the work you *should* do to give a good estimate to your stakeholders. However, you do have a few options for estimating (in a less than exact way) how long a project will last before you create the project network diagram.

Activity duration estimating, like the project network diagram creation, isn't a solo activity. You need your project team members' participation, because they are the folks that are closest to the project work; they're the folks who'll be doing the work. A better source of input than team member's recollections, however, is documented historical information.

Historical information comes from past project performance. This is assuming, of course, that historical information exists and that it is accurate and readily available. Keep accurate assessments of your project work and complete your lessons-learned documentation as the project moves towards completion. Your current project will eventually become your future historical information.

Identifying Activity Duration Influencers

Every project has attributes and influencers that may cause the actual activity durations to fluctuate. *Activity duration influencers* are any conditions that may cause the duration estimates you provide to be inaccurate, unstable, or subject to change. By documenting these influencers during your duration estimates, you're covering your, er, assets. Be sure to communicate which conditions can cause the project to last longer (or, on rare occasions, shorter) than planned. The following sections list the most common influencers.

Documenting project assumptions

Project assumptions include anything that you believe to be true, but that you can't prove to be true. For example, you assume that the vendor will deliver the hardware by a given date. Or you assume that if your team has to travel there won't be any extensive travel delays due to weather. Common project assumptions to consider:

- ✔ Hardware conflicts won't exist
- ✔ Software conflicts won't exist
- ✔ Technology interoperability won't hinder the project's progress
- ✔ The project team will deliver work as scheduled
- ✔ The project team will have access to needed systems
- ✔ The needed resources will be available throughout the project
- ✔ Changes to the project scope will follow a predefined change control system

Project assumptions must be documented as early as possible in the project planning phase to ensure that all of the stakeholders are working under the same set of assumptions. You document the assumptions in the project scope statement, which we describe in Chapter 3.

If an assumption is later proven not to be true, the assumption may be a risk to your project. One of the first places you go to identify project risks is the assumption log.

Documenting project constraints

A *constraint* is anything that may restrict the project manager's ability to get the project done. Constraints are usually identified as rules, regulations, or restrictions that the project manager must work within while completing the project work. For example, if you know that you must have the project completed by December 30, that's a schedule constraint. Here are some common constraints to consider:

- ✔ **Budget constraint:** You have a preset budget to meet an identified scope.

- ✔ **Schedule constraint:** You have a deadline for the project completion or dates within the project to deliver key components of the software.

- ✔ **Technical constraint:** You may need to program in a certain language, or build software that is consistent with legacy applications.

- ✔ **Regulations:** You may need to follow legal or industry-specific regulations that require your project team to do extra work, complete extra communications, and so on.

- ✔ **Resource constraint:** Your project team members may be on multiple projects at the same time, so they'll likely have conflicts within their schedule and your project's schedule. Resources can also include facilities, equipment, and materials that you may need to complete the project.

- ✔ **Organizational constraints:** This is a big bucket of constraints that your organization enforces on your project. Consider internal procedures, meetings, communications, quality assurance programs, and more.

- ✔ **Skills and competency levels:** If your project team members don't have the capacity to deliver the project scope, they will constrain your ability to get the project work done.

Like assumptions, constraints can turn into risks if the constraint impacts the ability to deliver the project.

Considering the project risks

You need to consider project risks when you create activity duration estimates, because if the risks do come into play you may face delays.

Consider a project to create and distribute a piece of software to 25,000 users. One of the risks involved is that a vendor may be late delivering its portion of the project. If the vendor is late, then there's a ripple effect, not only for the vendor's lateness, but also for your quality review of the vendor's deliverable, the possibility of rework, the time to incorporate the vendor's deliverable into your project, and on and on — your project may have many items yet to complete that depend on this single deliverable.

In addition to vendor delays, common risks include the following:

- ✔ Project team members' delays
- ✔ Errors and omissions that lead to reworking

> ✔ Scope creep
>
> ✔ Project resources assigned to too many project activities simultaneously

Considering resource requirements and capabilities

When you begin to estimate how long a software project will take to complete, you must consider the amount of labor you need to satisfy the project scope. If you think you need eight C# developers and you've only got three available, your project will either have to hire more developers or extend the project schedule to allow for your developer shortage.

Most software development projects are labor driven, which means that you can add more labor to drive the project duration down. However, as Figure 8-2 depicts, the *law of diminishing returns* restricts a project manager from adding infinite resources. Eventually, you reach a limit where the productivity actually goes down when you add more people. Just because 8 developers can finish a project in four months doesn't necessarily mean that you can add 16 developers to complete the job in half the time.

Getting a bird's-eye view of the law of diminishing returns

Did you skip Econ 101? No problem. Here's what you need to know about the law of diminishing returns:

✔ **There is a fixed amount of yield, and your yield is in proportion to the amount of labor assigned.** The classic example from Econ 101 is harvesting a wheat field. There's only so much wheat in the field, regardless of how much labor you add, so getting the field harvested in half the time won't pay off. You still have to pay all those extra laborers. The same idea applies to software development. More labor doesn't immediately equate to a better piece of software or more profits.

✔ **Adding labor doesn't guarantee time savings.** If you've ever heard the expression "Too many cooks spoil the broth," you may

know what we're getting at here. Maybe you have even experienced this phenomenon when you put a ton of developers on a project, only to realize that instead of working they argued with each other over how to do the project work. This isn't just a fluke — it's a likely occurrence.

✔ **Adding labor doesn't equate to relative productivity.** As more and more developers are added to the project, each developer will create slightly less code than the developer that's been on the project longer. In other words, the first developer will likely do the most labor because she's been on the project since day one, while the newest developer won't create as much code simply because there's less to accomplish in the project.

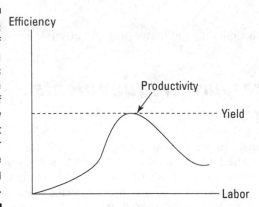

Figure 8-2:
The law of diminishing returns restricts the amount of productivity a project manager will realize by adding more labor.

Anticipating the first-time, first-use penalty

At the onset of each project, you need to consider the competency and talent levels of your project team. If the team is not proficient in the development environment, your time estimates aren't likely to be very accurate. If you're developing software in a new language or this is a type of project you've never done before, then your team may suffer from the first-time, first-use penalty.

The first-time, first-use penalty means that if you've never done something before, you're likely to not be very good at it. The good news is that you can accurately predict the penalty: It'll inevitably take longer to complete the work (and may cost more too) because everyone on the project team is learning as they go. Think of first-time, first-use as similar to the concept of the learning curve. The learning curve states that efficiency increases the more times a person repeats a task. Simply account for a bit more time on the project, because you know it's going to be bumpy.

Making the Project Duration Estimate

Management wants to know two things:

1. How much?

2. How long?

We discuss costs in Chapter 9. In the previous sections, we've discussed all the inputs you need to enter to find the time estimate, as well as all the risks and factors you need to take into account. Now it's time for politics. You must be smart when you consider what type of an estimate management is *really* looking for.

Creating a rough order of magnitude estimate

If you're caught in an elevator with your boss and he throws out some wild idea for a piece of software, fully expecting an answer about the project duration, chances are your estimate won't be all that reliable. After all, you're in an elevator, trying to guess at the project scope, the project requirements, and you've really got no clear idea on how many resources you'll need or their ability to complete the project activities.

At best, you can provide a *rough order of magnitude* (ROM) estimate. A ROM estimate can be wildly off target — from 25 to 75 percent off, or even more, so if you give one, be sure to add a disclaimer. We explain the relationship between ROM and your budget in Chapter 9.

Hallway estimates, elevator estimates, and coffee shop estimates are dangerous to offer because the second that management hears a timeframe, it becomes a guarantee. Always, always, always preface ROM estimates with, "This is a wild estimate and I would need to gather more definitive project requirements in order to give you a more reliable estimate," or you'll be haunted by whatever schedule you offer. Unfortunately, even with that preamble, you may still be haunted by the estimate.

Creating an analogous estimate

An *analogous estimate* is an estimate that creates an analogy between your proposed project and one that's been done in the past. Say you're managing a new project to create a database to track help desk calls. The project needs to track who's calling, how often they're calling, and what their issues are. If you managed a similar project a year ago to track sales calls, you can pull out that project's archives, lessons learned, and timeline to see what resource you think your current project will need to complete.

If your previous project took six months from start to finish, and it matches the current scope of your project, and you have approximately the same number and type of resources, you have a little historical evidence to create an analogous estimate.

Of course, there will differences in scope, so you'll have to use your expert judgment and input from your project team to determine an accurate timeline. Perhaps the new project is more detailed. If so, you may want to start out with nine months as your analogous estimate.

Creating a parametric estimate

A *parametric estimate* is one of the simplest estimates to offer (even if the term doesn't sound so simple), but you may not have many opportunities to employ it in software project management. When using a parametric estimate, you find a parameter, usually in the form of units. For example, you might say that it takes 8 hours per unit to install. If you have 500 units, you multiply the parameter (8) times 500 to get your estimate in hours (in this example, the job will get done in 4,000 hours, or ten 40-hour weeks).

Using parametric estimates in software project management is difficult because you're usually estimating time for the developers, not for units they're creating. It may be possible to use a parametric estimate when you're troubleshooting, fixing databases, or pushing software out to clients via a network, but usually you can find a better way to predict timelines in software projects.

If your shop completes projects for other organizations, you may have already developed your own parametric estimates. Some IT integrators do the same type of projects over and over, so they can predict how long that project will take based on the number of developers assigned to the project. They simply use the number of developers assigned to the project as the parameter for predicting time.

You have to be careful when using a developer as a parameter. On paper, you can reason that two developers can work faster than one, but that's not always true. One developer may have superior skills, better organizational skills, and a higher level of proficiency than the other.

In addition, there's the concept of a day's worth of work. A developer can bill for eight hours of labor every day, but meetings, phone calls, and distractions all steal time away from your project. Tracking metrics, such as time devoted to creating code versus time in meetings, planning, troubleshooting, and so on, can give you solid input to how many hours it'll take to complete a project, and then you can extrapolate from there how many days it'll take to get the whole thing done, but doesn't this seem like a lot of work?

Estimating Do's and Don'ts

Here are some tips to help you come up with the best timeline estimate possible:

✔ **Don't work alone:** Work with your project team to examine your project network diagram, determine the duration of each activity, and then determine when the project will be able to complete.

✔ **Don't work in a vacuum:** Even if you've got all your team asking questions and shaking it, a Magic 8 Ball will not help you come up with an accurate timeline.

✔ **Do get everyone onboard:** Let us repeat: No one on your team is allowed to use a Magic 8 Ball. Their time estimates must be as accurate as possible.

✔ **Don't bloat:** Every task estimate team members provide tends to end up being overinflated, and your project, on paper, looks like it'll take a lot longer than it should.

When you begin padding time estimates, you succumb to Parkinson's Law. *Parkinson's Law* states that work will expand to fill the amount of time allotted to it. So when Bob says it'll take 40 hours to do a task that should only take 30 hours, it'll magically take 40 hours to complete. Bob will take as much time as he's given, not because he's a bad guy, but because he's human. This is also called *students' syndrome.*

✔ **Do take advantage of management reserve:** *Management reserve* is a collection of time that's appended to the end of your network diagram. It's usually 15 percent of the project duration, although you can determine how much based on your comfort level with the project scope. All estimates, you should stress to the bigwigs, are accurate *without* padding. The reserve is there so that when real issues arise, you can take it if you need it.

Using PERT for the Most Accurate Estimates

One approach to creating an accurate time estimate is something called PERT. PERT means *program evaluation and review technique;* it's an estimating approach that requires three estimates for every activity to account for uncertainty:

✔ **Optimistic:** The best-case scenario

✔ **Most likely:** The most-likely time

✔ **Pessimistic:** The worst that can happen

With PERT, you just plug these estimates into a simple formula:

```
Pessimistic + Optimistic + (4 × the Most Likely)
```

Then divide the sum by 6. Figure 8-3 shows the formula in action. PERT is the only time-estimating technique that has a level of risk assessment built into it, because it considers the worst-case scenarios.

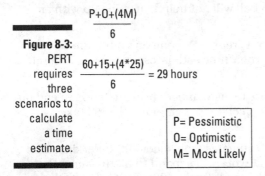

Figure 8-3: PERT requires three scenarios to calculate a time estimate.

$$\frac{P+O+(4M)}{6}$$

$$\frac{60+15+(4*25)}{6} = 29 \text{ hours}$$

> P= Pessimistic
> O= Optimistic
> M= Most Likely

Knowing What to Say if the Boss Wants an Estimate Now

Remember Susanna, the COO in the introduction to his chapter? If she wants answers to her questions, you should respond by covering the following details, without exception, before giving her any concrete answers (Memorize this list!):

✔ **Clarify that this is only an estimate.** Based on the information you've been supplied, WBS or not, you'll never really know how long it'll take to complete the project until the project is done. Every estimate you create should identify that this is an estimate, not fact.

✔ **List your assumptions.** You may be assuming that the project team will not have to complete the user acceptability testing. You may be assuming that the project will not require you to push the software image to every desktop in your organization. Or you may be assuming that your project team can work offsite. Whatever the assumptions are that you used to create the estimate, you need to provide them to the stakeholders.

✔ **Offer a range of variance.** A range of variance usually consists of that important phrase, "plus or minus. . . ." For example, you might say it'll take two months to complete, "plus three weeks or minus a week."

✔ **State the length of validity for the estimate.** If business is currently slow, your timeline might be shorter than when your developers are cranking through so many projects that they don't know whether they're coming or going. Put a length of validity on the estimate (say 30 days).

If you don't put a cap on your timeline, good old Murphy's Law states that the stakeholder will disappear until the minute you've booked your developers on seven different projects.

✔ **Provide some background on how the estimate was created.** If you used analogous data, then say so. If you based the estimate on your gut feelings, say so. If it was a rough day and you relied heavily on the Magic 8 Ball, then *really* say so (and take a vacation). Your background for the time estimate may simply consist of the scope the customer defined, but you should document it.

Understanding the Way PND Paths Interact

It's been said that the first 90 percent of the project takes 90 percent of time. The remaining 10 percent of the project takes the other 90 percent of the time. How often is that the case? Hopefully, not with your projects, but if you're like most software project managers, it is true.

Calculating the critical path

You should locate the *critical path* (or most time-consuming part) of your PND. The critical path is not the most urgent path in the PND; it's just the path that takes the longest to get from the first task to last task. What makes this path critical is the fact that if any projects on the path get delayed, the whole project will miss its deadline.

Figure 8-4 is a simple network diagram with all of the activity duration estimates completed. In this sample, there are four paths to completion:

1. ABEHJ = 10 days
2. ACGJ = 11 days
3. ACFIJ = 15 days
4. ADFIJ = 16 days

In this example, the path of activities ADFIJ will take 16 days to complete. Path ADFIJ is the critical path because if any of the activities on this path are delayed, the project will be late as well.

The other paths in the project have to be completed as well, and it is possible that delays on the other paths can change the critical path, but as it stands right now, the longest path of the project will last 16 days.

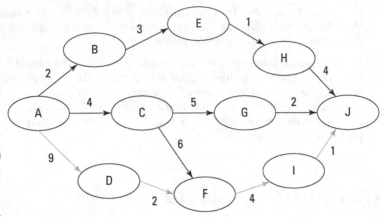

Figure 8-4:
Finding the
critical path
in your
project
network
diagram.

ABEHJ = 10 days
ACGJ = 11 days
ACFIJ = 15 days
ADFIJ = 16 days

You may notice activity C, which precedes activities F and G. This means C must be completed before F and G, even though C is not on the critical path. The point is that just because an activity is important doesn't mean that it's on the critical path — and vice-versa. The critical path only shows how long the project will last.

Most *project management information systems* (PMIS) software, including good old Microsoft Project, can find the critical path for you. However, PMIS is a tool to assist the project manager; it doesn't replace you.

Calculating float

Take a look at Figure 8-4. If path ADFIJ is the critical path and cannot be delayed without delaying the project, what does that say about all the other paths? If you guessed, or knew, that you could possibly delay these noncritical path activities without affecting the project end date, you're correct.

The other paths have what is called *float*. Float is the opportunity to delay an activity without affecting when the next activity is scheduled to start. Float allows the project manager to delay activities to move resources, wait for vendors, or use soft logic for resource scheduling, all without affecting the project end date. It's great.

Float is also called *slack*.

Again, most PMIS software can do all the math business for you and show you the float, but we're going to walk you through the process anyway. Here's the process for the first part to complete what's called the *forward pass:*

1. **Start with the first activity and assign an Early Start (ES) of 1, because you start the project on day one.**

2. **Add the ES to the duration of the activity and then subtract 1 to find the Early Finish (EF) of the first activity.**

   This number represents the earliest you can complete the task. The next activity's ES is the next day. In Figure 8-5, the EF of Activity A is 2, so the ES of Activities B and D are 3, the next day in the project schedule.

3. **Whenever an activity has two predecessors, such as Activity F, you take the largest predecessor and then add 1 to find the ES.**

   This is because all of the predecessor tasks must be completed before the project can move forward.

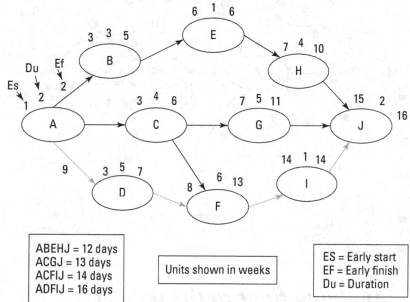

Figure 8-5:
The forward pass finds the earliest date activities can finish.

ABEHJ = 12 days
ACGJ = 13 days
ACFIJ = 14 days
ADFIJ = 16 days

Units shown in weeks

ES = Early start
EF = Early finish
Du = Duration

Now that the entire forward pass has been completed, you start at the end of the network diagram and work backward to find the Late Start (LS) and the Late Finish. Here's the process as shown in Figure 8-6:

1. **Start at the end of the PND and assign the LF as the last day of the project.**

   This is the latest it can finish without being late.

2. **Subtract the duration of the activity and then add 1 to equate to the latest the activity can begin.**

3. **To find the LS of the predecessor activity, simply go to one day before the LS of the current activity.**

   For example, in Figure 8-6, notice how Activities H and I both have an LF of 14, just one day before Activity J is slated to begin.

4. **Whenever an activity has two successors, as in Activity C, always choose the smaller of the two Late Starts.**

   This is because the activity must finish just one day prior to the scheduled start date of the successor.

5. **Complete the backward pass for all paths in the project.**

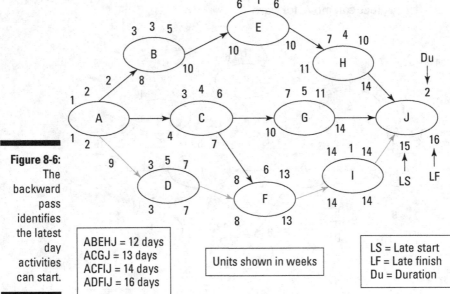

Figure 8-6: The backward pass identifies the latest day activities can start.

ABEHJ = 12 days
ACGJ = 13 days
ACFIJ = 14 days
ADFIJ = 16 days

Units shown in weeks

LS = Late start
LF = Late finish
Du = Duration

Applying float to the project

Knowing that you have a couple days of float here and there throughout your project network diagram can make a big difference. These are activities that can be strategically delayed without delaying the end date of your project.

If some activities are slipping behind schedule, or you need to move resources from one activity to another, you can take advantage of activities that have float and delay their start date — or expand their duration.

Here are some reasons to be glad for float:

✔ **You can reallocate resources:** Say you've assigned four developers to an activity that is scheduled to last ten days. If you remove two of the developers, you reason, the activity will take twice as long because there's only half the effort. If you examine the float on the activity and notice that you've actually got 12 days of float, you're in good shape; now you can move two of the developers to other work, allow the remaining two developers to work as planned, and still finish the activity before the next successor is scheduled to start. Float gives you scheduling options.

✔ **You can give people a break:** Sometimes, if your project team has been pushed to extreme limits, you can use float to examine where you have opportunities to give them a break. This is, to an extent, resource-leveling heuristics within float. In other words, you're flattening the amount of time project team members must work without extending the project scheduling.

✔ **You can work around unforeseen scheduling issues:** Maybe your crack developer has a long-planned vacation, or perhaps someone has a death in the family or an illness that takes him away for a few days. With float, you can make simple adjustments without any pain.

Creating the Project Schedule

Just because your PND says the project duration will be 18 weeks doesn't mean it'll *actually* be 18 weeks. You have lots of things to consider:

✔ Project dependencies, such as resources, vendors, materials, and people.

✔ Availability of resources, specifically the developers and stakeholder inputs for testing.

✔ Priority of the project. Sure, sure, your project is slated to last 18 weeks, but if it's not all that important, the work may be done sporadically over the course of 16 weeks.

✔ Weekends, holidays, lines of business, and other interruptions of the project implementation.

Working with the project calendar

The project calendar describes when the project work can take place. The project calendar is often defined by a manager or the customer, but it may sometimes be defined by the project manager. Most software development projects take place during normal business hours: Monday through Friday, 8:00 a.m. to 6:00 p.m. Nothing fancy.

Imagine a developer, however, who's been placed on-site to complete a portion of the project. The customer may request that the developer work only between the hours of 8:00 a.m. and 4:00 p.m. In this instance, the customer has set the project calendar working times. Now throw on top of this all the company holidays that your company has, and that limits the project working time even more.

You must examine the project calendar to predict when a project will be complete. That 18-week project may end up taking much longer than predicted because of interruptions like holidays and weekends. One approach you can use to calculate when a project will end is to use a *Gantt chart,* as Figure 8-7 shows. A Gantt chart is simply a project schedule smashed onto a calendar. Notice in Figure 8-7 that the Gantt chart does not include weekends for project activities.

Working with a resource calendar

Your project team members have a life beyond your project. They have vacations, doctor appointments, sick kids, and more. In addition, your project team members may be working on more than one project at a time and they can't allot all of their working hours to your project.

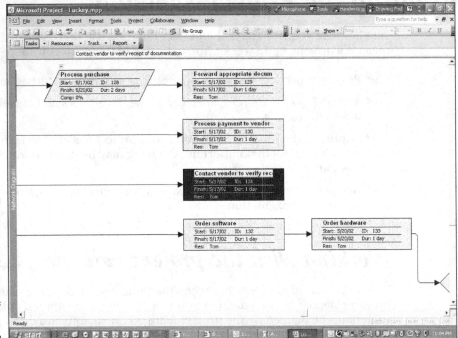

Figure 8-7:
A Gantt chart shows the project schedule against the backdrop of a calendar.

As you build the *resource calendar,* which identifies when the resources you need are available to do the project work, you need to bear these factors in mind. The resource calendar conveniently takes into consideration multiple projects, holidays, and time away from the project. Some project management software can also help you to coordinate the amount of hours per week allotted to your project versus the amount of time allotted to other projects within your organization.

After you create the resource calendar, you'll need to revisit the Gantt chart and rearrange the availability of resources. More likely than not, this switcheroo will increase the overall project duration, but not the amount of labor needed to complete the project.

Using resource-leveling heuristics

Resource-leveling heuristics is an approach to flatten the amount of time that employees work on your project. For example, consider a project that requires its project team members to work 75 hours a week for the next 15 weeks. There aren't too many developers who'd be happy to work 75 hours per week for the next 15 weeks (or ever, for that matter). Even if they were eager to do so, paying that much overtime would be costly, and after a while they'd be exhausted, disgruntled employees who produce poor-quality products.

In this wild instance, resource-leveling heuristics allows you to enter a value for labor, such as 40 hours per week, as a maximum value. Then the additional time that you've assigned for your project team is lopped off of the current schedule and appended to the end of the project.

Some project managers try to use resource leveling only for activities that are not on the critical path. In other words, if your project is slated to last 18 weeks and this requires overtime in order to complete the project activities, it's tough noogies! Resource leveling then takes advantage of float by only leveling resource overage on activities that have some amount of float. Noncritical path activities, of course, have no float, so the project team members will have to work the overtime in order to hit the target for project completion.

Your individual situation and your organization's policies will determine whether or not you use resource leveling. It isn't a good practice or a bad practice; it's just a tool you can use to make adjustments in your project schedule so that you can meet your deadlines.

Begging for more time

If you're overbudget and running out of time, you're more likely to get more time than you are to get more money. However, being in a position where you have to ask for either isn't very much fun. From your stakeholders' point of view, if you missed your target end date (no matter what the reason), it's your fault. When you ask for more time to complete the project, here are some things you should explain when you present your case:

✔ **Why the delay has occurred:** Don't assign blame or point fingers, but show why the delay occurred. For example, if you couldn't move forward with the project because the stakeholders wouldn't sign off on scope verification, milestone reviews, or other documentation, tell them so in a nonaccusatory way. But if the delay is because of your errors and omissions, be honest here as well.

✔ **What needs to happen for the project to be complete:** Often there's very little left for the project team to do to complete the project work. Include a status report of the project and explain why the project will need more time in order to complete.

✔ **If you have some deliverables to present to the stakeholders, show them:** You may have just a few deliverables to complete, but some immediate deliverables may help the stakeholders move ahead with their plans. Also, presenting deliverables demonstrates good faith.

✔ **Who needs to be involved:** Determine which stakeholders are affected by the project delay and communicate with them, even if they're not decision makers. Communication shouldn't be delayed just because the project is.

✔ **What you'll say when you compose a lessons learned document:** In your lessons learned document, be certain to explain why the project is running late so that you or other project managers don't repeat the same mistake.

✔ **Your confidence level in the new deadline:** You don't want to replace a bad date with another bad date (just ask our editors). You want to offer a good date that's honest and reflects what you're capable of completing, rather than what you hope you can complete.

Crashing and fast tracking your project

So your project is running late and no one is happy. Your customer needs the software you're creating, your project team won't get their bonuses if the work isn't completed on time, and you're aching to finish the project as promised. You do have options.

Crashing the project

Crashing the project means that you identify the effort-driven activity and you add more effort. In theory, the additional labor will reduce the amount of time it takes to complete that project work. Crashing a project, however, always drives up the cost of the project, because you have to pay for the additional labor. If you want to crash a project, identify

- The activities that are resource-driven and can be crashed
- Whether you have enough time for the newly added labor to ramp up the project
- What effect the new labor may have on the project team's cohesiveness
- What impact the additional labor will have on the project budget
- Whether the law of diminishing returns is in effect here
- How competent the newly added labor is to complete your project work

Fast tracking the project

Fast tracking sounds speedy because it is. Fast tracking is when you allow two activities or project phases that you'd ordinarily do sequentially to either be done in tandem or to overlap just a bit.

Fast tracking increases risks. Consider this example: If you allow the second phase of your development project to begin before the testing of the first phase is complete and there's a major error in phase one, you have major problems that won't save you any time at all:

- You lose the time you allowed for the second phase of the work to begin.
- You lose time because you have to go backward to do the rework.

Fast tracking increases risks. The more risks your project incurs, the less likely it is to be successful. Save fast tracking for those times when you can control or limit the risks that fast tracking is certain to bring.

Chapter 9

Building Your Project Budget

Projects cost money. Think about all the things you have to buy in order to make your software project successful:

✔ Developers' time

✔ Consultants' time

✔ Development software

✔ Hardware

✔ Pizza (food motivates people, especially programmers)

In order to predict how much a project will cost, you have to consider all the things that will be required in order to reach a successful completion. After you create the estimates, then you can commit the funds.

Your managers and customers, however, probably want to review your estimates before shelling out dough. They need to understand how you create the *project cost estimates,* and are likely to query you on the funds your project needs. In this chapter you discover how to estimate costs and spend the money in a fiscally responsible manner. We also show you how to react when things don't go as planned.

Creating Cost Estimates

A *project cost estimate* is pretty much a budget. You sit down and you try to account for all realistic costs so that you can give a stakeholder a fairly accurate ballpark figure for the project. To achieve accurate cost estimates, you and your customers need to recognize and understand everything a project requires.

All the necessary information isn't usually available until later in the planning process, but that won't stop customers and your managers from asking you cost questions that they expect to have answered right now.

After getting initial cost estimates, your customers and bosses will send you back to the proverbial drawing board for more research and planning. Eventually, you'll find yourself having a conversation in which you justify all your costs and your clients and bosses attempt to find areas to cut costs in your deliverable. You may go several rounds before everyone is finally in agreement with the project cost estimate.

Sometimes projects never get past the project cost estimate stage. A customer may see your initial estimate and scrap the whole project because it's too expensive. Sometimes, stakeholders are just fishing, or *running the numbers,* to see whether a solution is cost effective. Don't feel bad. Your estimate isn't to blame.

Using the right resources (and using them wisely)

Before you create an estimate you, should first know the rules of how your organization approaches estimating. Some companies may not have any policy or direction on creating cost estimates, but most have some guidelines the project manager should follow. Here are some do's and don'ts:

- ✔ **Do know your company's estimating policies.** You and the stakeholder must operate within the confines of your company's policy on cost estimating. Typically these policies define the contracts and documents that need to be in place before you even create an estimate. For example, you may need a *statement of work* (SOW), *statement of objectives* (SOO), or a project scope statement. These documents show how the estimate is created, who approves the estimate, and the refinement process for updating the project estimate.

- ✔ **Do use cost estimating templates.** You should love templates. They save time and keep documents uniform across the company. A cost estimating template captures the most common elements, standardizes the project costs, and streamlines the estimating process.

- ✔ **Don't ignore historical information.** History can be very helpful in cost estimating. Use any information within the organization that relates to the project scope or the product scope you're estimating.

Pay attention to lessons learned documentation from other similar projects. Lessons learned documentation can tell you where other project managers went wrong, discovered faster, cheaper approaches, and avoided pitfalls within their projects.

✔ **Do get project team input.** Estimating is rarely a solo activity. You should rely on the input of your project team. Be aware, however, that team member recollections aren't as reliable as documented historical information.

✔ **Do speak with other project managers who have worked on similar projects.** Using lessons learned documentation is great, but you can also gain a lot by actually communicating with those who have gone down the same path that you're heading. It's amazing what people remember when you get them talking about a subject.

Creating a rough estimate

If you're ever asked to give your best-guess cost estimate under less-than-ideal circumstances, then you've been a project manager for at least two hours. Staving off impossible-to-answer questions without seeming as though you don't know anything is one of your primary jobs as a project manager. It's important that you remind everyone that an estimate is not a guarantee.

Technically, this estimate is called a *rough order of magnitude* (ROM) estimate. Some folks call this a *hallway estimate* or an *elevator estimate*. These estimates usually have a wild qualifier, such as –25 percent to +75 percent on actual costs. You use these qualifiers because you provide a ROM estimate when you don't yet have enough detail to provide a more definitive cost estimate. Figure 9-1 shows the range of variance customers can expect with a ROM estimate; as you can see, it's not particularly reliable.

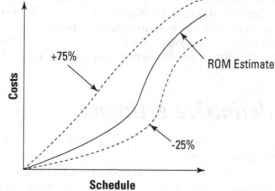

Figure 9-1: ROM estimates are wild and unreliable.

ROM estimates are unreliable, and some project managers, assuming that they have the power to just say no, won't offer them. Does it make sense to not provide a ROM? Sure. It's likeus asking how much it'll cost to build a house. Define a house. Define the materials. Define the time frame. And on and on the questions would have to go. It's difficult, if not impossible, to give an accurate estimate on anything if the requirements and scope of the project are not defined. As you progress through the project planning and gain more information about the project requirements, your estimates will be more reliable. Instead of a range of +75 percent to –25 percent, your next estimate may be +40 percent to –10 percent.

Traditionally, ROM estimates have a nice way of coming back to haunt project managers. There's something mystical about the first number management hears when it comes to estimates. Be wary of ROM estimates.

Creating a budget estimate

While a ROM estimate is nice for conversations, it's impossible to use for any substantial software project plan. ROM estimates are little more than wishes and blue sky. In order to create an accurate estimate, or at least a *more accurate* estimate, you need more information. The next level of estimating for a project is to create a *budget estimate*.

The budget estimate is somewhat more reliable because you've got a better grasp on what's actually to be included in your software as you spend more time gathering requirements. The qualifier for budget estimates is typically –10 percent to +25 percent.

Budget estimates are typically created based on historical information. If you've done a similar project in the past, you can use this historical information to predict what your current project is going to cost. Using historical information is called *analogous estimating* or *top-down estimating* because you start at the top of the project and you move quickly to the deliverables, drawing analogies to previous projects as you go. Again, although it's a great place to start, when used all alone, analogous estimating doesn't yield the most reliable results. We discuss analogous estimating in more depth in Chapter 8.

Creating a definitive estimate

The final, and most accurate, estimate type is the *definitive estimate*. Even its name sounds accurate. The definitive estimate requires a detailed decomposition of everything the project will create. It takes time to create and is also known as *bottom-up estimating*. Its qualifier is usually –5 percent to +10 percent. Figure 9-2 shows the range of variance customers can expect with a definitive estimate.

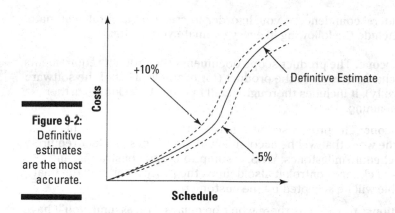

Figure 9-2:
Definitive
estimates
are the most
accurate.

To create a definitive estimate you need a work breakdown structure (WBS) in place. You have to examine every deliverable within the WBS. You also must consider all the needed materials, labor, resources, and risks that may influence project costs, as well as all the other elements that contribute to the bottom line of the project.

The reason you must consider project risks when you create your cost estimates is that if a risk materializes, it may negatively affect the scheduled activities and the costs.

Because so much of software development is based on labor, you may find that you're building your project estimates using a *parametric model*. A parametric model uses specific parameters, such as cost per hour, cost per line of code, or cost per network drop, to predict how much the project will cost. Parametric modeling is fine as long as you document how the estimate was created. In some organizations, parametric modeling won't work, because each developer's time is accounted for and billed independently.

Although it takes more time to create a definitive estimate, it's always better to spend time up front creating an accurate estimate than to spend time begging for more cash later (and explaining why your estimate was off the mark).

Creating an Accurate Estimate

Assuming that you have time and resources to create a definitive estimate (as we discuss in the previous section), you want to make sure that the estimate you create is as accurate as possible. An inaccurate cost estimate can upset stakeholders, make you appear foolish, put your project at risk, and shake your stakeholders' confidence in you. In order to create an accurate estimate, you need to include the following in every estimate you create:

- **Product scope:** The product scope documents the product requirements and the characteristics of the product (for example, a list of the software functionality). It includes thorough detail in order to facilitate further project planning.

- **Project scope:** The project scope describes the project deliverables and defines the work that will be accomplished. It includes product requirements, schedule milestones, WBS, assumptions and constraints, and methods of change control. It also defines the process for how the final deliverable will be accepted by the customer.

- **Assumptions:** You assume there won't be delays. You assume you'll have all the resources you need. You assume that this is an estimate, not a quote.

- **Constraints:** Any constraints that have been brought to the table at this point need to be documented. A constraint is anything that limits the project manager's options; examples can include

   - **Time constraints:** You must have the project done in four months.

   - **Resource constraints:** You can only use two developers on the project.

   - **Development environment restraints:** You must develop in COBOL.

   - **Budget restraints:** Your budget is capped at $250,000.

- **Timeframe:** We discuss timeframe in detail in Chapter 8. Essentially, you need to let stakeholders know that this estimate is a limited-time offer that depends on currently available resources. If the stakeholders want to do this project in five months when all your developers are wrapped up in other projects, you might have different numbers.

- **Range of variance:** The range of variance describes the +/– every estimate should have. For example, as discussed previously in this chapter, you create a ROM estimate for a project to create a new piece of software. You estimate the project to cost $150,000 with a possible variance from +25 percent to –10 percent. For input into the range of variance, you use any or all of the following resources: marketplace conditions, commercial databases, cost-estimating policies and templates, historical information, project files, team members' knowledge, lessons learned documentation, project scope statement, WBS, project management plan, schedule management plan, resource management plan, and risk register.

Considering Project Profitability

There are other approaches to estimating how much a project will cost. Software project management depends on the time your developers take to complete tasks. Obviously, the more time you estimate it'll take for your project team to complete the software, the more it'll cost to create the product. Your particular circumstances will vary:

- If you're billing just for the developers' time, then you need to consider the resource rates for the programmers that will be working on the project.

- If your organization completes projects for other organizations, then you have to consider the profit margin your project should create.

- If you're a software project manager completing internal projects, then you'll be considering the straight rate for the developers' time.

If you're completing a project for another organization (that is, you're developing software for another company that's paying your company a fee to develop the software), you're in this business to make a profit for your company.

The faster the team can successfully complete the work, the higher the project's profitability. As a project manager, you may have to consider the resource rates that you pay your project team members against what your company bills for their time. In other words, you want to have a higher variance between what you pay the developers and what you charge other companies for their time.

For example, Susan is a senior developer who earns roughly $50 per hour from your firm. Your company likely charges more than $50 an hour for her time. Now consider Sammy. Sammy earns roughly $30 per hour because he's less experienced than Susan. Some organizations bill more for Susan's time than for Sammy's time because of the difference in experience. Some organizations, however, don't differentiate between developers; they just offer an hourly rate for each developer's time.

If your company bills more experienced developers at a higher rate, you must examine whether it's more cost effective to utilize Sammy or more cost effective to pay more for Susan. For example, Sammy may take longer to complete a task than Susan would, but Susan could be better utilized on more higher-priority, more profitable activities. Making these decisions is called *value engineering* — determining which resource is best for the project activities and which resource is best for the project profitability.

On the other hand, if you're completing projects internally and not for organizations outside your own, it's likely you won't have to worry as much about the developers' hourly costs. You have to worry only about adhering to your project budget. Someone (the customer or project stakeholder) is paying for the developers' time, or their salaries are incorporated into the cost of doing business. You need to understand what approach your project should follow when it comes to accounting and billing for your project team members' time.

Planning for Contingencies

Estimates are usually based on idealized concepts of how things will go, while the actual project is full of conditions, risks, and (if you're smart) contingency plans.

Plan on dealing with known unknowns. A *known unknown* is any event that is governed by Murphy's Law. You know there will be problems; you just don't know exactly what those problems will be or when they'll crop up. If you don't accommodate for these snafus up front when you create your budget, things can go bad. Unfortunately, some problems may be unavoidable, but they can still devastate a budget:

✓ Errors and omissions in the product scope mean that the developers take longer than expected once they figure out what they've missed.

✓ Errors and omissions in the project work mean that tasks need to be performed that were never planned for.

✓ Miscommunications of all kinds can cause work to be undone and require reworking.

✓ Failure in user acceptability testing can mean you go back to the drawing board.

✓ Failure in quality control may mean that you have to recode a bunch of stuff.

✓ A hard drive crashes during a routine backup, and some development work needs to be done. (We know you would never forget to back up your work!)

✓ Poor requirements gathering means that your developers are working without all the necessary information.

✓ Project management errors mean that you spin your wheels a bit (hey, you'll get better with time).

What you need is a *contingency reserve.* A contingency reserve, sometimes called a *contingency allowance,* is hidden treasure, a set amount of funds that the project manager may use to respond to known unknowns throughout the project.

Don't get too excited. This reserve is allotted for uncertain events, risks, and issues that are anticipated but not confirmed. You can't use contingency funds as part of your project budget for execution.

Controlling Project Costs

Great news! Your project is moving ahead and you're making progress. You're spending the project budget. As your project team develops the software, their labor consumes the monies that were allotted to pay for their labor. You've also spent cash on resources such as training, support materials, servers and hardware, software, bonuses, and more.

Well, not so fast. You have to account for every red cent your project consumes.

Understanding accounting blue dollars

In some organizations, everything you spend is blue dollars. *Blue dollars* describe the funds that are internal to an organization and just shift between departments — no one's actually writing a check for the project work. If this scenario describes your organization, you still have to accurately keep an accounting of all the dollars you spend.

Understanding work-for-hire accounting

If you're a project manager in an organization that completes projects for other companies, then you've got a more evident responsibility to guard the project costs: the project's profitability. A common reason that organizations lose money on projects is due to poor fiscal management on the part of the software project manager. Don't let that be you.

If your company hopes to achieve a profit margin of 10 percent on every project you manage, errors, sloppy work, incomplete requirements gathering, late deliverables, and faulty judgments will quickly eat into that profit. If a software project is incredibly late, wrong, or buggy, the 10 percent margin begins to erode, and before you know it, your company is paying out-of-pocket to deliver the project.

A project manager who's losing money is a project manager who's on the way out.

Following simple strategies to manage project expenses

You need to take active steps to monitor and control the costs within your project.

Getting a plan together

The first step in managing costs is to have an accurate and reliable project plan. Projects often fail at the beginning, instead of at the end. If your project plan is skewed, faulty, or half-cocked, the implementation will be as well. Flip to Chapter 2 for further information on project planning.

One of the components of the project plan is a *cost management plan,* which describes how you will plan, estimate, budget, and control your project costs. The more detailed and accurate these estimates are, the less likely you are to have budget surprises.

Another component of the project plan is the *human resources management plan,* which details processes and policies regarding the members of the project team, such as roles and responsibilities, reporting structures, improving project team members' skills and enhancing their knowledge, accepted hiring and firing considerations, and staffing plans.

Although the cost management plan and human resources management plan are listed separately, in actual practice, they interact and overlap. For example, your cost management plan probably lists the cost of resources (people) required to complete the software project.

Reviewing costs and performance

When you've got a solid plan, then you need a method to review costs and performance of the project team. This is vital in every software development project because the project is built on how efficiently project team members use their time. You need to track and measure the team members' time to complete the project activities.

Just because you need to ensure that team members manage their time well does not mean that it's open season to micromanage. Everyone works his or her own way, and you need to allow staff to feel free to be idiosyncratic — within reason, of course. However, using historical information and analogous information, you can (and should) attempt to estimate how long various tasks will take (see Chapter 8). You can also set incremental deadlines for partial deliverables.

CASE STUDY

Knowing the actual cost of scope changes

Meet Marti. She's a software project manager for a financial advisement firm. She's managing a project to create a software program that will enable the financial advisers within her company to track clients' activities, portfolios, contact information, and communications. The software will interact with databases and internal and external Web servers, and provide real-time secure transactions with commodities, stocks, and bonds.

Marti and the experts on her project team have been working closely with Thomas Lippy, the chief operating officer and main stakeholder, to develop the project requirements. Thomas has signed off on the requirements document and is eager for Marti to get to work on the project. He believes that the software will help their company grow by 15 percent each year.

The rough order of magnitude estimate for the project was $750,000, +75 percent to –25 percent. The moment the WBS was created, Marti provided a definitive estimate of $1.5 million, +10 percent to –5 percent. Thomas approved the definitive estimate, and the team went to work creating the software.

At each milestone within the project, Thomas was given the opportunity to review the project's work and to inspect the timeline and the budget. This also provided Thomas an opportunity to tinker with the project requirements. At each milestone review, Thomas added more deliverables to the project scope. Over the course of the project, Thomas added the following requirements to the project deliverable:

✔ Field changes to the financial adviser's input screen

✔ Interaction with the company's IP-based telephone system for customer lookup

✔ Incorporation of a client Web site for customers to securely access their portfolios

✔ Integration with legacy databases for trend analysis

✔ Multiple views, searches, and tools for customers and financial advisers to access data

These changes increased the project scope, which, in turn, increased the project costs by $450,000. Remember the Iron Triangle? You can't increase the project scope without affecting either budget or schedule (or both). When Marti discussed the changes and their impact with Thomas, Thomas was unhappy that these changes could nearly double the original project budget. Marti explained that there are several factors that affect project costs:

✔ The time to research each change takes time away from doing the project work. Someone has to pay for the developers' time to do the research.

✔ Some changes require that progress be reversed in order to incorporate the new changes.

✔ Some of the requested changes would add time to the system testing phase of the project.

✔ Many of the changes required modifications to the training documentation.

✔ The legacy database change required Marti to hire a contractor because the project team did not have the skill set to configure the middleware to interact with the software.

✔ The project team had to expand to include a network engineer to configure the IP-based telephones to interact with the software the team was designing.

(continued)

(continued)

✔ The multiple views, searches, and tools increased the developers' work time, which also drove costs up.

✔ Bonuses for the project team are based on the budget for the project. As the project's budget grew, so did the bonuses for the project team. However, team members became frustrated that they had to change their work throughout the project, so the loss of morale likely affected project performance.

Marti and Thomas agreed that the changes to the project scope were value-added changes, but the changes' value may be marginal. Tracking the impact of the project benefits after the deliverable moves into production is the only method to analyze the true cost-effectiveness of the changes and their profitability for the organization.

Conducting variance analysis

Any time you experience differences between what was planned and what was experienced, you have a *variance*. Variance analysis enables you to complete *root cause analysis*. Your goal is to find out why the actual project costs are differing from your estimates so that you can stop the bleeding. You can even correct the overruns if you're good at root cause analysis. We cover variance analysis and root cause analysis in Chapter 14.

When you track and measure, you have opportunities to react. For example, if Bob is slipping on his assignments, but Jan is way ahead, you can balance the load by giving some of Bob's work to Jan. Your root cause analysis may tell you that Bob's not confident in this area of the project work, or that he's on seven other projects, or that his time estimates were over-optimistic. Whatever the reason, you can now react and make process changes to correct the problem.

Software project management tools, such as Microsoft Project, can help you determine where activities are slipping, complete trend analyses, and simulate what may happen if project costs continue to mushroom. The goal, of course, is to make corrective actions to get the project back on financial track and to prevent similar mistakes from entering the project again.

Having More Project than Cash

Ready for some bad news? Sometimes there's nothing you can do when it comes to your project being overbudget. Sometimes all your planning, hard work, efforts to control costs, attempts to keep changes at bay, and efforts to keep your project team on track all go down the drain.

Whatever the reason your project has begun to rival the budget for the movie *Waterworld* (we hope the product isn't quite as bad), you're stuck between a failing project and a hard place. You've got to fix this thing.

The first thing you need to do is sit down and revisit your plan so that you can consider your options. Yes, you do have options.

Completing root cause analysis

Before you pull your hair out or quit your job to run a dental floss farm, do some root cause analysis of the problem — or problems. Chances are, you probably have a hint as to the cause of your budgetary crisis. These things rarely crop up suddenly, but fester for a while. Root cause analysis enables you to map out problems so that you can respond. We cover this thoroughly in Chapter 14.

Just to be crystal clear, root causes are problems that you, the project manager, can control. Weather, for example, is not a root cause because you don't have control over the weather.

You don't need any fancy software to complete a root cause analysis. You just need to work with your team and the appropriate stakeholders to list the problem and all possible causes. But remember, time is money. Balance the amount of time you spend on root cause analysis with the time you will be away from the project. Obviously, for you and your team to spend an exorbitant amount of time away from the project determining cause without also using that time to come up with a plan to address the root cause is a little on the counterproductive side.

Here's what you should accomplish with root cause analysis:

- ✔ Identify what has happened, how it has happened, and why it was allowed to happen to prevent the problem from happening again
- ✔ Identify specific underlying causes and their effects so you can put steps into place that will improve overall performance
- ✔ Chart the causes and contributing causes through trends, data collection, and project analysis
- ✔ Facilitate a conversation on root cause identification to lead to a solution — and to prevent the problem from recurring

Collecting data

Your first step in root cause analysis is to collect the data that contributed to the problem. This process is the largest part of root cause analysis. Here are some common themes in software projects that you'll want to consider in your analysis:

- ✔ Time delays
- ✔ Rework
- ✔ Inaccurate time estimates

> ✔ Inadequate scope definition
>
> ✔ Performance issues during testing
>
> ✔ Risks and threats that have affected the project

Causal factor charting

Causal factor charting, as explained in Chapter 14, is a flowchart of activity sequences leading up to an identified issue and identified circumstances that affected the problem. This process is about more than finding a single, major blunder. You need to identify all the circumstances that led to the problem: competency levels, communication breakdown, lack of testing, and so on.

You begin causal factor charting in tandem with your data collection. It helps you and the project team identify the problems and how the problems have caused the project budget to be consumed faster than what was anticipated.

Identifying the root cause

Now that you and the project team have completed the causal factor charting, you need to identify why each causal factor existed. The answer to the question "Why did this problem happen?" tells you the root cause and where the project began to erode.

Yes, you have to do root cause identification with every single causal factor you've identified, and no, this is not an easy process. The point of the process, however, is to identify where the problems started, what trends may be running through your project, and how you'll prevent the problems from recurring. (Of course, you may also identify some positive trends in your project and use them to your advantage in the problem resolution stage of this process.)

Reacting to the causes

What good is root cause analysis if there is no response? You must react to the causes in the project or your project is bound to repeat the same mistakes over and over. Not addressing issues can cause your project to go deeper and deeper into the red.

The outcome of root cause analysis will help you, and management, determine what the best route for your project is. And that's what the rest of this chapter is all about. You cannot, must not, go to management with a problem unless you can clearly identify the problem. And then, of course, you must propose a solution. If your problem is simply "I'm out of cash," and your solution is, "Gimme some more money," you're setting yourself up for failure, dismissal, or, at the very least, a shake in management's confidence in your abilities.

You may identify some surprising positive trends (Lucy is always ahead of schedule and her work is always perfect; your team has really picked up the slack since Ralph was out sick; or Mary is chronically overworked, but Jon isn't) that can help you toward a solution.

Reducing the project scope

After you identify the cause of the project failure, one of the first options you can recommend is to reduce the project scope. This option may be a tough sell (and difficult to accomplish) because the client has already approved the deliverable. Reducing the project scope may not be an option if you have contractual obligations.

The Iron Triangle, which we discuss in Chapters 2 and 3, requires that all three side of the triangle (cost, time, and scope) remain equal for the project to be successful. Figure 9-3 shows what your Iron Triangle probably looks like at this point of your project. Notice that the line for the scope is much longer than the lines for time and cost. You can lop off parts of the project scope to be closer to the budget you've been allotted. This will allow you and the stakeholders to have a deliverable and to still be close to the original budget. Another option is to add to the cost part of the triangle or the schedule portion.

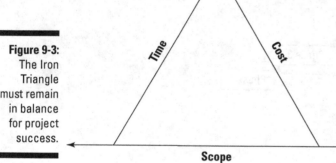

Figure 9-3: The Iron Triangle must remain in balance for project success.

The problem with trimming the project scope is that it's not always feasible. Chopping the scope leaves you with less of a deliverable, especially if the causes of the budget overrun are related to errors, rework, and rejections from testing.

But if the project team does have a deliverable — or at least part of the deliverable — it may be enough to move the project into production with a bit more work. And what of the remaining scope? You've got options:

✔ Live with the deliverable as it is if the project is a low priority and not expected to make much money. Of course, this may not be an option in every scenario.

✔ Live with the deliverable as it is if the software is a stop-gap tool.

> ✔ Live with deliverable for the short term and then move the project into versioning.
>
> ✔ Live with the deliverable as it is because there's no more cash available to sink into the project.

Trimming the project scope can be a great solution (okay, it's not great, but it is acceptable — sometimes) for projects that have never been attempted before. Projects with undertakings that have no historical information, no point of reference, and no expert judgment to rely on are projects that are just begging to run over on cost. By reducing the scope, you're able to create a deliverable and not go wildly over on cost overruns.

This approach, as Figure 9-4 illustrates, is most feasible if you have incorporated kill points into your project. A *kill point* is a point during the project where the project is slated for review. The idea is that management reviews the overall success of your project up to a certain deliverable. If your project is doing well, congrats! You get to advance to the next phase of your project. If your project is not doing so hot, then your project is cancelled or postponed.

Figure 9-4:
Kill points
are oppor-
tunities to
stop the
project.

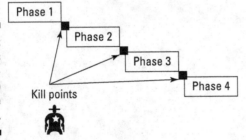

Begging for cash

If trimming the project scope is not an option (and often it's not), then your option is limited to asking for more cash to complete the project. Typically, it's easier to get more time than money, but because you're usually buying the developers' time to complete the project work, time and money are tied together.

When you're forced into this scenario, you really need all the facts about what has gone wrong and why. Most importantly, you need to be able to determine how you'll avoid making the same mistakes again. You can use your lessons learned document and your root cause analysis as tools to show what has caused the problem and how you'll prevent the problem from happening again. No one, especially management, wants to infuse your project budget with more dollars only to see the problem reappear over and over.

TIP

Tactfully remind management or the customers why the project was initiated. This may help steer additional funds to your project. If the project was worth initiating, then it's likely worth continuing.

Recognizing Budgetary Problems Before You Get to the Root Cause Analysis Stage

It should never be a huge surprise to you, your bosses, the stakeholders, your clients, or even your project team that your project budget is suddenly gone. The words *surprise* and *suddenly* shouldn't even be used in the same sentence as the word *budget*.

As the project moves through phases, milestones, and even deliverables, you should easily be able to track expenses against the amount of work you've completed for the dollars spent. Figure 9-5 shows a cost baseline project that's in month four of eight months. The solid line represents the project's cost estimate while the dashed line represents the actual costs of the project to date. The difference between what was estimated and what is being experienced is the variance. If this project continues on the same path, the project costs will likely continue to mushroom and move farther and farther away from the original estimates.

Figure 9-5:
A variance
is the
difference
between the
estimate
and the
actual
costs.

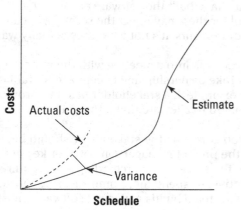

Costs

Actual costs

Estimate

Variance

Schedule

When costs exceed the estimates, you'll likely have to do a variance report for management so that you can explain why the actual costs aren't in line with your estimates. The *variance report,* sometimes called an *exceptions report,* details the cause of the cost. Get to work on this report at the first hint of a problem. Do not wait until you have completely run out of cash!

Dealing with a Budget Problem that Your Bosses Know about (But Haven't Addressed)

Your project is out of money and you need more funds to complete the work. You've completed variance reports, so management knows what's what, but your bosses haven't exactly jumped at the opportunity to pour more funds into your project.

When things get to that hysterical point, call a civilized meeting with management (bring all your documentation) so they are forced to examine the variance reports to determine whether the same problems have recurred throughout the project or whether new problems, risks, and other cost-eating monsters have crept into the execution.

Before you enter this meeting, prioritize the major problems that have consumed the project budget so that you can identify the cause of the problem and who may need to help pay for completing the project scope. For example, if one of the project stakeholders failed to provide accurate requirements, then your project team may have built the software according to the supplied requirements. The stakeholder then may reject the software because, while it matches their supplied requirements, it's not what they actually wanted.

Just be very careful to never walk into a meeting with the intent of placing blame or escaping blame. Take ownership and accept accountability when something goes awry. For example, if a stakeholder failed to provide accurate requirements, what did you do to alleviate that situation?

While this scenario is all too common, the stakeholder should bear some of the blame. But so should the project manager. One of your key activities is to communicate with, not to, the stakeholders regarding their requirements. It's easier, and more cost effective, to spend more time ensuring the accuracy of the requirements before your team builds a piece of software the stakeholder doesn't want.

After you and management have identified the cost problems, the stakeholders have to evaluate the overall worth of the project and determine what to do next. If the project is worthy, far enough along in the project deliverable, and you've done a good job of explaining the cost overruns and how you will react to them in the future, then you can probably expect to continue working on the project with more funds.

Part III
Executing Your Software Project Plan

The 5th Wave — By Rich Tennant

"Why, of course. I'd be very interested in seeing this new milestone in the project."

In this part . . .

Part III shows you how to put your hard work and impressive planning into action. You've created your project plans — now execute them. Discover how you can develop your team, and find out how to best manage conflicts. In this part, you also figure out the various types of vendor contracts and discover how to execute your quality management and risk management plans.

Chapter 10

Working the Project Plan

Do you want to create software project plans that other project managers talk about for years to come? Do you want to be the envy of your peers as they gaze longingly at your quality management plans and slobber all over your risk management plans?

To be the talk of the software project management community, all you need is to perform the proper planning, use the appropriate tools and techniques, and figure out how to make the most of what others have already done. If you're proactive in your software project management efforts, your project plans will be a success. In this chapter, we show you all the types of plans you must deal with and show you how to use them.

Authorizing the Project Work

You should have your work authorized before you ever start working on your software project. After all, no one wants to take a chance on working on a software project — or any project for that matter — that was never authorized. Your project is officially and formally authorized as a part of the project charter, which we discuss in Chapters 1 and 2. A *work authorization system* (WAS), one of the inputs to the project charter, is a tool that authorizes the work activities that need to be completed to ensure the success of your software project. Your organization defines who is responsible for authorizing the project work as part of the WAS; it may be your client, your sponsor, or a particular governing body within the organization.

Creating a work authorization system

Your organization probably has a pretty standard method for authorizing software project work, so you should refer to its outline for the exact procedure. The WAS is simply a document that includes information on

- ✔ Project tasks that need to be completed
- ✔ Sequence for completing required tasks
- ✔ Documents and/or deliverables that need to be developed
- ✔ Methods of tracking project progress
- ✔ Required approvals for authorizing work
- ✔ Project start date
- ✔ Project end date
- ✔ Required resources
- ✔ Special considerations

The work authorization system should be completed before a project begins and it may also be completed before the future phases of a project begin. When one phase of the project ends, your organization may have a phase-end review so that they can close the current phase of the project before starting the next phase. Such systems are sometimes called *phase gates*. During this process, the appropriate stakeholders for your organization authorize the next phase of the project.

Using a project management information system

A *project management information system* (PMIS) is a set of automated tools that enable you and your project team to gather information, develop and track the project plan, and keep track of the status of your software project and communicate that information to the appropriate stakeholders. These can be homegrown systems, off-the-shelf systems, or enterprise-wide systems.

PMIS enables you to:

- ✔ Track resources to find out whether team members are available, overextended, and on track with their deadlines.

✔ Control project changes, making updates as needed.

✔ Track project activities, such as writing specifications, documenting unit test plans, or creating CBTs.

✔ Report on the status of project activities using templates. The template may be a dashboard that is incorporated into the PMIS; it could also be a standard report set up in the PMIS.

✔ Compare the current status of your project to a baseline.

✔ Track risks associated with the project.

✔ Analyze project conflicts, such as a resource being overextended or two activities being assigned sequentially when they should be consecutive.

✔ View and share project calendars.

✔ Check the status of project costs and schedule.

PMIS software is handy because it allows you to view, share, track, and report on many project activities. In fact, some types of PMIS software enable you to share this information on the Web. Take a gander at *Microsoft Project 2003 For Dummies* by Nancy Stevenson (Wiley) for more information on Microsoft Project.

Ensuring Quality in Execution

Project quality management is one of the project management knowledge areas described by the Project Management Institute (www.pmi.org). The purpose of this knowledge area is to ensure that the requirements of the project are met. In other words, if the project quality is being effectively managed, then the software that you were contracted to develop is the software that you actually develop.

Avoiding the PMIS panacea

Although PMIS software can help you to keep track of the status of your project, even the best PMIS can't:

✔ Guarantee that you will have a successful project

✔ Think for you

✔ Solve problems for you

✔ Hide your mistakes from others

You must know how to be a successful software project manager on your own. Use PMIS as a tool — one of many tools — to help you keep track of project activities, control changes, align resources, and share relevant information with the appropriate stakeholders.

For information about how project quality management fits into the larger scheme of things, see the sidebar, elsewhere in this chapter, called "Remembering the nine project management knowledge areas."

The three processes from the PQM knowledge area are

- ✔ **Quality planning:** For quality planning, you use your firm's quality policy and its standards and regulations as input. You develop the quality planning during the planning phase of the project. Determining the quality standards for the project should be fully integrated into the rest of your project planning.

- ✔ **Quality assurance:** Quality assurance is one of the executing process areas and is concerned with performing quality audits so that you can ensure stakeholders that the quality management plan is being adhered to. Make sure that the software systems you are developing satisfy the quality standards that you and your stakeholders developed during the quality planning phase. The tools and techniques you can use for quality planning are benefit/cost analysis, quality audits, benchmarking, cost of quality analysis, and flowcharts. We discuss all of these tools later in this chapter.

Whenever you can, you should work smarter, not harder. You can save a lot of time and effort if you use templates for the quality tools. If your organization doesn't provide templates, be sure to create templates yourself as you develop your quality planning tools. Making templates may be extra work, but they pay off during your next project and on into the future when you can use the templates that you created.

- ✔ **Quality control:** Quality control is one of the controlling process areas, and it deals with monitoring your software project to ensure that it conforms to the appropriate quality standards. This phase also helps you fix the areas of your project that contain broken processes that are causing the project to fall short of the quality standards. The inputs for the quality control process are work results, quality management plan, operational definitions, and checklists. You should also conduct inspections, a trend analysis, sampling, and use Pareto charts.

Say that you're developing software that enables physicians, nurses, and other clinicians in a hospital to place lab, medication, and radiology orders. All of these orders need to travel to the appropriate corresponding systems quickly and efficiently. The hospital has specific needs:

- ✔ Orders must be delivered efficiently and quickly to the correct departments.

- ✔ When the departments receive the orders, they must correctly identify what's needed, for whom, and how fast.

TIP

Remembering the nine project management knowledge areas

In Chapter 1, we introduce the nine project knowledge areas outlined by the Project Management Institute (PMI). PMI is a nonprofit organization that sets standards and facilitates development for project management professionals. Here's an overview:

✔ **Project Scope Management:** Controlling the planning, execution, and content of the project.

✔ **Project Time Management:** Managing everything that affects the project's schedule.

✔ **Project Cost Management:** Cost estimating, budgeting, and controlling the purse.

✔ **Project Quality Management:** Ensuring that the product you are producing is a quality product and that it meets customer expectations.

✔ **Project Human Resources Management:** Hiring and managing the competent people working on your project.

✔ **Project Communications Management:** Making sure that the people who need information get it — when they need it.

✔ **Project Risk Management:** Anticipating and handling risks, as well as taking advantage of opportunities that can help a project.

✔ **Project Procurement Management:** Creating vendor contracts and purchasing goods and services.

✔ **Project Integration Management:** Ensuring the coordination of all the other knowledge areas.

For example, with your software, a doctor should be able to enter a complete blood count (CBC) lab order into the hospital order entry system; when the CBC order travels to the hospital's lab system, it must come into the lab system identified as a CBC order, and not as a pregnancy test.

You might perform the following types of testing to ensure the quality of your hospital system code:

✔ **Unit testing:** A unit test ensures the quality of the specific areas of the software. For example, when users click a particular button in the hospital software, they see the appropriate item.

✔ **Functional testing:** Functional testing ensures that the software functions according to the requirements. For example, when users click a tab, they are taken to the appropriate area of the system. The purpose of functional testing is to perform processes that a typical user would perform and is primarily concerned with identifying issues found within the user's logical workflow.

✔ **Integrated testing:** If the software interfaces with other software programs, integrated testing ensures that the two systems communicate appropriately. For example, a physician writes an order for a CAT scan in the hospital order entry system and that order flows to the radiology system as a CAT scan order and does not come through as a toe x-ray.

✔ **Volume testing:** If your software is to be used in a hospital where many clinicians will be using it simultaneously from any of several different computers, volume testing ensures that the software can withstand having multiple simultaneous users.

When you create the quality management plan, you document how you plan to measure the quality of the project and the product. As part of your quality management plan, you must spell out which specific types of software testing you will perform in order to ensure quality.

There are several quality management theories that may assist you in finding out more about project quality management, and each one has its own set of tools and techniques. We discuss them in Chapter 6.

Understanding the Interoperability of the Quality Management Plan

The quality management processes of quality planning, quality assurance, and quality control don't operate in a vacuum. It's a beautiful image (wouldn't it be cool to visualize these quality processes dancing around in a vacuum?), but not entirely accurate. In reality, they all work together, and are tied to other important planning, execution, and control processes in your project.

Actually, the processes interact with each other throughout the course of the project. There would be no point in having quality assurance if you didn't have quality planning, because there would be no processes to audit if you hadn't already planned those processes.

PQM is not just concerned with the quality of the project but also the quality of the product — that is, the quality of the systems you're developing. The aim for high quality is one reason that you perform software testing. Can you imagine finishing any software project without completing the appropriate software testing? You perform the various types of software testing to ensure the appropriate quality.

Using benefit/cost analysis and benchmarking

Preventing errors is usually more cost effective than fixing them after they make their way into the software. During your quality management planning, you can use a *benefit/cost analysis* to determine whether the benefit of meeting quality requirements is worth the cost to implement the quality standards. For example, the benefits for incorporating quality requirements such as system testing are that you'll spend less time recoding the software, your project will cost less (project team members won't have to spend as much time fixing bugs), your customer's satisfaction will be improved, and, depending on the software, unknown third parties will benefit. Consider those untold millions who could be affected if you're implementing software in the health care industry (failure of your software could affect patient safety) or the banking industry (people could lose real money

if your software doesn't know where to put the decimal).

Benchmarking is a quality planning tool that enables you to compare your project to other similar software projects so that you can have some standard to judge your project against. For example, if most projects like yours usually require two print servers and your project requires eight print servers, you are over your benchmark, at least in this area of the project.

Another quality planning tool that you may use in your software project is *flowcharting*. You can create flowcharts with a paper and pencil or with an application such as Microsoft Visio. You create a picture or diagram that shows the sequence of steps you might take for a particular quality planning activity. For instance, you might list the steps required for integrated testing.

Following Quality Assurance

Using the quality assurance process, you ensure that the project meets the project specifications that were set out at the start of the project in the planning stage. *Quality audits* are tools and techniques that you may use during the assurance process. For example, if, during the planning phase of your project, you documented that your project team would conduct unit testing before functional testing, one thing you'd determine during the audit would be whether you actually followed that predefined process. If a quality audit reveals that you performed steps out of order (functional testing before unit testing, tsk, tsk), you need to implement plans to correct this inefficiency.

Quality audits may also be used to ensure that your project team is following your organization's coding standards.

During the quality assurance stage of a software project, an independent review of your processes is used to ensure the quality of the project so that you can identify and eliminate inefficient processes and procedures. Quality assurance deals with making sure project work is being performed in an effective and efficient manner.

Audits are usually involved in quality assurance.

In addition to quality audits, another set of tools and techniques that you can use to ensure quality assurance on your project are the quality planning tools that you used when creating your quality management plans, such as benefit/cost analysis, benchmarking, and flowcharting.

If you have a choice, your approach to quality assurance should be proactive instead of reactive. You want to have adequate quality policies in place — testing, coding standards, and so on — before releasing code to your customers. Preventing bugs in your code is much more efficient than fixing bugs after they enter the code.

Following the Quality Policy

During the planning phase of all software projects, you define your quality management plan and outline how you plan to ensure quality in your project and your product. You document how you plan to confirm that the project will satisfy the stated requirements. You also outline how you can continue to make quality improvements.

Think of the consequences of not following your quality policy for your software project:

✔ Your team wrote code for a system (like the hospital software system we discuss earlier in this chapter) that allows physicians to place medication orders; this info gets passed to the pharmacy system. Your team did not perform sufficient integration testing and you discover that when a physician enters *mg* for a unit of measure on a medication, this appears in the pharmacy system as *gram*. Ouch! This is an extreme example just to demonstrate the importance of following your quality policy. Chances are, something this important would never get to the testing phase; a mistake like this would likely be caught during requirements gathering.

✔ Your team wrote the code for a banking program, but the team didn't do anything to address decimal points, and neglected to perform sufficient functional testing. Now, when a teller enters a customer deposit of $10, the software records a deposit of $100. Good news for the customer; unemployment for the project manager.

✔ Instead of planning for a smart inventory system for an online shopping firm, your team skipped out early. When the program was complete, you didn't perform sufficient testing. Now, whenever a customer orders a 40-watt light bulb, he or she receives a 12-ounce jar of spicy canned meat. Yum! Your customers might really enjoy the taste of the canned meat, but that won't light up the room, will it?

These are also examples of why the cost of quality should be built into the project plan. You should spend your time preventing errors rather than fixing errors after they occur. It is more cost efficient and no one will end up eating their meat in the dark. This concept is often referred to as *prevention over inspection*.

The cost of quality includes the costs of all your software testing, as well as any other steps you take to ensure the quality of your product and project. It is your responsibility as the project manager to ensure that your team follows the quality policy, and you have the ultimate responsibility for the quality of the final product.

You need to know your firm's quality policy, because it is an input to the quality planning process. The *quality policy* (as you may have guessed) states your organization's approach to quality. Quality is not a subjective component that can be decided upon by your team on a per-project basis. However, your team should understand and follow the quality policy determined by your organization.

Managing Software Project Risks

Everything you do has built-in risks. When you reached to pull this book off the bookshelf, you risked losing your balance and falling in the bookstore, becoming the laughing stock of the store. You also took a risk of discovering something new and becoming a better software project manager in the process.

Risk management is concerned with identifying potential risks for your project and then putting a plan together to deal with them if they occur. A risk to your software project is an uncertain event or condition that, if it occurs, affects at least one project objective, such as time, costs, scope, or quality. Risks are usually seen as negative events, but there is such a thing as a positive risk. A risk with a positive consequence is that a project that one of your developers is working on gets postponed or cancelled. This risk is a negative for some other poor, sad PM, but the effect is a positive for you that can translate into improved deadlines and code quality.

If you knew with certainty every scenario that could possibly happen with your software project, you would not need a risk management plan. But chances are, you will never start a project with 100 percent complete information at hand. Things change. Team members may leave to take other job offers, thus putting your schedule at risk. Your technology may become obsolete, thus putting the quality of your project at risk. One of your preferred vendors may go out of business, forcing you to seek solutions elsewhere at perhaps a higher price, thus putting your costs at risk.

Accept the fact that dealing with risks is just a normal part of project planning. When you're working on a project, you're creating a unique product or service. Because the product or service has never been created before, you can't possibly have all the facts.

Gathering the ingredients for a solid risk management plan

The best place to start when creating a risk management plan is to identify and document the risks that may occur and then strategize on how to deal with or avoid them. This plan should occur early in the project. Your goal is to increase the probability and impact of positive events while decreasing the probability and impact of negative events.

Here are the ingredients you need when setting up a risk management plan:

- ✔ **The project scope statement:** Because the project scope statement contains information regarding the products and services you are creating with the project and has information regarding what is and is not included in your project, you will need to use this in developing your risk management plan.

- ✔ **The project management plan:** The project management plan lists the activities, resources, task sequence, and schedule; you will use this to identify and plan for risks concerned with these areas.

- ✔ **Your organization's risk tolerance strategy:** You must also know your organization's general attitude toward risks when developing your risk management plan. If the organization tends to have a low tolerance for risk, you may not want to consider some activities that you would otherwise have no problem doing. On the other hand, if your organization has a high risk tolerance, you may want to allow for certain activities that other firms may never consider.

If your organization already has certain methods that they use for defining terms and concepts for creating risk categories, use them when defining your risk management plan.

Examining typical risks

The following list includes some examples of some of the risks you may encounter and should plan for during your software project:

- Key resources (materials and personnel) leaving your project
- Technology becoming obsolete
- Stakeholders attempting to enhance the scope of your project (*scope creep*)
- Leadership changing direction
- Labor disputes or strikes
- Schedule delays due to issues with off-site resources
- Personnel resources being squeezed because they are working on too many projects simultaneously
- Lack of commitment to project funding
- Software testing revealing major bugs that could impact the timeline

Getting a plan together

We're sure you can think of other risks for your specific projects. The more often you create project plans and risk management plans for your software projects, the easier it will become to develop risk management plans.

As we said in Chapter 1, there are nine knowledge areas, identified by the Project Management Institute (PMI), to consider in project management. These knowledge areas interact with and affect each another. The knowledge area that impacts risk is (unoriginally) called *project risk management*. Table 10-1 lists the six processes involved with project risk management, as well as a brief definition of each process.

Table 10-1	Project Risk Management Processes
Risk Management Process	**Definition**
Risk management planning	Planning on how to deal with project risk management activities
Risk identification	Identifying the risks that could potentially affect your software project
Qualitative risk analysis	Deciding on the priorities of each risk and determining the probability of a risk actually happening
Quantitative risk analysis	Assigning a number to each risk so that you can analyze its possible affects
Risk response planning	Planning how you will respond to each risk so that you can minimize threats to your project objectives
Risk monitoring and control	Tracking and monitoring existing risks as well as identifying new risks while you evaluate the effectiveness of your risk management plan and make appropriate revisions

Each of these risk management processes has particular tools and techniques that you can use as you develop your risk management plan. The tools and techniques for the first process — risk management planning — are planning meetings and analysis.

Gathering information to identify real risks

As you begin planning your software project, you need to hold meetings with appropriate stakeholders, such as current team members and associates in the firm who have worked on similar projects in the past. All these people, and others who may have information to contribute to the success of your project, can share their experiences and expertise. During these initial meetings, with your firm's risk tolerance in mind, you will begin gathering information to develop your risk management plan. Your organization may even have templates that you can use for these activities.

During the risk management planning phase, you're likely to be performing risk identification because you and other appropriate stakeholders will be reviewing project documentation, such as previous project plans and project files.

To gather information for your risk management plan, you may use some of the following techniques:

- ✔ **Brainstorming:** Be sure to document all ideas regarding risk identification. The idea that you omit because it sounds lame could end up being the best idea of all. Another reason to accept *all* ideas is so that no one feels that their idea is too dumb to be accepted. You never want someone with an idea to avoid raising his or her hand because this could potentially keep you from discovering some valuable information.

- ✔ **SWOT analysis:** This analysis documents the strengths, weaknesses, opportunities, and threats to your project. You'll be surprised at how much easier it is to identify risks after you've thoroughly explored each of these areas.

- ✔ **Delphi:** This strategy is sort of like anonymous brainstorming. You and others provide your input on risk identification but no one knows who submitted particular ideas.

One method of accomplishing this is to have people send an e-mail to a particular person and have that person consolidate the items into one document (without assigning names to each idea). Another method is to have everyone place his or her documented ideas into a receptacle (a suggestion box) and have someone take all of the documentation and consolidate it. One advantage of this technique is that those people who are shy or uneasy about providing input in meetings can speak freely without being concerned with how they look to others. You receive input from those that you might not otherwise hear from.

- ✔ **Root cause analysis:** You discuss risks and the likely causes of each risk. If there are many risks associated with a particular cause, root cause analysis provides you with the information you need in order to prioritize your risks. When you see that several risks are associated with a particular cause, you can make sure that you put more effort into minimizing those risks.

- ✔ **Interviewing:** Chances are, you already have access to several experts regarding risk identification. These are the people who have already created risk management plans for your firm. Don't be shy. Talk to them. They probably won't bite.

- ✔ **Don't reinvent the wheel:** You may already have contact with people who have already done all of this work before, so take advantage of their expertise.

As you gather the information regarding types of potential risks, the probability of each risk occurring, and the potential impact of each risk, you can start to develop a *risk probability and impact matrix* to show each risk and its potential impact on project objectives that deal with the Iron Triangle of cost, time, and quality. To obtain the risk assignment, you multiply the probability by the impact: P × I = RA. Table 10-2 shows an example impact matrix.

Table 10-2	Risk Probability and Impact Matrix		
Risk	*Probability*	*Impact*	*Risk Assignment*
Technology becoming obsolete	.6	.9	.54
Key resource leaving project	.3	.8	.24
Execs changing direction	.4	.8	.32
Major bugs in software	.4	.7	.28

The first column in the risk probability and impact matrix lists each identifiable risk. The second column, probability, indicates, in a decimal format, how likely a risk is to occur. For example, if you determine that there is a 60 percent probability that technology will become obsolete, you enter a .6 in this column. Probability should always be listed as a number between 0.0 (no probability) and 1.0 (100 percent certainty). The third column, impact, assigns a number to the impact of an event occurring. For example, your organization may say that any event that will have a high impact should be assigned a .9 or 1, and anything with a relatively low impact should be assigned a value somewhere between .1 and .3. To determine the probability and impact of a risk, you should use expert judgment and gather information from other stakeholders who have knowledge and expertise regarding your software project.

Monitoring and Controlling Risks

Risk monitoring and control is the last risk management planning process listed in Table 10-1. After you identify your project's risks, perform qualitative and quantitative analyses, document your risk management plan, and define your responses to the risks, you can start working on the project. Along the way, you will be monitoring and controlling your risks.

You may create a database or register to keep track of each previously identified risk, identify and document new risks, and track the response plans for each risk. There may even be instances where a risk that you documented at the start of the project is no longer valid; you should make revisions to your risk management plan to address this change.

You can use a risk database as part of your risk management plan to track and respond to project risks, as well as to monitor and control risks. However, you don't *need* a database to monitor and control risks. It's just an added tool that may assist you with your risk management planning.

These processes interact with each other and are ongoing throughout the life of your software project. You will continue to monitor and control risks based on whether or not identified risks are still valid, new risks have been identified, a risk probability has changed, or any other number of factors that could affect your risk management plan.

You don't need to overcomplicate what really should be a standard part of your project planning. You can track risks with a risk database or with a spreadsheet or even with good old-fashioned paper and pen (but who uses those things anymore?). The method you use is not as important as your commitment to following through on identifying, tracking, planning for, and responding to each risk.

Of course, if you do have a database where you can store project planning information such as risk management data, you may be able to easily report on the risk management aspects of the project. Here are a couple of benefits of creating a database for your risk management data:

✓ A database will enable you to keep the appropriate stakeholders informed of any issues related to risk management.

✓ A database will also aid you and your organization in creating a more solid risk management plan for future projects.

✓ A risk management database can become part of your firm's historical database, contributing to the company's overall risk management strategy. Who knows? They might even name the database after you.

Managing Secondary and Residual Risks

As you develop your risk management plan, you need to consider secondary and residual risks:

✓ A *secondary risk* is a risk that occurs because of a planned risk response. For example, you may identify as a primary risk the fact that Kathy, a key resource, is leaving your project. As part of your response to that risk, you hire a new programmer, Peter, when Kathy leaves. Maybe Peter stretched the truth on his resume and did not have the experience that he indicated he had. All you know is that he ends up causing more problems than solutions with the project. Peter's hiring is a secondary risk because it came about due to the planned risk response. You should identify secondary risks and create a response plan for these risks.

✔ A *residual risk,* on the other hand, is a risk that just won't get the hint and go away. It stays. You can't avoid it or get rid of it. For example, you identify declining team morale as a primary risk. After you implement steps to respond to this risk, such as team building activities, you still have one or two team members who continue to be miserable. Nothing you try will change the attitudes of those team members. You may have to accept that misery as a residual risk.

The bottom line is that you still need to manage these risks as well as the primary risks identified in the planning process.

Documenting Risk Management Effectiveness

How effective is your risk management plan? Why should you document the effectiveness of your risk management planning? Why do you care? Here are some reasons why you care:

✔ You can use the data that demonstrates your project effectiveness as you start developing the plans for your next software project. This information will help you (and others) to use your risk management effectiveness documentation as lessons learned documentation.

✔ You can use this documentation to improve the risk management planning on your current project and on the next phase of your current project.

✔ You can use this documentation to improve your chances of getting a promotion for being intelligent enough to create a strong risk management plan and the documentation to support it.

You should hold post *project reviews* (otherwise known as meetings) to gather feedback from stakeholders regarding the effectiveness of your risk management plan, elicit suggestions on how it could be improved, as well as discuss what areas of the plan were particularly successful. This information will be extremely valuable when you (or others) start planning for your next software project.

Getting it done

This is what project management is all about — getting the project to completion.

Getting your software project to a successful completion should not be a painful process. In fact, it can be quite enjoyable. You just have to think logically and remember the keys to successful project management. Use your resources; talk to other successful software project managers who have done this type of project already.

Find out what they do to ensure success. Chances are they will tell you they created a quality product by using the appropriate tools and techniques available to create a solid quality management plan.

No project is without risk, so remember to plan for the potential risks and identify responses to each risk. Risk management is an iterative process and should be performed at each project phase.

Chapter 11

Working with Project People

Projects are not solo endeavors. You have to let go, delegate responsibilities, and lead your project team to complete the job. People — the people you hire and the people you work for — are involved in each step of the project. You depend on those people to perform their tasks, and they depend on your help to lead them to project completion. Everyone involved has some stake in the success of the project, and cooperation is imperative to accomplish what must be done.

Chapter 7 introduces you to many of your responsibilities and duties as a software project manager. Taking these roles seriously will help you to find the optimal mix of human resources, so that you can then motivate, align, and direct the team. Chapter 7 also discusses how to build the project team and walk the fine line between leadership and management.

This chapter continues that discussion, with the focus now on the concept of leading your project team. Without further ado, here's all the information you need on facilitating your team's success.

Examining the Phases of Team Development

Remember your first college class? You sat in a room with a bunch of strangers and wondered what you were doing there. The temperature of the room was unbearable and no one spoke more than a muffled, "hi," to those who accidentally made eye contact with them for a split second.

Only one or two people knew each other from high school. They sat together and nervously discussed Frisbee golf, the weather, or the prospects of the local football squad while you all waited for class to start. No one was comfortable.

The professor insisted upon reading every single word of the verbose syllabus as if none of you could read it on your own. When the hour was over, you shuffled out and may have mumbled a few words to the person beside you before seamlessly disappearing into the crowd on the sidewalk again.

At some point in the semester, all of that changed. People in the room started talking to each other before the class began. They started talking to each other after the class was over. Occasionally, they even talked to each other during class — not just contributing to the class discussion, but making snide comments and jokes.

The strangers in the room became a *team* — a temporary group brought together for a short time (a semester) for the purpose of passing the class. Some members of the team valued being in that class more than others and some still wished they were anywhere else but there. Some contributed more — possibly because they grasped the content or were fascinated or stimulated by it, or simply because their personalities made them more gregarious than those around them. Some were not right for the class and left, while others transferred in a little late.

The professor was delighted to have some of those students. Others were more of a challenge, and the professor wondered why they were there. Some pesky folks may have needed more individual attention or additional resources to supplement what they already had, and one or two could not grasp the material at all.

This pattern of team building continually repeats itself. It plays out in every project team assembled in school, in business, and in life. Members start out being quiet and uncomfortable — eventually we all move away from that. Understanding this pattern — and ways to speed up the process — can make you a more effective software project manager.

A team is a group of people brought together temporarily for a determined length of time for the purpose of achieving a specific goal.

Understanding the life cycle of a typical project team

Being a team leader is a major part of your job as the software project manager. But just throwing a bunch of people into a conference room, pushing a project manager in front of them, and assigning them activities doesn't make them a team.

When they function at their best, teams are cohesive units of resources working together for a common cause. Get that? Working together. Not working against one another, for another, or on their own accord. Teams are fascinating entities when they're working properly.

For some project managers, a good team is any team that can get the work done. These project managers don't care if the team members like one another, the project manager, or even the project work. Sounds like a great time: a disinterested project manager lording over individuals cranking out code independently of one another.

Project teams have a natural process they go through to become cohesive. The process consists of four distinct phases, which, if you watch closely, you can see (or just check out Figure 11-1):

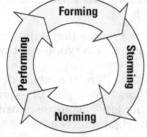

Figure 11-1: Project teams move through four phases.

1. **Forming.** At the beginning, team members gather together and introduce themselves. It's the "Hi, how are you?" phase of project team development. Everyone is polite, cordial.

2. **Storming.** Heated discussions, disagreements, and struggle for team leadership occur in this phase. Storming is the phase of the project when someone on the project team is going to take charge. You may see power struggles between team members. Someone with more seniority may feel superior to a junior team member, or someone with a specialized skill may feel that he or she has more to offer. A team member with advanced education may feel that his or her opinion is more valuable than others'. Conflicts and disagreements about the direction of the project are likely as team members struggle to work cohesively together.

3. **Norming.** In this stage, things settle down. Team members have gotten to know each other and start to deal more with issues on the project than with issues with other team members. You may still notice tension in the air, but for the most part, folks have accepted their roles on the project team.

4. **Performing.** Forget the power struggles and politics — we've got to get this project done! In this stage, performing is the primary goal. The project team members have accepted their roles and are working hard to meet goals and deadlines.

Making a team out of a group of people

The transition from individual to team member rarely occurs at the same time for any two people. It is, however, often accompanied by a number of things:

- ✔ A belief that everyone is working toward a common goal.

- ✔ A feeling that the goal everyone is working toward is worthwhile.

- ✔ The creation of trust among members of the team. The members feel as if it is okay to speak out and be noticed.

- ✔ An acceptance of responsibility. Members realize that if the goal (to complete the project) is to be accomplished, everyone must contribute.

Moving from individual to team member is something that some do quite easily — they are always looking for something to be a part of — and something that others do quite hesitantly. It is your job — your responsibility — to help this process along and lead them in the right direction.

Training the project team

Earlier in this chapter, we use the analogy of a college class to describe a team. Everyone starts out as strangers and then becomes a part of the group. The ideal is that when the group comes together, it does so in a way that enables each person to contribute positively. On occasion, however, the opposite happens.

Students sometimes form subgroups that impede the educational process. Whether this happens because the professor is incompetent, the students just happen to be overly rebellious, or for some other reason, the result is the same: The hour in the classroom is not conducive to learning and it ends up being a waste of time for the semester. Even though the professor may not be the reason that the negative subgroup formed, he or she is still the one who must deal with the situation.

You cannot afford to be the professor in this situation. You cannot afford to lose control of the situation, or become the butt of the joke or the person who represents a drain of time and energy. Professors have the enviable position of having a fresh start two to three times every year, and you do not.

Doing Some Fun Team-Building Exercises

Don't roll your eyes.

When many think of *team building,* they think of making a fool of themselves in some torturous exercise that doesn't seem to really have anything to do with the task at hand. You may hear apocryphal stories of teams that go hiking through the mountains so that they can bond. I'm still waiting for stories of project team members that were chased by bears and snakes, and wandered lost in the woods for hours.

You don't need the Smoky Mountains, however, to do some team building. At any library (read *Team Building for Diverse Work Groups* by Selma G. Myers, and published by Wiley), and at a plethora of Web sites, you can find information on simple exercises that can be used to build effective teams. These include everything from the aforementioned survival mission to being able to suspend countless tennis balls for a short period of time. When you look at these, you should ask but one question: Why are we doing this?

Here's a list of just a few popular team-building exercises:

- ✔ Golfing or putt-putt
- ✔ Bowling
- ✔ Geocaching (going on a geographically oriented treasure hunt)
- ✔ Outdoor rope courses (Check out *The Power of Team Building: Using Rope Techniques* by Harrison Snow, published by Wiley)
- ✔ Paintball
- ✔ Hide-and-go-seek

The reason for any team building is to help the members establish trust in one another and come out of their shells; you want to expedite the natural team-building process in order to make the team more cohesive and get results faster. The goal of team-building exercises is really simple: Build a cohesive team.

When choosing what type of exercise to employ, you should know something about the members of your team. If you take the wrong approach, you can end up with the wrong results. For example, taking a group of insecure programmers and making them play baseball against a college team probably isn't going to make them respect you much and feel as if they gained anything from the experience. Take that same group of programmers, give them a box of Lego blocks and a remote control car, tell them to create a city that the car can maneuver through, and they'll be off and running. This simple exercise demands the whole team be involved and work together towards a common cause. Its simplicity doesn't overpower the purpose of the exercise.

Be careful when choosing team-building exercises. Some activities require participants to compete with one another while others require members to work together to accomplish a common goal.

If you have more questions about team building, check out *Team Building for the Future: Beyond the Basics* by Steve L. Phillips and Robin L. Elledge for more information on team building. You should also check in with your organization's HR or Organizational Development department. The smart people in this part of your company may have more information about team development than you realize.

Managing Project Conflicts

Will you complete your project without a single problem or hitch? Absolutely — and then you'll wake up. If projects were easy enough to be completed without any problems, there wouldn't be a need for project managers. Your primary job would become updating your resume.

Too often, we tend to think of conflict as a bad thing. Life would be better if everyone would just think like you do and agree with you. So much more would be possible. In reality, conflict enables greatness.

If there wasn't any conflict, would anything ever get better? What a bland, boring project it'd be without any challenges or disagreements.

It is all right if team members sometimes disagree, feel passionate about the project, and take a stance on an issue. You want them to express those opinions, share them, and explain why they are important. When team members use their skills of arguing logically and thinking critically to examine issues, they contribute to the project's success by coming up with original ideas to solve problems. When dynamic people express their ideas and opinions, especially in complicated projects, creative solutions arise.

Of course, you also want them to disagree in a civilized manner, to follow directions when asked, to be willing to compromise, to see the point of view of others, and to accept that their opinion may be just that. When this happens, the team wins, the project improves, and everyone benefits from it.

Still, sometimes conflicts need your attention. In the following sections, we address the methods you can use to address conflicts with various stakeholders involved in the project. Here's a teaser: The first rule is to listen before you respond.

Dealing with stakeholders

You are the iconic representation of the project. When there is a disagreement, you are the one that others turn to for solutions. Stakeholders have an important interest riding on the success of the project, and they are looking to you to make their vision a successful reality.

When stakeholders feel that a project is in jeopardy, or that it runs the risk of not being as successful as it could be, they are going to come running to you like a crime victim runs to a police officer. They want you to solve any conflicts and make it all okay.

Your first job is to listen, and your second job is to act. In that order. Don't try and immediately jump to any conclusions on how they feel or how highly they value what they are concerned about. Repeat back what they've said so that they feel assured that you get what they're saying.

After you have assured them that you do understand their issues, begin to address them. Every situation is different. Sometimes the stakeholder is correct — the project must proceed this way because that is the mandate. Other times, the stakeholder simply does not have all the information; that's when you need to introduce the relevant information and persuade the stakeholder about why your position is the best one.

Of course, the best thing to do is to be proactive so that you can prevent being in this unenviable position in the first place. Stakeholders may be upset because they don't have all the pertinent information or they are seeing a situation through their eyes only. Documenting, implementing, and following a thorough communication plan to ensure appropriate stakeholders receive the appropriate information at — you guessed it — the appropriate times can help you prevent some of these conflicts.

If the stakeholder is correct, don't be afraid to say so. Few things go so far today as admitting that you might be wrong and that someone else might be right. The progress of the project also has some bearing on the outcome of the disagreement, as Figure 11-2 demonstrates. Early on in the project, the stakeholders' influence on changes and scope verification should be high, but as the project nears completion, their influence should wane. During the early phases of the project, when the stakeholder influence is high, the stakeholder conflicts or issues may be more prominent than at times when the stakeholder influence is not as high.

If the stakeholder is wrong, say so. Delicacy is paramount — there are many ways of letting people know that they are wrong, but few are as successful as education (and avoiding use of the phrase "you're wrong"). Explain why your thoughts differ and focus on the end result.

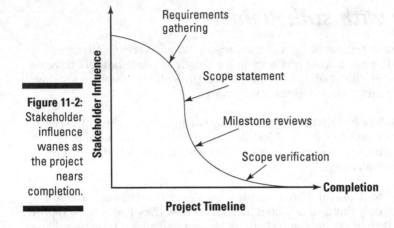

Figure 11-2:
Stakeholder
influence
wanes as
the project
nears
completion.

Few issues are truly black and white, which means that using phrases like "you're wrong" or "I'm right" just serve to create unnecessary contention. You can express your reasonable conclusion based on your intimate experience with the project, but if a stakeholder still disagrees, you may have to implement plans that you don't like. You expect your team members to follow your instructions even if they disagree. As part of a larger team, that's also your job.

In all cases, whether right or wrong, the stakeholder wants assurance — assurance that the project will be successful and that they made a good choice by choosing to be involved in it.

Dealing with project team members

Fire them all. (Kidding.) Although firing difficult members of your team is an approach that has been employed by many a manager, it is the wrong tactic to take. Conflict can be a sure sign that members within the team are comfortable enough to express themselves — and that's something that you can exploit for greater success. Isn't greater success what every project manager hopes for?

Some experts in project management advocate moving team members to various teams over time. As the members become more comfortable with each other, they tend to disagree less often, so mixing up the dynamics by adding new members can be beneficial.

The members of the team should know that it is okay to disagree with each other, and they should be comfortable doing so. However, they should also know that you will often make final decisions.

As a general rule, we like to take a democratic approach to project management: The team members are the experts, with the SPM approving their decisions and providing direction when necessary. Sometimes, however, you have to yield to the circumstances of your project, and you may have no other choice but to become more autocratic. And in rare situations, your pleasant democracy could become a dictatorship. You obviously want this to be the exception, not the rule. Teams that lead themselves with some oversight are happier; and happier times get more work done.

When a conflict arises that demands your involvement, you should listen to each party individually and weigh what they are saying — paying particular attention to why each person is passionate about the issue. You need to know whether the conflict and solution are in the best interest of the customer, a stakeholder, or the party voicing the issue.

After you have weighed the matter, gather the parties in a meeting and explain the decision that you have come to. Here are some conflict resolution do's and don'ts to consider when you have this meeting:

- Do make sure to address each and every concern that was expressed to you.

- Don't let things get emotional. Let the parties cool down, and don't let them rehash the issue in this meeting.

- Do clearly state the reason why you elected to go with the solution that you did.

- Don't let the parties walk out of your office before you tell them that you understand that they may not be pleased with the decision. Reiterate that it's the best decision and that they need to accept it for now.

- Do make sure that the parties understand that they need to let things go and get back to work.

- Do make certain that the team members leave knowing that when another conflict comes up, you will listen to it openly and objectively and make the right decision again.

Documenting project conflicts and resolutions

Conflicts should be looked upon with the same weight and value of every other part of a project. You should document specific conflicts, the parties involved, and the resolutions. This info can be helpful on future projects, as well as when you need to make changes to this project at a later time.

For example, suppose a team member felt adamantly that the user interface should have a different look and feel, but you decided to go with the one that the focus groups preferred. If the final software product fails to gain acceptance with the end users, and interface is brought up as a potential cause for the failure, you can talk to the team member who disagreed with your decision. That person can do a detailed study in to what changes could be made. In the following section, "Using Your Super Magic Project Manager Powers," we get into more specific scenarios for resolving conflicts.

Using Your Super Magic Project Manager Powers

You're the boss, darn it! You don't have to go any further than that — every time an issue comes up, just stamp your fist and make that proclamation. Let your team know that you're the one getting paid the big bucks and storm out of the room.

Oh, wait. That might have worked in the production era of Henry Ford, but that approach doesn't work so well in the workplace of today.

The reason tantrums fail is because we no longer can stand behind someone assembling parts on a line and make sure they are not tarrying — speeding up the line if it is suspected they are. In today's world, work is far more mental. You speed up the line with motivation, rewards, and praise.

As a software project manager, you have several powers at your disposal. Every manager, and in fact, every team, has varying degrees of success utilizing these powers.

Your greatest power is your knowledge and understanding of your team members. Know what drives them so that you can apply your other powers strategically to match every situation.

Forcing a decision

As much as we all love democracy, there are times when someone just has to make a decision. You are that someone.

You don't have to be so bold about it as to demand that your every whim be obeyed; you can be more subtle. Your manner and your focus can steer decisions in the path that you want them to take. You have to be careful about forcing everything to go your way, because everyone else should have a say if you want to maintain team cohesiveness. You don't want an army of ants, but sometimes you need to force the decision and move on.

The following discourse shows you what we mean:

Team member 1: *Before we go any further, we need to test this part of the software on every Linux platform currently shipping and make sure that there are no issues.*

Team member 2: *We have tested it on three Linux platforms already! Those are the ones that most corporations are using. We've found no issues, and as long as they are using the same kernel, the software should run the same on every implementation.*

Team member 1: *We can't afford to wait until the project is finished to find that it doesn't work on every version. We need to find and identify the problems now.*

Team member 2: *If we do that with every single module as it is developed, that will slow us down and we'll never make the dates.*

Project manager: *I can understand what you're saying. We can't afford for the final build to not run everywhere, but we are a long way from that. Let's check each module, as it is finished, on three versions and alternate those versions — always using two of the most popular ones. That way we stand a good chance of catching issues early on and adapting to them. Now, about the interface. . . .*

In this discourse, the project manager listens to both parties and respects what they are saying before quickly making a decision and moving on to the next topic. In making that decision, the PM references the key points of both discussions, offers a compromise, and ends the discussion. This is a highly effective strategy in many instances because it addresses both the serious quality assurance issue, as well as the crucial timeline issue while also keeping everyone happy.

Relying on expert power

One rule of life is that expert opinions have more weight than others. You may not realize it, but you have expert power because you have valuable experience and knowledge to make sound decisions.

Consider this discussion:

Team member 1: *I think we're crazy if we don't stop and check every module on every platform. Unless we are doing that, there is no guarantee that the final product will run without error for every customer.*

Team member 2: *We don't have the time or manpower to check every module in that way. A better solution is to just wait and check the final product on every machine.*

Team member 1: *I'm not about to go along with that! If it doesn't work, we wasted all of this time creating nothing.*

Project manager: *When I taught at MIT, we recommended checking each module on a few platforms. I used that method when I developed the DST and it worked well. Let's go with that — it's worked for me over and over in my experience.*

By bringing into the conversation the name of a prestigious school, and by conjuring up past projects, the project manager has been established as an expert in the topic. If you follow this technique, you can make a decision and quickly move on.

Be careful with this technique. While you may demonstrate your expertise, if you use the wrong tone you may come across as an elitist and your team members may get the impression that you're working too hard to establish that you're better than they are. You need to find the right balance between showing team members that you're an expert while identifying with their day-to-day issues.

One of the best ways to praise a team member is to acknowledge the individual as an expert. We all like to think that we know more than anyone else in some category, and there is nothing so rewarding as hearing someone in a position of power say, "Hey, you really know your stuff."

Using coercive power

Usually, coercion is defined as compelling a person to act by employing a threat.

The coercive power that remains at your disposal typically involves repercussions directly related to job performance. This coercion can be as simple as demanding that team members work weekends if the project falls behind, or as complex as threatening to transfer an employee to another department or telling individuals that their work practices may warrant a note in their HR file. Of course, you never want to overstep your boundaries or abuse your power when it comes to HR issues, so be sure to understand your firm's human resources policies.

One of the most feared threats for employees today involves the *performance improvement plan* (PIP). Contrary to the name, it's not really viewed as a map for improving employee performance as much as it is viewed as a means of documenting any weaknesses in the worker's performance and sending a message that termination is a distinct possibility. Consider the following exchange:

Project manager: Evan, I understand that you haven't been finishing your assignments on time.

Team member 1: That's not my fault. I didn't get the software I needed from Kristin until Thursday. When I got it, it didn't work right and I had to basically redo everything she did.

Project manager: You got it on Thursday, but when did you request it from her?

Team member 1: Thursday.

Project manager: Don't you think you should have requested it sooner? Isn't this pretty much the same thing that happened with the last project, and the one before it, as well?

Team member 1: I had to spend all my time redoing what should have been done in the first place.

Project manager: That is not your assignment, is it? If anything that reaches you is not ready, you need to bring that to my attention. I don't see any record of you ever documenting any changes you've made to the stub files. Can you show me what you did?

Team member 1: I didn't write down the changes.

Project manager: Did you save them?

Team member 1: No. I just did what I needed to do; then I started in on my part of it.

Project manager: Again, this isn't the first time this has happened, is it?

Team member 1: No.

Project manager: Do you know what your deadline is for turning over the next phase?

Team member 1: This Friday.

Project manager: Are you going to make that?

Team member 1: I am going to try.

Project manager: I need you to do more than try. I need you to make that date or else the whole project might slip. I've started working on a performance improvement plan. I don't want to go that way, but if you don't make if by Friday, you're going to be in here looking that over. Do you understand what that means?

Team member 1: Yes, but . . .

Project manager: Let's talk about the "but" on Friday. I want you to get out there and start working on that module.

Notice the large number of questions the project manager is asking. These are all questions that the project manager already knows the answer to but is asking in order to get the team member to acknowledge that there is a problem. After the team member agrees that the problem exists, the natural outcome seems to be the PIP — or, more specifically, the threat of it. As long as the team member does not want the negative consequence, the coercion works.

Rewarding the project team

You can still be a tough boss (as described in the previous section) and do kind things, as well. Being the one who gets to reward people can be very rewarding for you, too. Rewards are a wonderful motivator, if properly applied, and can give you results like no other form of inspiration. Not only do rewards make the team members happy, but they feel good to give.

When you begin planning for the project, include a few lines in the budget for rewards. These do not have to be expensive (forget about that new car!) because you'll be surprised at how hard some will work for very little. If you don't believe us on this, just think back to the last time you went to a county fair or carnival. Some people will spend hundreds of dollars playing impossible games to win a prize they could easily purchase at the dollar store. They value the prize, not because of the worth associated with it, but because of the task they had to do to get it. Then there are those people who respond to public recognition. They just want to know that others recognize their efforts and accomplishments.

One of the best rewards anyone can get is praise. It costs nothing but can generate immense loyalty and commitment — but you have to mean it. No one likes a fake who offers fake kudos.

Using this train of thought, you can create relatively inexpensive prizes that employees want and will compete to get. For example, you can offer tee shirts, hats, or other clothing items with the company logo (or team logo) to employees who finish their tasks ahead of schedule. You can also offer pizza parties at lunch for teams who have zero defects, dinner gift certificates, or other thoughtful rewards for a job well done.

If you do not have any money set aside for rewards, offer intangibles — the ability to take a day off if some arbitrary criteria are met. Give the gift of leaving early or coming in late, parking in a special spot in the lot, or using the new monitor to the workers who keep the project on (or ahead of) schedule.

The one thing you have to be careful of with rewards is that they have to be valued by those receiving them. One way to devalue them is to give too many. If everyone gets a reward — or if they get a reward without having to do much of anything — then the rewards fail to be a motivator.

Another issue with rewards is that once they are given, they come to be expected. Giving $100 to each team member at project completion fails to motivate anyone after doing it for a few years. If you fail to give it after one project, because budgets are tight, the entire team will revolt — they've come to see the reward as part of their pay, and not as a reward.

You and Your Positional Power

Sometimes you just have to be the manager. It feels good to pass out rewards. It feels good to offer praise. It feels good to sit back with your feet on the desk and your hands behind your head.

That isn't all there is to management, however. As a project manager, you'll find yourself in situations where you simply have to step in and assume the tough role. You'll have to remind someone that you're in charge of the project and that your decision is the one that matters.

This is not a role that anyone relishes. No one wakes up in the morning looking forward to facing a team member who wants to challenge every decision and make accusations about lack of leadership.

Someone had confidence in you, or you would not be in the position that you are currently in. If you feel shaky, you need to find that confidence within yourself and let it exude. The only way to face a challenge of your position is to face it head on — immediately.

Theories of human resources

The field of human resources, in general, and motivational theory, specifically, is nothing new. A great many of the best minds in the world have turned their attention to this area. The following five theories offer insight to this topic.

Hertzberg's Theory of Motivation: In 1959, Frederick Hertzberg wrote *The Motivation to Work,* which focused on what people want from their jobs. Convinced that it is not just a paycheck that we crave, but also positive experiences, he did a study asking engineers and accountants what parts of their jobs pleased and displeased them.

(continued)

(continued)

He took the results and divided them into two categories: hygiene factors and motivational factors. Hygiene factors, also known as maintenance factors, are those that serve basic (animalistic) needs. They include supervision, salary, physical working conditions, job security, company policies, and so on.

Motivational factors serve specific human needs. These needs can be specific to individuals. He argued that hygiene factors are not enough to motivate anyone (but the lack of any of them can lead to lack of motivation), and only motivational factors can encourage people to devote themselves to a cause.

McGregor's Theory X and Y: Douglas McGregor formulated ideas about management by talking with those who practiced it. What he found is that managers fall into two camps — those who think people are inherently lazy and dislike work *(Theory X)*, and those who think work is a natural part of life *(Theory Y)*. He created a set of assumptions for each and a kind of continuum upon which they lay.

For example, within Theory X, there are those who believe that scientific management is the only answer *(hard X)* and those who think human relations can be of great help *(soft X)*.

Ouchi's Theory Z: William Ouchi thought that McGregor's X and Y needed something more added to them and came up with *Theory Z*. This theory essentially pulls in and combines management practices from the United States and Japan. Instead of saying only the two ends of the spectrum exist, it offers the importance (as motivators) of job security, individual responsibility, career paths, and the like — in other words, it looks at work as part of the whole picture instead of looking at it independent from everything else.

Halo Effect: A number of researchers have devised what is known as the *halo effect*. In essence, this theory states that we tend to view a person in all areas the way we see them in one. Thus, if Spencer is a wonderful team member who always gets his work done on time and without problem, we tend to think favorably of Spencer in all areas — he probably has a great home life, and would make a wonderful manager.

On the other hand, if Roy can't turn his work in on time, we tend to think that he would make a bad manager and probably has a bad home life, and so on.

Many cues are used in determining how to decide whether a person is one thing or another — someone wearing glasses is often thought of as being smart, a company is thought to be successful if it has one popular product, and so on.

Expectancy Theory: Victor Vroom is the father of the *expectancy theory*, which states that people decide whether or not to be motivated by three criteria. All three criteria must be present, or motivation is foregone. The first of the criteria is the perceived importance of the reward that could be had. The second is the feeling that actions will lead to the result (performance is a factor). The third criterion is the actual connection between the performance and the reward. For example, a person believes that the team will only achieve its results if everyone participates more than they usually would and that the result would be a bonus for all.

Chapter 12

Procuring Goods and Services

. . . .

. . . .

*Y*ou've put a lot of work into determining your project's scope, documenting your project plan, and creating a super change control system. You have the cream of the crop for your project team. What's left to do? Well, lots. In order to complete your project to satisfy your stakeholders' requirements, you need an application for software testing. Yes, that's right, you need a software-testing doohickey.

You've already decided that it is out of the scope of the project to create the testing doohickey yourself, so you must purchase the software-testing system for your project. This is called a *make or buy* decision. You've decided to buy, so now you start the procurement process, which includes all the activities involved when you purchase goods or services. Although you have lots of options when you participate in the procurement processes, they all have one thing in common: *Procurement* (the art of buying resources) is usually a formal written process.

To get back to our procurement scenario, you know that several testing-services firms are in the market, but you need to find just the right one for a reasonable cost, and you only want to deal with a reputable vendor. You must go in search of the perfect vendor for this project, or at least the perfect vendor for you.

If all this sounds like it makes sense, but you're still not sure how to do it, don't worry. We're going to tell you everything you need to know. Keep reading, Weedhopper, and the solution will appear before your eyes. This chapter tells you about vendors, SOWs, contracts, and more.

Finding a Vendor

If your customers or stakeholders already have a list of preferred vendors, then much of your work is already done for you. You just choose a vendor from that list. Assuming, though, that you have to start from scratch, here is a starting list of what you need to consider when seeking a vendor (this list applies whether you're seeking a software vendor, a hardware vendor, or any other type of vendor for your project):

- **Risk tolerance:** In Chapter 5, we discuss risk tolerance. An organization's risk tolerance is defined as its ability and willingness to take on risks. If your firm has a high risk tolerance, then you can consider vendors that someone with a lower risk tolerance wouldn't consider. For example, a vendor who is new to the field of software testing may be acceptable to you, whereas a firm with a lower risk tolerance would want only established software-testing vendors.

- **Cost:** If cost is one of your biggest considerations, you need to find a software-testing vendor who can get you the most bang for your buck.

- **Time:** If time is your biggest concern, you must find a vendor who can successfully complete the work within a tight timeframe. Unfortunately, if you want something done in a hurry, you usually have to pay big bucks for it, so be sure cost isn't too big a factor.

Your choice in vendor depends on the priorities and requirements of your organization and your stakeholders.

As you search for your vendors, your process works a little something like this:

1. **Send out a Request for Information (RFI).**

2. **Set up a bidders' conference.**

   A bidders' conference is optional, not required.

3. **Send a Request for Proposals (RFP).**

4. **Review proposals and make your final decision.**

After you've navigated these waters, you're almost done acquiring the service or product you need for your project.

Using RFIs to solicit vendors

Say you've made the decision to outsource or purchase a portion of your software project work (perhaps the software testing) and now you're ready to start soliciting vendors. How are the appropriate vendors going to find out that you need something they can provide?

Because the entire procurement planning process is usually formal, you need to prepare appropriate documentation for all phases, including the phase at which you solicit vendors. You need to ask for information from various vendors so that you can ensure that you're getting the best software testing system. By asking for information from more than one vendor, you enable yourself to explore and compare capabilities of various systems and vendors, and to ensure that the process remains competitive.

The best way to solicit information from vendors is to create formal documentation to request information. This formal request is appropriately referred to as a *Request for Information* (RFI).

In the RFI, you present your wish list, which details your best-case scenario (list of your most desired software requirements) of what you'll need for your software testing. In addition to asking the basic questions about price and cost, for example, your RFI might contain the following list of requirements and questions:

- The software testing application must integrate with the development database residing on our on-site servers.
- Is any specialized hardware required on our end?
- How long has your company been providing application-testing services?
- What are the general qualifications of the personnel who would be providing software-testing services?
- Can you perform the software testing on-site, or do we have to come to you?

After you receive satisfactory answers to these and the other questions in your RFI, you're on your way to Happy Testingville!

Hosting a bidders' conference

Remember when you were in high school and you had those parties in your parents' basement? All your friends came and tried to impress each other. Ah, those were the days. Well, a *bidders' conference* is similar to those basement bashes, but now they have a fancier name and no Spin the Bottle.

In high school, each party was different and had its own tone: You had after-game parties, parents-are-out-of-town-for-the-weekend parties, and post-prom parties. Well, the same is true for bidders' conferences — each one is its own adventure. In your own practice, you may run into different types of bidders conferences, and just like those high school festivities, each one can have its own advantages and disadvantages.

There is more than one correct way to host a bidders' conference.

The bidders' conference is the second-best opportunity for vendors to impress you; the best opportunity, obviously, is a knock-you-out-cold proposal that you can't turn down — but that comes later. You can set up a bidders' conference as an informal meeting, where you sit around a conference table and have a discussion with a couple of vendors, or you can set up a formal round-table forum with several suitors vying to outdo each other.

In any meeting, however, it is imperative that you maintain control — all vendors think that they have the best solution to every development issue and they will take every opportunity to gain control of the meeting and convince you that they are the best. If vendors take over, you'll end up hearing sales pitch after sales pitch. That's okay, but you need to have control so that you can ask the hard questions. You get the picture.

You know who you consider to be viable vendor candidates, and you can control the conference by controlling who you invite. Whether you send formal, written requests for vendors to attend, or simply invite the vendors by e-mail or phone, control of the meeting begins with who you invite. Occasionally, a vendor may hear of your project through the grapevine, contact you, and ask to attend. The decision is yours, but know what the vendor offers before you extend an invitation. If the vendor doesn't understand your process, it is unwise to bring him in at the last minute.

A day in the life of a bidders' conference

The bidders' conference is the place for all parties to ask questions regarding your project and the various offerings. As the person hosting the conference, you must make an opening statement that outlines your agenda and high-lights specific areas that you would like the vendors to address concerning their product or service. Members of your team and other stakeholders you have invited should also express any specific interests or concerns that they would like the vendors' solutions to address. The software vendors may have questions for you to clarify your requirements and wishes. By the time the vendors are with you, you can determine the commonalities in their offerings and address specific differences in each supplier's capabilities.

Often, when a vendor provides an explanation to one of your questions, one of his competitors may jump in to challenge or one-up the explanation. This is where the process can get interesting, and also where you must exert your control.

Ideally, a bidders' conference is the mechanism to discover in greater detail each provider's true abilities, as well as any new developments in his offering since the RFI was returned. Keep your exaggeration detector well tuned; in the heat of competition, many of the vendors' offerings suddenly gain greater powers, as when Mr. Gadget yells, "Go, go, gadget!" and all manner of fantastic gizmos and abilities suddenly manifest in his arms and legs.

Finally, give the vendors the opportunity to make a final statement as to their capabilities and continued interest in working on your project. At the close of the meeting, present each of the interested and eligible parties a *Request for Proposal* (RFP) package and give them an overview of the logistics for the presentation of all proposals, including due date and any unique requirements you are placing on the bid process. At this point, you can sit back and wait for the real information to come in.

Setting up criteria for RFPs

A Request for Proposals (RFP) is your request for various vendors to provide the down-and-dirty, cut-to-the-chase offer to sell you their products or services. In the RFP, you specify exactly what you want vendors to supply. You also provide the logistical and service requirements that must be provided to accomplish your objective.

Logistical requirements are the delivery and installation timelines for any equipment and products; *service requirements* are contracts concerning warranties, maintenance, and upgrades after any warranties expire. Because the offerings in the proposal become incorporated in the contract for the purchase, what the vendors offer are what they truly believe they can provide, and they may vary significantly from their RFIs. They're likely to differ from any statements made at the bidders' conference.

In a perfect world (and we know there is one out there somewhere), what suppliers propose to sell and what they have discussed prior to the actual offer will be exactly the same. That's the perfect world, and it's out there, but we aren't living in it.

Evaluate all proposals carefully, because the second you accept one, any terms and stipulations included in the proposal may be included in the purchase contract and may override any terms and conditions you may have negotiated outside the vendor's boilerplate purchase quotation form.

Selecting the Vendor

After you get some proposals, get out your magnifying glass and detective hat and get ready to investigate all the offerings to arrive at a vendor selection. The devil is in the details. As you read through the proposals you've received from the vendors clamoring for your business, you can clearly see that all of the offerings handle the big stuff — the main items that you want to purchase — pretty much the same. Only the details differ, and these details (and the differences) can make or break the proposal.

What happens if you select a supplier to provide an application, but in the small print of the contract is a disclaimer stating that all support for the application will be provided through the crew of a pirate ship anchored off the coast of Sumatra? Well, the first time you need support, you'll discover that you would like to be the captain of that ship, because when the application doesn't perform and your project falls behind schedule and encounters cost overruns, you'll be swimming for your professional life. There's got to be a better way. Well, we can give you some tips for evaluating the proposals for applications you commission. Read on.

Considering market conditions

Market conditions may influence the desirability of your contract to purchase. If there is a booming market for software development, the software vendors may have all the business they can handle. If that is the case, you're dealing with a seller's market and probably won't get the terms and concessions you would expect in other times. If, however, business is slow for the vendors, you can realistically expect to get some good deals on performance guarantees and payment terms.

Even in the best of times, be sure to thoroughly read the contracts before committing to anything. Sometimes, and not usually intentionally, the terms agreed to in writing don't match what was discussed and agreed to orally.

The written terms almost always win in any contract dispute.

Everything in life is negotiable, and in slow times for the suppliers, negotiations can be favorable for you. If you are offered a good deal, or you just plain negotiated the deal of a lifetime, get it in writing as fast as you can and get the job done. You'll look good for negotiating a good contract, look better when your project is running like a precision clock, and look great when you bring the project in on time and under budget. That is the plan, isn't it?

Using a screening system

Remember the devil — the one hiding in the details? Start to get rid of it by using a screening system to sort through all the ins and outs of the proposals before you. A screening system can be something as simple as making a plus/minus (or pros and cons) list on a legal pad. Or, you may use a database with artificial intelligence for filtering all the offerings. Any screening system should, in the end, give you a clear idea of the advantages and disadvantages of each vendor. Sometimes, one vendor shows a clear advantage over the others and makes the selection simple; unfortunately that doesn't often happen.

In any system, be sure that you can tally and evaluate the minutiae of the contracts, as well as the major items. Know how tech support functions and where it is supplied. Technical support must be available when you need it, not when it's convenient for the vendor.

Using the help of others

It's also beneficial to ensure that your system involves other people. Though the final decision is yours, you might as well have more than one set of eyes looking into all the facets of a proposal. Team members may see something you missed, or may verify a pertinent detail you weren't sure of. An evaluation committee using a screening tool such as a product comparison spreadsheet can provide essential input and insights as you approach decision time. A properly used screening system can greatly diminish the chances of signing up to a less than desirable stipulation in a purchase contract.

Implementing a weighting system

Any screening and evaluation system you use should incorporate a weighting system. A *weighting system* looks at all the criteria. Some features of an application may be considered absolutely essential for your use, while others may not be as necessary. Those features deemed essential should have greater weight than other functions so that as you investigate and rank the vendor proposals, the essential functions play a larger role in determining the outcome of your selection process than the less important functions.

In systems using a weighting function, the various requirements of the system are assigned numeric values indicating how each evaluator sees the system meeting the particular feature. That number is then multiplied by a *weighted factor* to arrive at the true value of that feature in relationship to the other features in the system.

The weighting factor is generally a percentage of 1, so that if a weight is .4, that value is seen as more important to the overall value of the system than a feature that is weighted as .2. In theory, all the features should be assigned a numeric value related to how well the evaluator perceived the feature to fulfill its function. The numbers would be multiplied by their weighting factor; then those outcomes would be totaled to provide a single numeric rating for the software testing system. See Table 12-1 for an example of what you may see in a weighting system that you might use during vendor demonstrations.

Table 12-1	Weighting System		
Vendor: Testy McTesty			
Demonstration Item	**Weight (0–0.5)**	**Your Score (0–5)**	**Total**
Ease of use	0.5	5	2.5
System security	0.4	5	2.0
User configuration	0.4	4	1.6
On-site support	0.5	3	1.5
Vendor experience	0.2	5	1.0
Documentation	0.3	3	0.9
Interfaces	0.4	4	1.6
TOTAL			**11.1**

If your selection of a vendor is based solely on a weighting system, then the testing system garnering the highest numeric rating would be the automatic selection. But that isn't usually the case. Sometimes other factors play into a selection, but using a weighted screening system can provide valuable input into the ability of the system being evaluated to do what you need it to do.

Negotiating for the Best Solution

You've considered the market conditions, used an elaborate — or not — screening system that incorporated a well thought out weighting system, and selected a winner from all the vendors who came begging for your attention and business. That's the end of it, right? Not hardly. Now you have to negotiate the final contract and get the ball rolling on the actual implementation of the system.

What? You thought that after the evaluation process was done, and the vendor was selected, that you could just sign the contracts and move on? Well, think again. You can't just take the vendor's offer at face value, unless you want to risk leaving money on the table and setting yourself up for some substantial heartache when the fine print in the vendor contract kicks in. Now is when the real negotiation begins, starting with the price of the system. Everything else — remember everything is negotiable — comes later.

Starting with price

When you requested a proposal from vendors, you may have specified that you wanted their best and final price for the products they were offering. And, of course, when the proposals came in, vendors said that the offer was the vendor's best and final price. Yeah, right. That might have happened once, but nobody in the history of the planet remembers it.

As you know, because you develop software, there's a substantial profit margin in software after it's released and matures. That "best and final" price you were offered is so heavy on profit that it wouldn't float if it was loaded on a super-tanker. You always have room to negotiate pricing for a software product.

Also know that every component offered in the vendor's bid has a monetary value attached to it. Even if the vendor won't budge on the actual price, you can negotiate extended warranties, additional services, or other items that add value to the deal. The big margin is in the actual software, and a vendor can afford to drop the price of the software and not take as much of a loss as if time is added to the warranty or support hours are extended.

Negotiate! That's an order! You can get a better deal than the original proposal, and you can be assured that the vendor expects to have to negotiate the price. Ample margin was built into the pricing to give you a discount on the price and still hit his profit targets. Pretend this software is a brand-new car, and that the vendor is a cheesy salesperson at the dealership.

Considering time, cost, and quality issues

When negotiating your contract, don't focus solely on pricing. You have to consider the rest of the Iron Triangle. You have targets to meet for your main project, and whatever application solutions you choose must be able to fit in with your project timelines, budget, and quality requirements.

Your chosen vendor must be able to provide a timely installation of the contracted, properly working application when you need it. For example, if you use a vendor to create your testing application, and the time comes when you're ready to test your software, but — oops — the testing application isn't ready, you might as well not have any testing ability at all. You've paid for something that isn't available, and the delay in testing your product will cost money in lost time and lost productivity for your development team. If the timeline slips significantly, it may also cost you your career.

Here's what you need to negotiate as far as the Iron Triangle is concerned:

 ✔ Be sure that your agreement with the software vendor includes timelines and benchmarks that are realistic regarding your needs.

 ✔ Include penalties for not meeting targets.

   Don't jeopardize your project by allowing the vendor to provide a product at a time that is clearly out of touch with your reality.

 ✔ Factor in all the costs when purchasing your application.

   Be sure you know what is covered under your warranty and what services you might be paying for in areas where the warranty doesn't apply.

 ✔ Spell out how much support in manpower and equipment you need to assure a smooth implementation.

 ✔ Make sure that other resources with costs are accounted for in writing, including such items as room space for testing, extra computer servers, additional power capabilities, and cabling for the testing equipment.

All of these costs come out of someone's budget, and if you don't specify that they are coming out of the vendor's budget, they're coming out of yours.

✔ Make sure there's something in writing that gives you an out if something doesn't work as specified. You must be able to control the quality of the product you are producing, and therefore you must also be able to rely on the quality of the software application you are buying. Be sure that it works as advertised; call the vendor's user references and be sure you receive a working demonstration of the system before you buy. Verify that the software package you see demonstrated is the one you will be buying. Don't get caught buying a new version of the application software that hasn't been tested and debugged.

Unless you are really adventurous, you don't want to be fixing the vendor's software at the same time you're attempting to fix your own. Avoid beta versions of an application or "bleeding edge" releases of software. Let somebody with a higher risk tolerance be a guinea pig. You don't need the headaches, the poor press in your employer's office, and the possibility of slowing down or ruining your project.

Administering Contracts

If your company has a legal department, be sure to have one of its representatives review the contract first and alert you of any potential problems and help you negotiate the terms if necessary. Now you're ready to administer the contract. But first you must consider which type of contract is best for you.

The type of contract you negotiate determines whether you bear most of the risk or whether the vendor bears most of the risk. Ideally, you want the vendor to shoulder most of the risk; of course, the vendor wants you to bear the bulk of the risk in any agreement. The truth is, you'll meet somewhere in the middle.

In unusual circumstances, for instance, when an application you purchase is a new version or is otherwise untested (and we told you not to buy that), the risk in a transaction is shared between the parties. Extenuating circumstances can shift a larger portion of the risk to one of the parties of the contract, but in general, because both parties have a vested interest in the success of the product and its use, risk is usually split on a more or less equal basis. Of course, part of negotiating the contract is an effort to shift some of that risk away from yourself and your sponsor, and with a little luck and a lot of skill, you can accomplish that task.

Selecting the contract type

Some of the most basic contract types are listed in Table 12-2. Just keep in mind that this is not an exhaustive list, but it's enough to whet your appetite.

Table 12-2	Contract Types Defined	
Contract Type	*Definition*	*Who Bears the Risk?*
Fixed price contracts (contracts with a single fee)	You pay the vendor an agreed upon price for the work	The vendor bears the risk here because he's getting paid the same amount whether he has to spend more time on the project than expected or the project goes as planned.
Reimbursed costs contracts	The vendor is reimbursed for all costs incurred	The buyer bears more of the risk here because if prices increase after signing the contract, the buyer still has to reimburse for the higher costs even though the buyer doesn't get extra goods or services for the increased price.
Time and materials contracts	The vendor is reimbursed for the time and materials during completion of the project	The buyer bears more of the risk because if it takes the vendor longer to complete the project, the buyer has to pay for that extra time. Also, if the price of the materials increases, the buyer pays more for those materials.

Writing the terms and conditions

Terms and conditions are the details of a contract that define every aspect of its implementation and how its requirements on all parties are performed. Some of the items usually covered in the terms and conditions of a contract

Understanding how contracts and risk management coexist

All contracts come with some built-in risk. If you want less risk you have to pay for it. Risk is just like any other commodity in a contract that you pay for. If you engage in a fixed fee contract, for instance, the vendor assumes most of the risk, because the vendor gets paid the same amount whether or not he has to spend more time on the project. To compensate for this risk, you are expected to pay more for that type of contract.

were mentioned in the section called "Solving problems and compromising," later in this chapter.

The terms and conditions don't so much cover what you are buying (that information is spelled out in the purchase agreement), but address the issues surrounding your purchase, such as how and when payment will occur, where delivery is considered to occur, how long the warranty and any extensions will be, and who is responsible for any extraneous work and materials outside the basic package being bought by you, the fearless project manager. While some of these items seem like no-brainers, you would be surprised at the impact they can have on your transaction. For instance:

- **Free On Board (FOB) point:** Otherwise known as the place where delivery is considered to occur. We have no idea where the term originated or what that means, exactly. What we do know is that FOB origin means that the title to the product transfers to the buyer at the point the product is manufactured and shipped, and FOB destination means that the title transfers at the buyer's location.

  "So what?" you ask. Well here's what. If the title transfers at the point of manufacture and shipping (FOB origin), then technically the buyer owns the product at that point and is responsible for its transportation, insurance, and so on immediately upon its release from the sellers location. If the truck carrying the product is snatched by space creatures, you're still responsible for the product, even though the space creatures are enjoying your software. Hey, you can't control the space creatures!

  Negotiate the best FOB clause you can get. If the seller insists that the FOB be origin, agree to it if he agrees to insure and deliver the product. Often, the seller wants the FOB to be origin for bookkeeping reasons — the vendor can claim revenue for the product after the title transfers, which looks good at the end of a fiscal quarter. The person you talk to may be very accommodating in that situation.

✔ **Payment terms:** Should you pay the entire purchase price at the contract signing? Nope. Most contracts involving software are structured so that payment occurs in stages. Typically, some portion of the purchase price is paid with the signing of the contract, and other portions are payable at certain points during the installation and implementation. Some usual pay point triggers are

- At product delivery

- At initial installation

- Upon first use

- After completion of installation

- At product acceptance

Graduated payment works for both sides of the agreement; the vendor gets payments at various milestones, insuring that he gets income from his investment in his product to help cover his costs; the buyer gets to hold on to his capital longer and has some leverage to insure that the vendor continues to provide the product and services he has agreed to provide.

Nothing says leverage like withholding payment for incomplete or inadequate services and products. The final payment, usually at product acceptance, happens when both sides agree that the work was completed satisfactorily and the contract is fulfilled. This step usually includes a formal sign-off, which documents that the contract has been successfully performed.

✔ **Extraneous work and materials:** This is work that's not included in the product purchase unless otherwise specified. In many cases, software vendors provide only the software of which their product consists. Usually, they specify that any hardware, cabling, air conditioning, infrastructure or other factors necessary for the successful implementation of their product are to be provided by the buyer.

This works for both sides of the agreement because the vendor doesn't have to provide components that may not be compatible with the standard requirements, and the buyer can control the environment in which the application runs. This part of the contract should be specified, however, and the company providing the software should provide a list of recommended equipment that is compatible with its application.

Creating the statement of work

The *statement of work* (SOW) is a written document that details the scope of the work that the vendor will perform and is an output of the procurement planning process. The SOW can either be written by the buyer or by the seller.

Usually, the SOW is written by the vendor, because the vendor will perform the work. The buyer may have input into the SOW, and in some cases may actually write it with the input and consent from the vendor. No matter who writes it, the SOW needs to contain enough detail so that full expectations for the project are understood by all parties. As with most of the other project management processes, the SOW may be revised after more information is obtained.

The statement of work, at a minimum, should include in detail

- ✔ The product that is being installed

- ✔ The process and procedures for installing the product

- ✔ A specific statement about who will be doing the work

- ✔ A specific list of resources that are necessary for completing the project

- ✔ Specific milestones for marking the advancement of the project

- ✔ The expected amount of time to achieve completion of the project

The SOW is a formal document and should be incorporated in the contract for the software application that you have purchased.

Solving problems and compromising

Problems? Issues? What are you talking about? You bought the application that fits your needs and negotiated a great contract that covers all your bases. Or so you thought. Despite the best intentions of both you and your chosen vendor, problems sometimes arise during the application of the terms of your agreement.

Usually, the vendor is very accommodating in working through issues with the customer. After all, unresolved problems are terrible for attracting repeat business and can be deadly if customers discuss the problems in public forums within an industry. It is extremely hard to sell a product after one or more respected users have aired unresolved issues to their colleagues, so vendors generally work diligently to resolve disagreements before they reach a critical stage.

Sometimes, despite everyone's best intentions, disputes can't just be talked out. Accordingly, all purchase agreements and product warranties include stipulations for dispute resolution and remedies for disagreements between the contracting parties.

Arbitration is a common remedy for resolving disputes that involve performance and implementation issues, and it's a better way to address these issues than a good old-fashioned lawsuit.

Most, if not all, contracts also specify where the arbitration or legal proceedings arising from a dispute will be administered. Typically, software vendors want disputes to be resolved in the vendor's home state, and you (the buyer) probably want them to be handled in yours. This can be an important point in contract negotiations because the available remedies and penalties under contract law can vary from state to state. Be sure that you can live with whatever jurisdiction you agree to use. Your employer or sponsor may have strict guidelines regarding these issues, and you should always be aware of their needs.

Know what can and what can't be disputed under the terms of your agreement. Most contracts contain clauses releasing either party from their obligations under certain circumstances, such as damage due to monsoons, falling meteors, or other natural disasters.

In general, anything other than these factors, as well as terms of delivery and performance, are considered negotiable items in the contract and can be altered with the agreement of both parties to the contract. Issues such as when delivery occurs, who insures equipment and product, who owns the code, and how the product is delivered can all be negotiating points, and they can all affect your satisfaction with the contract you sign. When done correctly, a well-negotiated contract addresses all these issues and leaves little to chance concerning what is expected from you and your vendors.

If all parties know what is expected from your agreement, there should be little need for dispute resolution. Compromise and working through issues are always better than going to arbitration, being sued, and creating a hostile and tense working environment that you might have to endure due to a poorly executed contract.

Be flexible in dealing with issues, but also be firm in insisting that the provisions of the contract be upheld. It's just good business, and neither party should be upset with conforming to their responsibilities under their mutually agreed upon contract.

Closing the Vendor Contract

Time flies when you're having fun, and boy, have you had a ball. *Tempus* has *fugit* and you're at the end of the implementation of your software application.

What now? Through the whole process of acquiring your application, you have conformed to a system in which you monitored and documented every event related to your system acquisition. Now is the time to review your findings, get together with the software application vendor, and close out the contract. Read on for some insight into what you need to do to conclude your contract.

Auditing the goods and services

As the project manager, you need to ensure that the software application you purchased performed as agreed upon. If you have some of the vendors' employees perform areas of the system testing, you're expected to demonstrate the results of the audits of these testing services.

If you have a dispute — either you don't agree that the vendor adequately performed the software testing or their application was down longer than agreed upon percentages — you need to take the appropriate action. Some typical responses include withholding payment, insisting that the vendor rectify the situation, or (in serious situations that can't be resolved) going to arbitration.

But one way or the other you need to audit the products or services that you receive in order to make sure you get what you paid for. It's best to make auditing an ongoing process (hint, hint, build it into the project timeline) instead of waiting until the end of the project to announce that the vendor didn't meet an agreed upon objective. This auditing process may include scheduled meetings with the vendor to discuss outstanding issues, written status reports from the vendor, and acceptance of predefined deliverables at scheduled due dates.

Signing off for the procured goods and services

There are trigger points for contract payments at defined times or accomplishment targets in the contract. The final trigger is your acceptance of the system as a complete and functioning product. When you and the vendor agree that the goods and services you received are the goods and services you expected, you can sign off that the vendor has met its obligation.

Signing off is a formal transaction with full documentation indicating both your and the vendor's agreement that the project is complete to the satisfaction of all stakeholders. At this point, and only at this point, is the contract complete. Great job on managing a subproject to your main project, but hold the champagne — this is a business transaction, after all. Wait until you're off the clock!

Part IV
Controlling Your Software Project

The 5th Wave   By Rich Tennant

"And tell David to come in out of the hall. I found a way to adjust our project budget estimate."

In this part . . .

Every time you work on a big software project, things tend to get slippery. Stakeholders want changes, contractors miss deadlines. Exerting control is a significant factor in successful software project management, so Part IV helps you understand the importance of managing and tracking changes to your software project with an eye on reining things in. You discover how to create effective change control plans while proactively tracking project performance.

Chapter 13

Managing Changes to the Software Project

In This Chapter

▶ Planning for and managing project changes

▶ Managing your project's scope

▶ Creating and following a change control system

▶ Getting a handle on project costs

▶ Dealing with variances in your schedule

▶ Expecting and accepting changes

*P*lan for changes. That's right; you will encounter changes during your software project, so accept these facts, and just plan for them. Maybe a key team member will be removed from the project at a critical time or your stakeholders will determine that some of the functionality that they didn't want at the beginning of the project is now critical. Or perhaps an outsourcing portion of your project that you planned to have completed in six weeks will now be extended for three more weeks. Don't blow a gasket.

Encountering changes during your software project is not a sign that you planned poorly; it's a sign that you are living in the real world where people change their minds, risks are encountered, and stuff happens. You're better off accepting the fact that you will encounter changes so that you can plan accordingly. That's why the title of this chapter is "Managing Changes to the Software Project" instead of "Trying to Eliminate All Changes to the Software Project."

Introducing the Controlling Process Group

According to the Project Management Institute, the project management process group that deals with managing change is the *controlling process group.* You will discover a lot more about process groups if you decide to move forward in your career and take the PMP (Project Management Professional) exam (see the appendix for information about this certification exam).

The controlling process group is used to measure and compare where you are with where you planned to be. The controlling process group is concerned with monitoring and controlling the following factors:

- ✔ Scope
- ✔ Schedules
- ✔ Costs
- ✔ Risks
- ✔ Communication
- ✔ Team member performance
- ✔ Contract administration
- ✔ Quality

Controlling the Project Scope

As the project manager, it is your responsibility to remain constantly aware of all the details surrounding the scope of the project. The best way to get off to a good start in this department is to clearly and thoroughly define the scope at the start of the project. In this section, we talk about controlling the scope you set up earlier (if you want more information on defining project scope, check out Chapter 3).

If you have a thorough, well-planned scope to begin with, others will find misinterpreting the scope later more difficult.

You need to be aware of the potential for *scope creep,* which is an odd phenomenon in which some stakeholders lose perspective and begin to make requests that were never part of the original plan. You can recognize scope creep when you begin hearing people express expectations that certain functionality — that you never planned for — ought to be included.

With project management experience, you will start to notice the types of activities that precipitate requests for changes. For example, during project meetings, certain stakeholders may start talking about functionality that wasn't included in the scope. They may talk about these extras as if adding them is no big deal. They may even act as if everyone knew that this functionality was expected all along.

If you're past the planning phase and you ever hear a stakeholder say, "Why don't we consider adding something new to the interface," or other words to that effect, such as "Well, while we're doing X, we might as well do Y," beware. The stakeholder may make it sound as if both activities go hand in hand, but only one of the items is actually part of the project scope. It's up to you to manage and control the scope before you end up having to add all kinds of unplanned bells and whistles. With each project that you manage, tactics like these become more obvious and easy to recognize. Just be aware of them and add them to your very own lessons learned document so that you only have to deal with them once.

Also keep in mind that scope refers to all the work — and only the work — that your team needs to accomplish to successfully complete the project. If an item isn't part of the documented scope, then your team shouldn't be doing it. Any other response to scope creep can get you into trouble. The biggest dangers, not surprisingly, have to do with the other two sides of the Iron Triangle, the timeline and the budget. Additional factors include adding chaos and disharmony to your team's dynamic. Can you say "new job search?"

Examining the project scope

The project scope includes all of the work and only the work that needs to be completed to successfully bring the project to fruition. You have several opportunities to examine your scope as you *progressively elaborate* the project scope. Progressive elaboration occurs when you develop the scope through several stages — making the scope more complete with each pass-through.

You and your stakeholders must continue to examine the project scope, which is actually what you and your customer agree at any particular point in time is the work that needs to be completed.

As an example, at the start of the project when you are beginning to gather project requirements, you and your client may agree that the project scope is to generate a software program that constructs online report card applications for a local school system. Initially, you and the client agree that the project should include methods for

- Allowing each teacher to document scores for individual students
- Preventing a teacher from adding or changing scores of students who are not in his or her class
- Enabling teachers to print individual reports for their classes
- Sending automatically generated reports to the principal
- Generating reports that show trends in students' scores, as well as classroom averages
- Allowing teachers to input scores for both midterm and final grades
- Permitting parents to log on to view daily homework assignments

Later, after facilitating several of the efficient customer meetings that you documented so thoroughly in your project communication plan, you and your client agree that the scope of the project now must also include new methods for the following:

- Generating communication to parents when a student's average score for any class goes below a predefined level
- Generating e-mails to the principal and department chair whenever a teacher has a classroom average that reaches a predefined level (for instance, the average student grade in one teacher's class is 72 percent)
- Allowing teachers to input documentation from parent/teacher conferences
- Allowing teachers and guidance counselors to document student behavior problems
- Forcing teachers to change their passwords every 30 days
- Creating a password-controlled, secure area where parents can log on to view their child's grades and progress
- Dialing the pizza parlor on the corner to have them automatically deliver a large sausage and mushroom pizza to the teacher's lounge each Friday (just wanted to see if you were alert)

Now that you and the client have reexamined the scope and agreed that it needs to change, you should document these changes and follow a predefined change control process.

Every time the scope changes, you must, must, must document the change — as well as its potential impact on costs and timelines — and then make sure the client signs off. This is significant because it forces both you and the client to examine and progressively elaborate the scope, agreeing on changes before they are documented as part of the scope. But most importantly, you have proof for later, when the client acts surprised that the project took longer and cost more than originally planned.

Creating and following a change control system

You must create an effective change control system because changes are inevitable and even at times necessary. One way to prepare for these changes is to create and follow (and set the expectation that others will also follow) an effective *change control system*.

The purpose of the change control system is to identify, monitor, and learn from the changes occurring in your project. Your change control system may consist of tools, such as a database or spreadsheet to record your proposed changes, and you may also have a *change control board* (CCB) to review and approve changes in your firm. Project team members would document their proposed changes and present them to the CCB for evaluation and approval. If you do have a CCB, then all project changes would need to go before the CCB. The CCB might have just two members or it could be a large committee. The number of members varies from firm to firm. If you have too many members on your CCB, though, making decisions may take longer.

Although you may only be concerned with your own proposed change, the CCB is aware of all project changes and could determine whether your change may affect other portions of the software project. In effect, the CCB keeps everybody honest.

Instead of, or in addition to, a CCB, you might also track changes with a change control database where project team members or other stakeholders may enter their proposed changes. The CCB or SPM can then review and either approve or deny each requested change.

If your software project is relatively small, you may not need a whole database. Why bother with all that infrastructure stuff when a simple spreadsheet will do? Stakeholders simply record changes on the spreadsheet, and later the CCB (or another review body) lists each project change request as approved, rejected, or on hold for further investigation.

You can use a spreadsheet to further track the changes after they've been approved. You can record when changes are implemented into the various system environments so that you can monitor the consistency of the different system environments. This documentation could also be used for a root cause analysis if you encounter system problems after changes are implemented.

As an example, a typical change control spreadsheet could look similar to Table 13-1.

Table 13-1			Change Control Spreadsheet			
Change Request	**Owner**	**Accept/ Reject**	**Factors**	**Date in Test Environment**	**Date in QA**	**Date in Production**
Add functionality for secure e-mail of student progress reports	Sara K.	A		05/02	05/15	05/17
Remove `Discipline` field from teacher conference page	Amanda M.	R	Would affect other areas using `Discipline` field	N/A	N/A	N/A
Create report to notify principal of teacher's average classroom grade of 72%	Adam D.	A	Approved by client, stakeholder, and sponsor	08/22	08/30	08/30

Define your change control system early in the project. You don't want to be confronted with proposed changes without having the appropriate processes in place to deal with them. Also, make sure that all of the appropriate stakeholders are aware of and understand the steps to take in order to follow the appropriate change control processes.

Don't forget to include *emergency change requests* in your change control system. Although normal changes may require CCB approval during its regularly scheduled meetings, you may want to create a separate process for emergency changes. For example, a stakeholder who has a change that is considered an emergency may be able to take the change request to one of three or four individuals who are authorized to approve the emergency change. Even though you may have a separate approval process for this, make sure that stakeholders complete the appropriate documentation so that you have a record of who approved the change and why it was implemented without CCB approval.

Be sure to define what constitutes an emergency change:

- ✔ If you're creating software in the healthcare industry, an emergency change may be anything that, if left alone, could affect patient care or patient safety.

- ✔ In some firms, an emergency change is anything that, left alone, may cause the organization to lose money.

  The project team members need to understand the attributes that cause a change to be considered an emergency.

Documentation is crucial in the event of a system problem. You can quickly view the documentation for all changes that were done just prior to the problem and use the information to perform a root cause analysis.

Determining the value of the proposed change

When project changes are proposed, you need to determine the cost of implementing the change, as well as the value that the proposed change will add to the project. For example, if it will cost $500 to implement a change but that change will add a value of $10,000 to the overall project, you may have a better chance of getting that change approved than if the cost of your change is $10,000 and only brings $500 in added value.

Of course, you're not guaranteed that a change will get approved just because it adds more value to your project than it costs. You still have to consider the other parts of your Iron Triangle — time and scope. Maybe your proposed change will add $10,000 in value to your project, but if it completely changes the scope or adds six months to an already tight timeline, then those areas will also need to be taken into consideration when determining whether or not to implement a change.

Correcting mistakes

At times, you'll be required to make project changes in order to correct mistakes — either in coding or software testing or because of misunderstandings, miscommunications, or any number of other reasons. If you have the appropriate change control system in place and you complete the appropriate project planning processes, making corrections is a more manageable experience.

You can take certain steps to keep potential mistakes to a minimum:

1. **During the planning processes, spend the appropriate amount of time gathering project requirements.**

   You may be tempted to hurry through this phase so that you can quickly get to the fun stuff, but the time you spend here will save you time later.

2. **Follow your well-defined communication management plan.**

   You can avoid many mistakes if you proactively communicate with the appropriate stakeholders.

3. **Create a comprehensive risk management plan.**

   When potential risks materialize, you will be ready to deal with them instead of being caught by surprise.

4. **Define and document your scope management plan.**

   Your project team will be less likely to misunderstand the scope and potentially make mistakes if the scope is clearly defined, documented, and communicated.

One way or the other, you and your project team members will probably make mistakes during the course of your software project. The main thing to know is that (usually, anyway) no single mistake is the cause of a major disaster. Of course, lots of little mistakes are never good for a project either.

Controlling Project Costs

Earlier in this chapter, we mention the Project Management Institute (PMI) project management process groups. The project management process group that is concerned with controlling project scope, costs, schedule, quality, and risks is the controlling process group.

Just like the other parts of the Iron Triangle, scope and timelines, controlling costs is essential. In this section, we talk a little bit about the methods you can use to control your project costs.

You can't change one of the sides in the Iron Triangle without affecting the other sides. For example, if you start cutting costs by eliminating personnel, you will probably increase the timeline. If you add bells and whistles to the scope, then you will most likely increase the time and the cost of the project. Get it? By the way, we talk about costs in more detail in Chapter 9.

If you allow your costs to vary from your original plan without going through the appropriate processes to identify the need for changes, gain the appropriate approval, and follow the identified change control processes, you won't just affect the cost of your project, but you could also negatively affect other areas of the project as well. You could also use this documentation as part of your lessons learned.

Managing project cost variances

During the planning phase of your software project, you gather information you need to create your cost estimates, budgets, and baselines (see Chapter 9). Chances are that with a software project, most of your costs will be associated with resources required to complete the project, including programmers, analysts, software engineers, application testers, and other personnel.

Throughout the project, you need to be aware of variances in what you planned for your project to cost, compared to actual costs. For example, if you planned to have a certain percentage of experienced programmers and a certain proportion of junior or associate programmers, this ratio will be affected if a junior programmer is removed from the project and you replace her with a senior programmer. This action will affect your project costs and create a variance.

Aside from the cost of resources creating project cost variance, other actions or decisions can also potentially create a project cost variance. For instance, say you start to run out of time on your project and instead of creating a thoughtful and innovative plan of corrective action, you decide to sweep the problem under the rug by just eliminating one phase of system testing. After all, if there were bugs or problems in the software, wouldn't they have been caught in one of the previous phases of testing? "Besides," you say to yourself as you justify this craziness, "I'll be the hero of Projectville when the client sees how much time and money I'm saving by skipping one small system testing phase of the project!" This ingenious decision to eliminate some system testing could result in added time to the project due to recoding, eliminating bugs, and then more thorough testing.

Adding and removing resources creates cost variances, but your bad decisions can also create cost variances. Be careful of the project decisions you make; they can, and probably will, have lasting implications, not just for this one particular part of your project, but also for future phases.

Estimating the cost of change

When you estimate the cost of a change, you should consider not just the part of the project that you're changing, but also other affects of this change. For example, making a change to the project schedule could affect project costs with either a cost increase or cost decrease, depending on how you are modifying the schedule. Likewise, making a change to the project costs may also affect the quality of the project or product. Take all of these costs into consideration when estimating the cost of any change.

During the planning phase of your software project, when you create your cost management plan, you identify the methods you might use to identify cost changes in your project. Don't forget to also identify ways to have these changes approved, and don't forget to identify who's in charge of approving these changes (perhaps you need a CCB, as described in the section "Creating and following a change control system," earlier in this chapter).

It would be a harmonious idea to also identify during the planning phase the methods you would use for estimating the cost of project changes. This should all be decided and documented during the project planning phase in your cost management plan.

Forecasting variance

In Chapter 14, we tell you how to measure and monitor your costs (and schedule) using *earned value management* (EVM), so now you have something to look forward to. At any point in time during your project, you should be able to determine how much your actual costs vary from your projected costs. Forecasting variance can be useful for several reasons, but the most important is that your stakeholders will expect this information from you and you will want to know whether and when you need to take corrective action to bring your project costs back in line.

If you know your *earned value* (EV) and you know your *actual cost* (AC), then you can calculate your *cost variance* (CV). Here's the least you need to know:

✔ To determine the AC, simply add up all the costs for the time period that you are measuring.

✔ To determine the EV, look at the amount you budgeted for the work your team has completed at a particular time in the project schedule.

✔ To determine the CV, subtract the AC from the EV ($CV = EV - AC$). This difference is how much you vary in the costs that you expected to incur at this point in time and your actual costs for the same time period.

When you know your cost variance, you can start taking steps to get the costs back in line, if necessary. Along with bringing the costs back in line, don't forget to follow the meticulous communication plan that you documented during your planning phase. In that communication plan, you indicated the appropriate stakeholders with whom to communicate regarding costs variances, and more.

Controlling the Project Schedule

When creating the project schedule during the planning phase of your software project, you probably spent a large portion of your time gathering information. You probably did most or all of the following:

- Spoke to project managers who had managed similar projects

- Gathered requirements from appropriate stakeholders and worked with them and your project team to prioritize and sequence the tasks

- Built the schedule from the ground up focusing on each of the project activities, their definition, their sequencing, and estimating their durations

- Considered the appropriate resources required to complete the project successfully in the desired timeframe

- Built in contingency time in the event that a phase of the project runs over

- Created a schedule management plan that defined how you would control the project schedule and manage project time variances

Taking your time with gathering requirements, speaking to the appropriate resources, and crafting a thoughtfully considered schedule management plan will save you a lot of time in the long run. Armed with these requirements, you can proactively ward off schedule issues and variances before they get insurmountable.

Managing project time variances

Say you did everything right: You created an extremely thorough work breakdown structure (WBS), you spoke to the appropriate people to gather their insight and wisdom, you spent a suitable amount of time gathering requirements, and you created your project network diagram. Everything should flow flawlessly, right? Right! In the Ivory Tower Project World everything would go like a dream, but you're here with us — in the real world — and sometimes stuff happens.

Maybe you did all the right things during your schedule development, but let's just say that something has gone amiss and your schedule is no longer on track. Don't panic. There are steps you can take to manage project time variances. Because you're already here and you're already reading this, we may as well tell you what those steps are.

Before you manage your project time variances, you would of course need to determine that you actually have a project time variance. As part of the controlling processes, you will be monitoring your project schedule and determining if where you are now is where you said you would be when you created your schedule. The schedule controlling processes are concerned with

✔ Using the project schedule as an input to compare your actual results with your plan

✔ Using your performance reports (part of your communication plan) as an input to compare where you are in the schedule with where you planned to be in the schedule

✔ Looking at your approved change requests to determine whether the changes that have been approved and implemented have impacted your timeline

✔ Reviewing the schedule management plan to specify how you will track and monitor changes to the schedule

You will use all these criteria above as inputs to monitor and control your software project schedule and manage the variances. There are also useful tools and techniques to use in monitoring your schedule. One of these tools is a project management information system (PMIS). There are many good ones on the market, but we're most familiar with Microsoft Project. You can find out more about this software by reading *Microsoft Project 2003 For Dummies* by Nancy Stevenson (Wiley).

PMIS is only as good as the information it's fed and will never replace an effective project manager. Don't expect the PMIS to manage and control your schedule for you just as you would not expect a hammer to build a house for you; it's only a tool.

Some of the other tools you might use to manage and monitor schedule variances include the following:

✔ **Schedule change control system:** Devise a system (spreadsheet, database — whatever works for you and your particular project) where you can receive schedule change requests, assess their impact and value, and document their acceptance or denial. This doesn't have to be something fancy or technical; it just has to be a process that works for your project.

✔ **Performance measurement methods:** Use these to produce your schedule variance and *Schedule Performance Index* (SPI), which you can find out more about in Chapter 14. The bottom line is that these numbers, your schedule variance and SPI, will tell you how big of a deal a particular change really is and will help you determine if you need to take corrective action.

✔ **Variance analysis:** Use this to determine whether where you planned to be in the schedule is the same as where you really are in the schedule. This will also help you in determine what (if any) corrective action to take.

This is not an exhaustive list of all the tools and techniques that could possibly help you in managing schedule variances and controlling your schedule. This is just a list to get you started and point you in the direction of knowing that there are ways to monitor your schedule; you need to decide which methods are right for your project.

Estimating impact of change on the project schedule

When a stakeholder submits a change request using the change control system that you defined and communicated, you will need to determine the impact of the potential change. The requested change may impact the project costs, schedule, and/or scope, but for the benefit of this section we are just focusing on the impact to the project schedule.

Instead of providing some fancy-schmancy formulas (although we do love formulas, especially the fancy-schmancy kind), we're just going to go over some practical advice based on our experience as project managers. When someone submits a change request, you would be wise to discuss each change with a change control board or some other body so that you can gain insight from others as to what impact this change could have. There may be others involved in the discussion with the CCB who can offer some wisdom as to other areas this change could affect. As you go through the proposed change requests, you may want to ask yourself (or the CCB) some of the following questions:

✔ **What happens to the project if we don't implement this change?** For example, if you don't implement the change, and something you need won't function, this change could have a higher priority than other changes.

✔ **What are the implications for the system testing if we do implement this change request?** In other words, when you implement a change to your software project, you not only have to test that particular code, but you need to test other areas of your application that may be affected. Also, you need to extend the schedule in order to accomplish all the testing.

✔ **If we implement this particular change, what other areas of the actual project will we be affecting?** Consider each of those areas to determine whether you need to change the project schedule.

✔ **Are there other changes in the project that I can implement in order to reduce the impact of this particular change?** For example, if you move forward with this change, you can prevent schedule delays by adding a programmer to a portion of the project.

✔ **Is there enough positive impact in implementing this change that can counteract the negative implications?** For example, maybe you add three weeks to your schedule, but the actual change will increase the value of the product.

Forecasting schedule variances

In Chapter 14 we discuss *Schedule Performance Index* (SPI), which is used to trend the performance of your project and allows you to forecast how efficient your project is operating. Determining your SPI permits you to forecast schedule variances. We don't want to ruin your fun in reading Chapter 14, so we won't go into painstaking detail on SPI and trend analysis, but we do want to whet your appetite.

Forecasting schedule variances enables you to look ahead to determine whether you're on schedule. Having this knowledge provides you with an opportunity to show your creative talents and start defining corrective action to bring the project schedule back in line with your plan.

In a previous portion of this chapter we showed you how to calculate your earned value, actual costs, and cost variance to determine whether your actual costs were in line with your plan. There are some similar formulas to use for forecasting schedule variances. Here they are:

✔ If you know your planned value (PV) and you know your earned value (EV), then you can calculate your schedule variance (SV).

✔ Your PV indicates, for a particular period, how much work was supposed to be completed.

✔ Your EV indicates the work that was really completed during a particular period.

✔ To determine your SV, you subtract your PV from your EV ($SV = EV - PV$). This difference is how much you vary in where you are in the schedule compared with where you expected to be for the same time period.

After you know your schedule variance, you can start taking the necessary steps to get the project schedule back to where it needs to be. Again, after you determine that you have a schedule variance, and you've gone through the correct processes to get the necessary approvals to implement the changes, you should follow your scrupulous and carefully defined communication plan that you documented during your planning phase.

Follow your communication plan to communicate with the appropriate stakeholders regarding the schedule variances and corrective action.

Knowing why you should expect changes

No matter how diligently you gathered stakeholder requirements and how detailed your project plan is, you will, at some point(s) in your software project, experience a need for project changes. Changes are to be expected; that's why you have risk management and communication plans and change control. In software projects, changes can mushroom into expensive, time-munching beasts, but with the proper planning, change control processes, and expectation setting, you can manage the changes.

Chapter 14

Using Earned Value Management in Software Projects

*Y*ou never want to lose track of the notion that you must measure your performance throughout the duration of your software project. Even if everything appears to be rosy, the project team is having fun, your stakeholders adore you, and your sponsor is turning cartwheels in the hall, you still need to measure performance so you can quantify whether or not your project is progressing as expected. When you measure a project's performance, you give yourself the opportunity to proactively eliminate molehills before they become mountains by figuring out where the moles are hiding.

Defining Earned Value Management

Earned value management (EVM) is a way of measuring your performance (and the performance of your project team) at any given date or point in the schedule. As your project progresses, you should take the opportunity to analyze costs, the schedule, and other issues (in this chapter we just focus on costs and schedule). You use the EVM measurements to compare your projected progress with your actual progress on a certain date.

You use EVM to answer the question, "What is the value of the work that you and your team have completed as of today or as of some other particular date?"

When you perform EV analysis on your project, you assign a number to the progress of your cost and your schedule. As you put value into your project, you should be getting value back from your project. Analyzing your earned value enables you to determine the difference (if any) between how much value you *planned* to add to your project and how much value you are *actually* adding to your project.

During the communication planning phase of your project, you should create plans that define how your performance measurements are reported and how often you need to create and distribute that information. For a project lasting several years, you may have designated in your communication plan that you will prepare quarterly performance measurement reports. For a project lasting less than a year, it makes more sense to distribute this information monthly.

Using EVM, you put these plans into action by reporting the status of your project as of a particular point in time. Always communicate your progress to appropriate stakeholders. You don't necessarily have to report findings to all stakeholders.

Understanding what earned value is (and isn't)

Earned value is a means of measuring your performance on a project by evaluating the status of your project costs and schedule. You can also perform EV analysis on other areas of your project, but in this chapter we focus on the two big ones.

When you use EV analysis, you compare where you are with where you planned to be, with an eye on taking corrective action, if necessary, to realign costs and schedule.

Discovering the other pieces of the EV formula

To complete this analysis, you need to calculate a few formulas. Don't be scared; these are very simple computations. If you can add and subtract, you can perform EV calculations. Here are the primary terms and formulas you need to understand:

- ✔ Planned value (PV)
- ✔ Actual cost (AC)
- ✔ Earned value (EV)

If you studied or read a version of the *Guide to the Project Management Body of Knowledge* (PMBOK) that was published prior to the year 2000, you may have seen different terms for these formulas. Since 2000, the PMBOK has updated its terminology, as you can see in Table 14-1.

Table 14-1	Earned Value Terms, Then and Now
This Is the Current Formula	*This Is the Old-School Formula*
Planned value (PV)	Budgeted Cost of Work Scheduled (BCWS)
Actual cost (AC)	Actual Cost of Work Performed (ACWP)
Earned value (EV)	Budgeted Cost of Work Performed (BCWP)

Calculating EV doesn't solve all your project's problems. This analysis won't solve all of your cost and scheduling issues and it won't take a disastrous project and turn it into a gold-standard project. It is simply a way of measuring your project's performance at a certain point in time; you can use the results of the earned value analysis to find the root cause of your cost or schedule variances so that you can decide if these need corrective action.

Determining a project's worth

Many project managers say that a project is worth nothing until it creates something; a software project takes on value when it adds value to your stakeholders. Well, that's only partially true. Your project is always worth something. From the first second you invest time and money in your project, it has value because of that investment. Even if your project fails, its worth can be determined by other factors:

- ✔ **How much the team and other future teams learn from the mistakes made or opportunities that arose:** (Information about lessons learned documentation is available in Chapter 17.)

- ✔ **How much you can use the code in future projects:** You may be able to take parts of the code that did not work in this project and pour them into another software project, thus saving time and resources on the new project.

- ✔ **How much you can make by selling the salvageable parts of your project:** You can take the parts of the code that didn't work, sell them to another organization, and then use that money to fund more viable software projects at your own firm.

But when discussing worth or value of a software project, in this instance we are talking about the value you get from a project compared to what you put into it. Your project should create value to your stakeholders, and throughout the project you should periodically evaluate the value of your project.

Discovering the Earned Value Management Formulas

In this section you discover the meaning of each of these EVM terms, as well as how to calculate the formulas. Please keep in mind that there are many other terms and formulas related to EVM; we just focus on the most basic ones. If you're looking form more information about EVM, check out *A Practical Guide to Earned Value Project Management* by Charles I. Budd and Charlene S. Budd (Management Concepts).

Memorizing formulas when you understand what they mean is better than memorizing them in a void. After you understand the main concepts, you will be better off.

For our example, say your imaginary company has been contracted to create a software program that can be used in vehicles to alert drivers to oncoming radar. In fact, the software can automatically bring the car down to the correct speed limit. The program can be positioned to preconfigured settings to recognize whether the driver should be driving the city speed limit or the highway speed limit.

You have budgeted $120,000 for the cost of the project and you are in the third month of the 12-month project.

You've done a great job on all your project planning, communication planning, scope management, and schedules, and you've won awards for your risk management plan; now, it's time to report the status of the costs and schedule for the project to your sponsor and stakeholders.

Just keep in mind that you are comparing planned results to actual results. During the project planning process, you determined what you expected the costs and schedule to be at particular points in time, and now you are figuring out whether your cost and schedule plans were accurate.

The following is an explanation of some of the basic earned value terminology:

> ✔ *Planned value (PV):* Planned value refers to how much you planned for particular activities to cost during a certain stretch of time. You created these estimates when you started your project planning. Planned value is the cost for activities that you expected you and your team would have completed as of a particular time period, and it answers the

question: "What did we say would be the value of the work that the team completed as of this particular date?"

✔ *Actual cost (AC):* Actual cost refers to how much the project work actually costs as of a certain date. It answers the question: "How much have we spent on this debacle — I mean project — anyway?" Actual cost includes the indirect costs of the project as well as the direct costs of the project if you considered these in your project planning process.

The direct costs include all monies spent directly for your software project. For example, wages for resources assigned to work only on your software project are direct costs. Indirect costs refer to monies spent on resources or other items that may be shared among several projects, such as overhead.

Subtract the AC from the PV (or the PV from the AC). The difference between these numbers tells you how much over or under budget you are.

✔ *Earned value (EV):* EV provides you with a measure of your project's progress as of a certain date. EV answers the question: "What is the value of this project work as of this particular date or particular point in the schedule?"

To determine your project's EV, combine all the costs budgeted for work that your team has accomplished at this point.

The formula for figuring the EV is total budget multiplied by the percentage of work complete. For example, if you have completed 50 percent of a $300 project, your EV is $150.

You can plot these values (PV, AC, EV) on a spreadsheet so that you can easily see (and show stakeholders) the variances. If all the lines on the graph line up on top of each other, you don't have a variance — the work is progressing exactly as you said it would, and you're up for the Supreme Project Manager of the Universe award, the envy of all the other project managers who now grovel at your feet and constantly seek your advice on estimating costs. Table 14-2 gives you a quick understanding of how these formulas work.

Table 14-2	Earned Value Formulas
Term	*Meaning*
Planned value (PV)	Planned percentage complete × the amount Budgeted at Completion (BAC)
Actual cost (AC)	Indirect costs + Direct costs + All other costs from your original project plan
Earned value (EV)	Actual percentage complete × the amount Budgeted at Completion (BAC)

✔ **Budgeted at Completion (BAC):** This refers to the amount that you planned for the cost of the project. In our example, we budgeted $120,000 for the cost of the entire software project. When you add all the planned values for all the project activities, you get a total BAC. In our example, your BAC is $120,000. BAC is the total cumulative PV at completion.

✔ **Estimate at Completion (EAC):** Looking at where you are at this point in time, how much work do you estimate it will take to complete the scheduled activities? The answer to that question is your EAC. To gather your EAC data, use what you know about where things stand right now to estimate what your costs will be when the project is completed. You evaluate your project's performance as of a particular point in time.

Playing with Values

When you understand how planned value, actual cost, and earned value relate to your project, you can start figuring out how to calculate these numbers so that you, your sponsor, and your stakeholders can have a meaningful snapshot of where your project stands with regard to costs and schedule.

Calculating your PV

How much did you plan to have completed at this point in time? Your percentages may vary, but for our example, we say that you planned on having 25 percent of the code completed by June 29. But you've actually completed just 20 percent.

If your BAC is $120,000 and you planned on having 25 percent of the project completed, here's what the math yields:

```
PV = Planned % complete × BAC

Planned % complete = 25%

Budget at Completion (BAC) = $120,000

PV = .25 × $120,000 = $30,000
```

You had planned on your project having a value of $30,000 at this point in time.

Calculating earned value

After you know the planned value, you can calculate the earned value (the value that you have earned on your project) of your software project relatively easily. First consider what earned value means — how much work your team completed at a particular point in time. Just take the actual percent of the project that your team has completed and multiply by how much you said you would spend for the entire project.

Multiply the actual percentage of the project complete by how much you planned on spending (BAC).

In our example we have completed 20 percent of the project, so here are the details:

```
EV = Actual % complete × BAC

Actual % complete = 20%

Budget at Completion (BAC) = $120,000

EV = .20 × $120,000 = $24,000
```

At this point in time, your project has an earned value of $24,000.

Because you planned on your project having a value of $30,000 at this point in time, but it only has a value of $24,000, you have a $6,000 *variance* (which we discuss later).

Calculating your AC

You add your direct costs to your indirect costs to determine your actual cost (AC). Say for the sake of argument that the AC is $25,000.

Now that you understand all of these terms and you know how to calculate the formulas, you also know whether or not your team is ahead of or behind the planned schedule. You now know whether your costs are more or less than you planned and you have been able to quantify your progress.

With this knowledge, you not only can plan for what changes you need to make for the rest of the project, but also report your progress to your sponsor and stakeholders in a language that they can all understand. Maybe. They should. Oh, they will.

Understanding this information also aids you in determining if you need to make changes to your cost and schedule estimates.

Creating a new EAC

When your project sponsor or stakeholders ask about your Estimate at Completion (EAC), they are asking you to forecast the total value of the project based on project performance thus far. EAC answers the question, "What do you expect the total value of the project will be when all the work activities of the project are completed?"

You use the EAC to forecast the total value considering how efficiently you are completing project activities. There are many formulas out there to aid you in determining your EAC, but for starters just consider one.

You must take into account two things when determining your EAC: your BAC and your CPI. We explain how to calculate your CPI later (see "Finding your cost and schedule performance indexes"), so just take our word for it now that your CPI is 0.96. The ideal CPI is 1.00 or more.

Your CPI tells you how much you are getting for every dollar you spend. In other words, you consider how much you expected to spend and how much you are getting for each dollar you expected to earn.

To calculate your EAC, you divide your BAC by your CPI.

```
EAC = BAC ÷ CPI
```

In your example, this would be EAC = $120,000 ÷ 0.96 = $125,000. Seems logical, doesn't it? You budgeted $120,000, but you know your project isn't going as efficiently as planned because your CPI is less than one. If it's not as efficient as you planned, then you know you're spending more money than you expected. If you continue going at this rate, then instead of spending $120,000 as you originally budgeted, you should expect to spend $125,000 at completion.

EAC answers the question, "How much do you expect the project to cost based on where you are in relation to the cost and the schedule?"

There are many variations of each of these formulas. If you plan on studying for the PMP certification, you should memorize the formulas in the *Guide to the Project Management Body of Knowledge (PMBOK)*. The primary point to keep in mind is that you want to figure out how much your cost and schedule vary from what you had originally planned.

Determining the estimate to complete the project

When you determine the *estimate to complete* (ETC) your project, you estimate how much more you should expect to spend for the rest of the project activities based on your performance thus far. You can do this mathematically without a lot of swanky formulas.

Say you already know that your actual costs are $25,000, and that you know that your EAC is $125,000. So you can expect that to complete the project activities you will have to spend $125,000 – $25,000, which is $100,000.

You expected to spend $125,000 and you've actually spent $25,000 thus far, so you have $100,000 more costs to completion if the variances you've had thus far can be considered typical and you expect future variances to also be typical. Knowing that you have $100,000 left in your budget to spend is not enough information to tell you whether you're over- or underbudget. But you need to know where your project stands at this moment if you want to determine whether you're within your budget. We explain what to do with these numbers in the following sections.

Uh-oh! What's your variance?

Of course, there's no point in calculating all these formulas unless you determine how much the values vary from your project estimates. You use *variance analysis* to start figuring out if your variance is significant, what the reason for the variance is, and what, if anything, you should do about it.

First you should determine your cost variance (CV). You perform a variance analysis to determine whether you're over- or underbudget and ahead of or behind schedule. This analysis provides you with the information you need to proactively make changes to get your project back on the right path.

Usually, variance analysis is performed on the cost and the schedule, but you could also perform a variance analysis on project scope, risks, quality, or other measurable areas of your project. In this chapter, we focus primarily on variance analysis for costs and schedule.

Table 14-3 summarizes the variance formulas we discuss in the next couple of sections.

Table 14-3	Variance Formulas
Concept	*Formula*
Cost Variance (CV)	CV = EV - AC
Schedule Variance (SV)	SV = EV - PV
Variance at Completion (VAC)	VAC = BAC - EAC

Calculating cost variance (CV)

How much did you plan to spend? How much did you actually spend? What's the difference? CV just tells you how much your actual costs were compared to how much you planned to spend.

How much did you spend compared to how much you planned to spend? You find the answer to this question by looking at the difference between your earned value (EV) and your actual costs (AC).

For example, if your EV is $24,000 and your AC is $25,000, here are the numbers:

```
CV = EV - AC

EV = $24,000

AC = $25,000

EV - AC = -$1,000
```

The difference between the EV and the AC is -$1,000. In this example, you spent more than you planned to spend, so you end up with a negative number.

A negative number indicates that you are not doing as well as you planned; your actual costs are higher than you estimated. A positive number tells you that you are doing better than planned; you are not spending as much as you planned to spend.

Because your cost variance is -$1,000, your actual costs are $1,000 more than you budgeted. You have a negative cost variance, which is no reason to go out and buy party hats and paint the town purple.

Calculating schedule variance (SV)

Where are you in your schedule? Where did you actually plan to be in your schedule? What's the difference? SV tells you how much your schedule differs from your plan. Even though we are talking about a schedule, the variance is displayed in dollars. After all, time is money. To determine the variance, take the difference between the earned value and the planned value.

For example, say your EV is $24,000 and your PV is $30,000.

```
SV = EV - PV

EV = $24,000

PV = $30,000

EV - PV = -$6,000
```

Because your SV is –$6,000, your team isn't doing as well as you had planned with regards to the schedule.

A positive number for your SV indicates that your team is ahead of schedule. You know that you're behind schedule when you have a negative number for your schedule variance.

Evaluating your Variance at Completion

We show you several variance formulas in the previous sections. A variance just tells you how much you vary from where you expected to be. One other item to evaluate is your Variance at Completion (VAC). VAC is the difference between what you budgeted to spend when you documented your original project plan and how much you *expect* to spend by the time you complete your project.

To determine the VAC, you need to consider how much you budgeted to spend and, considering where you are right now, how much you estimate you will spend by the time the fat lady sings. The difference between these two is the VAC.

Say your budget at completion is $120,000 and your EAC (considering where you are in the project right now) is $125,000. Here's what you do to determine the VAC:

```
VAC = BAC - EAC

BAC = $120,000

EAC = $125,000

VAC = $120,000 - $125,000 = -$5,000
```

You can probably guess that because you have a negative number for your VAC, the current numbers indicate that the project will cost more than you originally planned. A positive number for your VAC indicates that your project is going better than you expected. A value of 1 indicates that you're right on budget.

Finding your cost and schedule performance indexes

You can do several calculations to determine whether your software project is progressing as efficiently as you and your stakeholders expected. Use these performance indexes to trend your project's performance and predict how efficient your project will be for the duration. An *index* indicates how efficiently your project is progressing and may be used to predict your project's future performance. Table 14-4 summarizes the index formulas we describe in the following sections.

Table 14-4	Index Formulas
Index	*Formula*
Cost Performance Index (CPI)	$CPI = EV \div AC$
Schedule Performance Index (SPI)	$SPI - EV \div PV$

Calculating your Cost Performance Index (CPI)

Cost Performance Index (CPI) answers the question, "How much are you getting for each dollar you are spending on your project?" To determine CPI, divide the earned value by your actual cost: $CPI = EV \div AC$.

For example, if your earned value is $24,000 and your actual cost is $25,000, finding your CPI looks like this:

```
CPI = EV ÷ AC

EV = $24,000

AC = $25,000

EV ÷ AC = 0.96
```

Okay, now that you have your CPI, what does it mean? It means that you're getting $0.96 for each $1.00 that you expected to earn.

Whoop-dee-doo! What does this mean to a software project?

Calculating PV, AC, and EV, along with variances, enables you to determine whether your project is on the right path. These calculations help you to predict how your software project will progress based on where you are now. The variances compare where you are with where you expected to be.

Now that you know how to calculate all of these numbers, what does that mean? A CPI of 1 means that your project is costing you exactly what you planned for it to cost. So, logically, if the CPI is less than 1, you are spending more than you expected, and if your CPI is greater than 1, you are spending less than you expected. For example, if your CPI is 1.25, you're getting $1.25 for every dollar that you expected. If your CPI is .99, you're getting 99 cents for every dollar that you expected.

Similarly, if your SPI is 1, your schedule is 100 percent where it should be. So, if the SPI is greater than 1, that's good. If your SPI is less than 1, that's bad. For example, an SPI of 1.25 indicates that the project is performing at a rate of 125 percent, and if your SPI is .99, the project is performing at 99 percent of where you expected to be with regards to the schedule.

What does all this mean to your software project? These calculations are necessary to determine if you are over- or underbudget and if you are over or behind on your schedule. This gives you the information you need to determine if your variance is enough to make significant changes such as increasing the number of programmers or revising timelines.

If your CPI is 1, then your project is right where you expected it to be. If your CPI is greater than 1, your project is doing better than you expected; you're getting more than a dollar for every dollar that you expected to earn. If your CPI is less than 1, you are not getting as much as you expected on your project.

In our example, you are earning less than $1.00 for every dollar you expected to earn. Still, 96 cents isn't too far from the mark.

Calculating your Schedule Performance Index (SPI)

SPI answers the question, "Where are you in the schedule compared to where you expected to be at this point in time?" To calculate your SPI, you divide EV by the PV. Here's an example, with some made-up numbers:

```
SPI = EV ÷ PV

EV = $24,000

PV = $30,000

EV ÷ PV = 0.8
```

Because your SPI is 0.8, your schedule is progressing at 80 percent of the rate that you planned.

You guessed it! If your number is less than 1 for your CPI or your SPI, that's not a good sign. A number less than 1 indicates that your software project is either overbudget or behind schedule. If the value of your SPI is 1, that would mean that your schedule is going exactly as planned.

Chapter 15

Tracking Project Performance

*Y*our project is underway and things appear to be going well, or so you think. How do you know how things are really working? Is your project on time, within budget, meeting not just your, but also your stakeholders', expectations? Unless you have a system for measuring and quantifying the performance of your project and all its components, you really don't know whether you're moving things in the right direction.

To be sure that you can show that your project is progressing as planned, you must be able to not only measure the various items involved in getting the project to closure (see Chapter 14 for information on one kind of assessment, earned value management), but also to communicate to the appropriate stakeholders that things are going as anticipated. After all, if stakeholders aren't convinced, you may find yourself with a plan and no project to go with it. You might also find yourself at an employment agency trying to finagle a new software project management position.

So how do you prove that everything is as it should be with your project? Well, that's why you're reading this chapter, isn't it?

Planning Project Metrics

Setting up metrics is Step 3 of a fool-proof, four-step plan:

1. **Set your project goals.**

2. **Use your leadership capabilities, project management skills, influence, and problem-solving skills to meet those project goals.**

3. **Create project metrics to tell you whether you've reached those project goals.**

4. **Use your communication management plan to disseminate that information to your project stakeholders.**

But what are metrics? Here's a quick-and-dirty definition: Your project *metrics* are the processes, tools, and techniques that you use to measure the progress of your software project. The reason measuring your project progress is so important is because metrics enable you to proactively recognize whether

- ✔ You're on track with your software project

- ✔ You're ahead of or behind schedule

- ✔ You're under- or overbudget

- ✔ You're performing to the quality standards defined by your organization

- ✔ Your project team members are performing to their maximum ability

- ✔ The potential risks you've identified have materialized and could potentially adversely affect the project

- ✔ You need to intervene to bring the project back on track

As you plan your software project metrics, keep in mind that you should be proactive; find problems before they find you. That's the point.

Establishing project goals

Before you establish the project goals for your software project, you should become familiar with the goals of the organization. A good software project plan supports and aligns with the strategic goals of the organization.

After you define the project goals, all of the other project management processes should support those goals. For example, the quality management plan should support the quality goals of the software project and the product. Have you ever heard the expression, "If you don't know where you want to go, then how will you know when you arrive?" The same concept applies to setting project goals.

Planning for project metrics

Here are some of the project metrics you might use with your quality management plan to determine whether you're meeting the quality goals defined in your quality management plan for your software project:

- **Benchmarking:** This process compares your current project activities to those performed in other similar projects. For example, you might compare the development phase of your project with the development project, similar in size and scale to yours, that's already complete. The benchmark for completing the development phase may be three months less than what you scheduled. Similarly, you might use a benchmark for comparing the number of errors found during the system testing phase of a project similar in scope to yours. If the other project found fewer errors than yours, you may have a problem. You can display benchmark information in a manner that makes sense for your project. It could be as simple as a bar chart with one bar displaying a ten-week testing phase for your project and another bar showing a seven-week testing phase for a similar size project.

- **Pareto *(pa-ray-toh)* charts:** These are *histograms* (or bar graphs) that display project issues and rank order of the causes of those problems.

- **Control charts:** Charts that show processes that are not reliable or stable.

- **Project audits:** Audits that are used to determine whether particular project processes conform to defined parameters.

- **Procurement metrics:** Metrics that are used to evaluate contractors and vendors.

- **Earned value management:** A tool that allows you to ascertain whether you're on schedule, within budget, and on track with your software project (see Chapter 14).

Your organization may have other specific project metrics that you need to become familiar with. You have several options out there, and some may be better for a particular project than others. In general, we think it's helpful to be familiar with a broad range of project metrics so that you can determine what will work best in any given situation.

The project metrics that help you succeed in the software project you're currently managing may not be the same project metrics that will work in your next software project. Be flexible and open to using a variety of project metrics that suit the needs of each individual project.

Determining realistic project milestones

Consider the major events or accomplishments in your life; these are considered milestones. Some examples are

- ✔ Turning 21
- ✔ Landing that first project management job
- ✔ Getting hitched
- ✔ Buying a car
- ✔ Earning a promotion

You may have different milestones, but a project milestone list should consist of realistic, attainable milestones such as the following:

- ✔ Contract signed
- ✔ Project team in place
- ✔ Phase 1 development complete
- ✔ Unit testing complete
- ✔ Project acceptance sign-off
- ✔ Final payment received

You're better off setting realistic project milestones that you can successfully meet than you are setting unrealistic project milestones and missing every deadline, overrunning your budget, and fighting scope creep every step of the way.

Sometimes the organization or the client may impose unrealistic schedule milestones. Unrealistic deadlines are a great example of a *project constraint* — something that limits you or your project team. But when you have the power to do so, create realistic project milestones. Work with your project team, other project managers who have completed similar projects, and other stakeholders to help you in setting realistic milestones. Don't be hesitant to use the resources available to you to assist you in setting realistic milestones.

Implementing a Tracking Plan

Hey, are your metrics working? How do you know? By implementing a tracking plan, of course. A *tracking plan* puts all the metrics you've determined are important to work for you.

Using project baselines

As you start working your software project plan and progress through the scheduled activities, you will undoubtedly encounter differences between the plan and the work that's actually being completed. You can use your project baselines to compare where you are with where you should be. Your cost baseline includes your project costs for all of the software project activities. Your schedule baseline is a particular version of the approved (by the project management team) project schedule with the project start and end dates. Your quality baseline details the quality objectives of your software project. You use your quality baseline to measure your project performance with regards to quality. You use all of your project baselines as metrics to determine whether your project is on track.

The project baseline describes what you should be delivering, so it makes the most sense that you use the WBS and the project scope statement as your project baseline. Why reinvent the wheel? If you change the scope, you change your project baseline. Here are just a few of the changes that could potentially occur and affect your baselines:

- Programmers resign in the middle of the project, creating changes in resource allocation.

- Vendors don't meet their deadlines, causing you to push back some of your own deadlines.

- Contractors create unexpected costs that must somehow miraculously be covered by your project budget.

- Risks that were unknown prior to creating your project plan suddenly materialize.

- Technology becomes obsolete, necessitating a change in methodology.

During the planning process, when you set up your *change control plan* (which we explain in Chapter 13), you identify changes (by type and by severity) that require change request submissions and must be evaluated by the change control board. If you encounter any of these or other unexpected changes during your software project, you will need to make changes to your project plan and you may need to establish a new software project baseline.

Do you recall, starting in Chapter 1 and continuing in almost every other chapter, where we discussed the project scope statement and the work breakdown structure (WBS)? Well, the project scope statement and the WBS are what should be considered as the project scope baseline for your software project; the project scope baseline details the work that you are to complete.

If someone requests an activity or deliverable that is not contained within your WBS or project baseline, you should also expect to see a *project change request;* no doubt, you will need to modify your baseline if the project change request is approved.

Only implement changes that have been approved by your change control board or follow the specific change processes defined by your firm; otherwise, you will jeopardize the integrity of your project baseline schedule.

When you receive the change request and it is approved by the change control board, you will change your software project scope statement and now have a new project scope baseline. Easy as pie, right? Well, at least easy as a cupcake.

Stressing accuracy in reporting

A solid communication plan spells out how specific types of information should be spread to particular stakeholders. Your project sponsor and other executives may require a high-level report or summary of the software project status, whereas another project stakeholder — the software training manager, for example — may only need info about, and screen prints of, items to be included in end-user training. Sometimes, knowing what to communicate (and to whom) is pretty obvious. You would not go into an executive steering committee meeting carrying a handful of screen prints of each item to be included in end-user training. That would be too much detail for an executive steering committee meeting. (In general, when talking to executives, be brief and limit the discussion to a view from 30,000 feet unless you are asked to provide specifics.)

In Chapter 4, we discuss performance reporting as a part of your comprehensive communication management plan. *Performance reporting* is just a term used to indicate what you do when you provide appropriate stakeholders with the information they need regarding the status of your software project.

Look at Table 15-1 for examples of types of performance reports typically distributed to selective stakeholders.

Table 15-1	Performance Reporting
Stakeholder	*Communication*
Executives	Presentation at steering committee meetings; status summary reports; milestone reports; risk summaries
Client	Cost reports; budget variance reports; schedule reports; resource reports; budget reports

Stakeholder	Communication
Project Team	Status reports; schedule change reports; issue review meetings; project team meetings
Functional Managers	Project team performance; milestone reports

In all of the examples in Table 15-1, you should consistently strive for accuracy. If you must give a presentation to your company's executives, it's understandable that you may be nervous and even a little scared to provide them with any negative news on your software project. Maybe you think it's better not to tell them that you've missed a major milestone because they might start to question your project management skills.

Don't be tempted to misrepresent the facts; it will catch up with you in due course. Seriously, do you think you could miss a major milestone and no one would notice?

It's imperative that you are completely accurate in all of your performance reporting for the following and a host of other reasons:

- ✔ Your client, executives, team, and other stakeholders will appreciate your integrity and come to count on you as someone who tells it like it is.

- ✔ The truth will always catch up with you sooner or later. Wouldn't you prefer to be the one to give the facts instead of telling a tale and being exposed later? Who would trust you then?

- ✔ Your truthfulness demonstrates your leadership ability. If your team members know that you lie, then why should they be honest about their own progress (or lack thereof) when they provide status reports? Your team will follow your example of integrity.

- ✔ The performance reporting you complete will be used to make other project decisions regarding budget, cost, scope, schedule, resources, and so on. It's crucial to the integrity of the project that your performance reporting be completely accurate at all times so that you and others don't make bad decisions based on inaccurate data.

- ✔ Being inaccurate in some of your performance reporting may result in schedule slippage, cost overruns, scope creep, and the immediate need to update your resume.

Your mother was right; always tell the truth, even when it hurts. And even if she didn't tell you to be accurate in your performance reporting, do it anyway.

Take the time to gather all of the pertinent facts for your specific performance reporting requirements before providing project reports, summaries, or presentations. The information that you omit because you ran out of time could be the information that your client deemed crucial to hear.

Using a Project Management Information System

A Project Management Information System (PMIS) is an automated program that can assist you in some of your software project management activities. PMIS software can definitely make things easier for you, but it will not do your job for you and it will not correct you if you make a mistake.

You can use PMIS software to do the following:

- Create performance reports, resource reports, tracking reports, status reports, and progress reports

- Schedule resources and view resource constraints

- Create a project baseline

- Track project progress

- Track and report on project issues and risks

- Organize and schedule tasks

- List task predecessors and successors

- Publish and share project information with your project team and other stakeholders

- View project calendars, charts, and network diagrams

- Perform other project tasks or calculations, depending on the specific PMIS that you use

PMIS software, such as Microsoft Project, usually includes many useful tools and techniques that you and your software project team can use to gather, track, share, and communicate project information. You can discover more information about Microsoft Project by perusing *Microsoft Project 2003 For Dummies* by Nancy Stevenson (Wiley) and by visiting www.microsoft.com.

You should be able to find several good PMISs on the Web that will meet your needs and are free, or you can complete some research and, depending on the needs of your software project, purchase a solid and reliable PMIS. Just don't expect even a top-of-the-line PMIS to do your job for you or make you appear more competent than you really are.

Tracking Project Performance

You should be proactive in tracking project performance to find problems before the problems find you. At any given time you should be able to provide information on project performance regarding schedule, costs, scope, and quality. You should at least be tracking your project performance thoroughly enough to know whether your software project is

- ✔ Ahead of or behind schedule
- ✔ Over- or underbudget
- ✔ Within the confines of your scope baseline
- ✔ Meeting the requirements of your quality management plan

Read on to discover some ways that you can track your project performance so that when your client stands beside you on the elevator for two minutes, asking how the software project is going, you can provide a quick summary.

Using earned value management

In Chapter 14 we discuss how you must track and quantitatively measure project performance throughout the life of your software project. You can't just count on your gut feeling or intuition that all is right with the project.

Earned value management (EVM) is a means of quantifying your project performance. That means you put a value, like 20 percent, on your progress. That 20 percent can represent the amount of work completed. If you planned to have 40 percent complete, that's not great progress.

Earned value management is a handy way of measuring your project performance so that you can determine whether you're where you said you would be at a particular point in time. You can use EVM to track and monitor project performance and then use your communication management plan to distribute this information to your stakeholders. See how all these pieces are coming together now? Check out Chapter 14 for more information.

Creating Pareto charts

A *Pareto chart* is a quality control tool that you can use to track items or processes that don't conform as they should. This chart helps you see where your problems are and where you should be focusing the work efforts of your project team. The logic behind this tool is that, usually, a small number of causes (20 percent) create a large number (80 percent) of the issues in a project. Ever hear of the 80/20 rule?

Here's a fun little history lesson for you. Vilfredo Pareto was an Italian economist who, in the early 1900s, wrote a mathematical formula to explain that 80 percent of the wealth in his country was owned by 20 percent of the population. Other economists, scientists, engineers, and professors have applied this same principle to many other areas, including project management.

Say you have 100 project issues in your issues database. Pareto's rule says that 80 of them are the result of 20 of the causes. The Pareto chart enables you to easily see what types of issues are causing most of the problems on your project. Some typical causes of problems in a software project include

- ✔ Inadequate software testing
- ✔ Vendor noncompliance
- ✔ Improper end-user training
- ✔ Lack of defined scope
- ✔ User error
- ✔ Technical issues
- ✔ Technology becoming obsolete

Keep in mind that every project is different and the problem causes we list here may not be typical of every project. These are just examples for instructional purposes. Also keep in mind that even though we use the Pareto chart for looking at the causes in system testing, training, and implementation, you can use Pareto charts as a metric in other areas of your software project.

Table 15-2 shows a list of issues, causes, and ranks for a software implementation in which physicians and nurses enter their patients' medication and laboratory orders into a medical software system. These problems and causes are related to the testing phase of the project, but you can use the Pareto chart to review the causes of problems in other areas of your project.

Table 15-2	Data Collection for Creating Pareto Chart	
Issue	*Cause and Explanation*	*Rank*
Nurse could not find chest x-ray order.	Training: End user was not looking in the proper place for this order.	2
Lab test report did not print.	Technical issue: Printers not set up correctly.	1
Nurse Manager requests a patient summary report to be written.	Training: This report is already in production. Nurse Manager needs training on how to find the report in the system.	2
Physician reports that her computer screen is freezing up while placing orders.	Technical issue: Programmer needs to make configuration change.	1

Issue	Cause and Explanation	Rank
Nurse states that patient report is not printing.	Technical issue: Report is printing but the printer is configured to print at the incorrect nursing unit.	1
Unit Secretary cannot locate a patient in the system.	Security: Unit Secretary doesn't have the appropriate security clearance to see this patient's information. Programmer will make change in security setting.	3

We've ranked the causes in Table 15-2 from 1 to 3 to show that the number 1 cause of the issues listed in the table is technical issues. Based on this data, you now know that you should focus more of your efforts on fixing these technical problems so as to eliminate the majority of the issues.

To set up your own Pareto chart, you should create a table similar to the one in Table 15-2. The table doesn't have to be too elaborate, but it does need to show the issues, causes, and rankings of each cause for each listed problem. When your table is complete, you can put all of the data into a Pareto chart to visually illustrate the issues that are causing most of the problems.

The visual nature of a Pareto chart is one of its most useful features. You can show your project team and other stakeholders why the team needs to focus its efforts in particular areas. See Figure 15-1 for an example of a Pareto chart derived from the data gathered in the above table.

Having fun by snooping through the issues database

Have you ever just randomly reviewed a software project issues database or issues spreadsheet just to look at the trends in the issues and the causes? Some Saturday night when you're really bored and you could be going out to some goofy party with friends, stay at work and review as many of your project issues as you can in, say, 30 minutes. Make a chart listing each issue and its cause. We bet that you will have lots of issues listed but the cause of each project issue won't be unique. You will probably be able to categorize each cause into just a few main categories.

Then you can display these categories into a lovely Pareto chart where the problems are listed in order by rank. The most frequent issue is ranked first; the second most frequent is ranked second, and so on.

You can group specific categories based on common causes: training, technical issues, and security, for example.

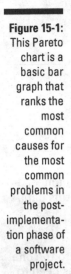

Figure 15-1:
This Pareto chart is a basic bar graph that ranks the most common causes for the most common problems in the post-implementation phase of a software project.

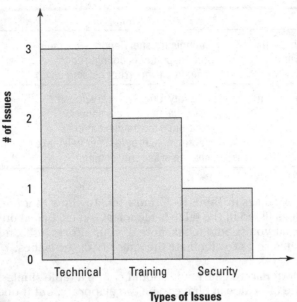

Pareto charts can also help as you continue to strive to understand how you can accomplish each of your future projects more efficiently and document your lessons learned.

Creating control charts

Like Pareto charts, *control charts* perform quality control functions on your software projects. A control chart can assist you in determining whether particular processes fall above or below a specified *control area*. If a process falls outside of the control area or beyond acceptable limits, it probably is not a reliable or consistent process and may require some tweaking (that's a technical term).

The control chart contains three horizontal lines:

- ✔ One line represents the acceptable upper limit.

- ✔ One line represents the acceptable lower limit.

- ✔ One line, in the middle, represents the mean.

The data points that you plot outside of the upper and lower limits represent issues that may be the result of special causes. After you identify a special cause, you can attempt to eliminate it so that it doesn't result in future errors.

By defining your acceptable upper and lower limits (your organization may determine these), you plot your data points on the control chart to reveal which data points fall above or below the acceptable limits representing potentially inefficient processes. These processes that display beyond the acceptable limits need to be fine-tuned.

Control charts help you determine variation of processes and diagnose problem areas in projects. The benefits of control charts are (nearly) endless:

- To show whether schedule variances are within acceptable limits.
- To identify the volume of scope changes.
- To evaluate the number of days of variance in your schedule (are you 22 days behind where you said you'd be?).
- To give a visual representation of dollars spent outside of budget.
- To show which problem items were found during individual phases of system testing.
- After the product is complete, you can use a control chart to show whether the number of configuration issues discovered during unit testing is outside of acceptable limits.

  You use your organization's or the client's quality standards (or a combination of both) for determining the upper and lower limits. Ask your project sponsor for the organization's quality standards.

Look at Figure 15-2 for an example of a control chart.

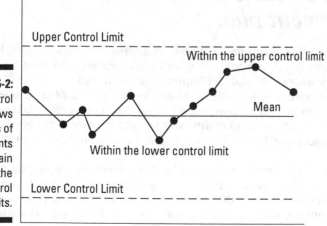

Figure 15-2:
This control chart shows a series of data points that remain within the control limits.

Upper Control Limit

Within the upper control limit

Mean

Within the lower control limit

Lower Control Limit

Because the purpose of this book is not to make you a quality management guru or a professor of quality management techniques, but to give you the basic software project management information that can help you become a tremendous software project manager, we don't go into microscopic detail regarding control charts. In fact, loads of publications have been written regarding both of these quality control techniques as well as other quality management tools and techniques. You may benefit from reading more about Walter Shewhart, who is widely credited with being the first to use control charts.

As with all other project management processes, tools, and techniques, you should use control charts, Pareto charts, and other quality management tools as part of your lessons learned documentation. These charts (and the associated documentation) improve your chances of making each project more effective and efficient than the last. You will amaze yourself and your friends with your superb competence.

Communicating Project Performance

Okay, so you've used lots of fancy-schmancy data analysis and quality control tools and techniques to show you if you are on track, behind schedule, overbudget, underbudget, or within the defined limits of your project scope. Now, what are you going to do with all of that information? Well, chances are you are going to rely on your thorough and brilliant communication management plan so that you can provide the appropriate stakeholders with the information they need.

Relying on the communication management plan

When you created your communication management plan, you defined how you would communicate, with whom you would communicate, and what information each stakeholder required. In Chapter 4 we discuss that there would probably be more communication at the beginning and at the end of the project, but not as much during the execution phase of the project. This idea makes sense when you consider the amount of time you spend gathering requirements at the start of the project; you have a lot more communication needs at that time.

As the project winds down, you have a lot of performance reporting requirements; you must show project status, resource plans, contract closure, and more. And, of course, during the execution phase of the project, especially during milestones, your project will require you to do more communicating than at other points.

Automating project communications

If you could automate all of your project communications, life would be swell. But no amount of automation is likely to ever take the place of the water cooler or the coffee machine. Those informal methods of communication, where a few (or more) people gather to discuss the status of the project, are crucial to a project's success. The only potential for problems occurs when people start rumors, or when more talking happens in the break room than in the project status meetings. (As far as we know, no one has invented the technology to completely eradicate rumors.)

Even though you may not be able to — or even desire to — eliminate all informal and formal communications, you can automate some of your software project communication. Here are just a few reasons why you should:

✔ To save time

✔ To enable stakeholders to receive particular communications at regularly scheduled intervals that they can anticipate

✔ To provide standardization in automated project communications (if you provide templates, some forms of communications will follow a standard format that excludes unnecessary information)

✔ To reduce the amount of noise in communications (if you can provide online reports instead of presentations in meetings, you avoid long meetings filled with side conversations and other interruptions)

The most important point to remember about project communication, whether it's automated or manual, is to clearly and concisely provide the information to the *appropriate* stakeholders. (See "Stressing accuracy in reporting," earlier in this chapter, for more information.)

Some examples of automated project communications are

✔ Project status reports, sent via e-mail, that are always due by 1:00 p.m. on Wednesdays, to a specified number of stakeholders.

✔ Project event alerts for certain predefined project events, such as team meetings or critical issues update meetings.

✔ Automatic pages to remind stakeholders of project activities. For example, a team member may receive an automatic page if he is past his due date on his input to an issue resolution.

✔ Automatic e-mail alerts when a project schedule (or other predefined project management tool) has been updated. Only the stakeholders affected by the change would receive the e-mail. For example, a stakeholder would

> receive an e-mail alert if a change control request has been approved for his area.
>
> ✔ Project information that is automatically sent from PMIS software to a lessons learned document.

With a little imagination and the help of solid PMIS software, you can come up with other ways to automate some of your project communications.

Hosting status meetings

There are some tricks of the trade that you can employ to hold an effective and dynamic status meeting; good status meetings are crucial to project success because you will have important information to communicate during these meetings and you need to hold everyone's attention.

One of the most important points to remember regarding hosting a project status meeting (or any meeting) is to sufficiently prepare for the meeting. You would never invite guests for dinner, and then, when they saunter in the front door, shamefully utter, 'Uh, hi, guys . . . maybe I should decide what I'm fixing you for dinner now, right?" Your invited guests would rightfully expect to walk in the front door and be pleasantly confronted with the aroma of your fine, tasty cuisine. Well, the same principle applies to hosting stakeholders at a project status meeting except that they should not expect any aromas. The food would just be a bonus.

In order to adequately prepare, prior to the status meeting, understand why you are holding the project meeting and what you do and don't want to take the time to discuss. This is important because people may start to discuss topics that are not within the scope of your project meeting. If you let them talk, your 30-minute meeting may become a two hour free-for-all.

Getting an agenda together

Prepare and distribute a meeting agenda prior to the meeting. We usually distribute meeting agendas at least 24 hours prior to the status meeting so as to provide all stakeholders sufficient time to review the agenda before arriving at the meeting. People should walk into the meeting knowing what is going to be discussed.

To help maintain everyone's focus, there are certain items that you should include on every meeting agenda. You can get a sample agenda by skipping ahead to Chapter 19.

For obvious reasons, be sure to always include the meeting purpose and objective when you write up your agenda. Attendees need to know why they are coming to that project meeting so as to make better use of everyone's time. This will also provide attendees with the opportunity to send someone else from their team in their place.

You should also include a list of attendees so that everyone invited may gauge the necessity of his or her presence at the meeting. For example, if you're a functional manager, you may be interested in knowing why you were invited to a project meeting where the list of attendees included technical people only. People do make mistakes, right? There's always the possibility that you were invited in error. This would give someone the opportunity to call and find out if they were invited accidentally.

It's obvious why you would want to include the start time of a project meeting, but you should also include the end time of the meeting on the agenda so that people know when to leave!

Document the names of the facilitator and minute taker for every project meeting so that all attendees know that someone is in charge of the meeting and so they understand that minutes will be recorded. And then make sure that person does take minutes — when meeting attendees understand that what they are saying is being documented, they stay more focused on the topic at hand. Don't forget to distribute the meeting minutes as soon as possible after the meeting.

If someone does inform you that there is a mistake in the minutes, be sure to distribute a corrected version of the meeting minutes to the entire group of invitees (even those who did not attend). This is also documentation that will become a part of the project records, so it's important that everything is accurate.

Parking off-topic discussions

If something comes up during the meeting but it isn't part of the agenda, you should park that idea to be addressed at a later time. A *parking lot* is merely a list of topics that need further discussion or review but are currently being parked.

It helps to efficiently move the meeting along if the attendees know that the purpose of the meeting is to discuss a defined list of topics; if a topic is not on the agenda, it should be parked to either be discussed later or added to the next meeting's agenda.

Sharing good and bad news

As the software project manager, you can expect to have the fabulous job of communicating both bad and good news at various times throughout your project.

In Chapter 4 we explained the different styles of communication — formal and informal, automated and manual, written and spoken — and they are all appropriate at different times and with particular stakeholders. For example, you would not expect (usually) to provide informal communication during an executive steering committee meeting. We're sure that could happen at times, but usually that would be a more formal communication.

However, when speaking with your team about a small issue, you may send an e-mail or individually drop by everyone's cube for a chat.

Communicating bad news

But there is one absolute regarding sharing bad news with your project team or other stakeholders: Never ever share bad news in an e-mail. If you have some negative news to relate to your team or to other stakeholders, do this in person if possible. Of course, if your project team contains members from all over the world, that may be impossible. But if at all possible, give bad news in person, or at least on the phone.

If, for example, your deadline just got pushed forward two months and your project team now must work 16-hour days instead of its usual 12-hour days, spreading the word in an e-mail may lead to a mutiny — and that's a whole other book.

If someone is absent when you deliver bad news, be sure that you follow up with that individual as soon as possible. The last thing Susie needs is to hear from the janitor that all her work needs to be redone in half the time because of a slight error on her part.

Communicating via e-mail

People can't see your body language or that smile (or smirk) on your face when you communicate via e-mail. When someone reads an e-mail from you, he or she can only guess what you really meant if you are not perfectly clear. Don't try to flower up your writing or try to make it cute. Just say what you have to say in a professional manner and be concise, as well as unambiguous.

If you try to make a joke in an e-mail and the receiver doesn't understand what you're trying to say, or doesn't get your sick sense of humor, the results are invariably the same: misunderstandings, resentment, and hurt feelings. Don't try to be funny; it's safer to just consistently maintain a sense of professionalism in your communications — after all, you get paid to be a software project manager, not a comic.

Communicating good news

When you communicate good news, it doesn't matter as much which platform you use. You should still be clear, concise, and unambiguous, but positive messages are almost always well received no matter what form of communication you choose.

The one area where you may have a problem with good news is leaving someone out of the loop or forgetting to give credit to someone who deserves it. Be generous with your praise, and be sure to follow up with individuals who, for whatever reason, missed your announcement.

Part V
Closing Your
Software Project

The 5th Wave — By Rich Tennant

"You ever get the feeling this project could just up and die at any moment?"

In this part . . .

Part V supplies you with the knowledge you need to bring your software project to a successful and systematic end. Look here to sharpen your project documentation skills, write excellent historical documents, and figure out your lessons learned. You also find information that can help you tie up loose ends regarding vendor contracts. Also find tips on making product documentation and help files all the easier for end users to understand and navigate.

Chapter 16

Finalizing the Project Management Processes

The goal of any software project is successfully building the software you've been commissioned to create. Therefore, everything you do, even at the beginning, builds toward the goal of closing the project. Setting expectations with vendors, preparing your scope management plan, and starting your lessons learned documentation — all activities you start early in the project — are things you must do to close the project. In this chapter, we discuss all the important chores and functions of closing down a successful software project. The only topic that we don't cover here is the lessons learned documentation. Never fear: Lessons learned are covered in Chapter 17.

Closing the Software Project

The end of the software project is an exciting time for the software project manager. Along with planning a festive celebration with your team, you're busy performing the actions that go with the closing process group of project management. These activities include ensuring that the appropriate stakeholders are satisfied with the final product, closing out vendor contracts, completing and distributing your lessons learned documents (see Chapter 17), performing audits, and releasing your software project team. Primarily, you need to tie up all loose ends and bring all activities to a clear, crisp end.

Before you consider your software project closed, you may also want to make sure that all project issues are resolved or turned over to the support team. If you created a database to track issues that affect the project, you can run reports to demonstrate to the appropriate stakeholders that all issues are closed. There's also a possibility that during the planning phase of your software project you set the expectation that at project closure, the only open issues would be those with a low priority.

Just make certain that you are meeting the requirements that were set at the beginning of the software project. You should create a checklist for project closure to ensure that nothing is forgotten and to make sure that all closing activities are handled in a timely and effective manner. The following is a list of items that you need to consider in your project closure checklist:

- ✔ Met with help desk to review system
- ✔ Met with appropriate operational staff to turn over software
- ✔ Reviewed system training requirements with operational staff
- ✔ Received sign-off from operational staff
- ✔ Completed and distributed performance reports
- ✔ Completed and distributed system documentation
- ✔ Completed quality audits
- ✔ Completed vendor audits
- ✔ Completed performance review or offered performance input for project members
- ✔ Distributed to team members questionnaire on project management performance
- ✔ Received sign-off on scope verification and formal acceptance of all project deliverables
- ✔ Closed vendor contracts

Create a checklist with all appropriate action items included so that you can go through this project closure checklist with your project team. Your list is likely to have quite a few more items on it — this one's for example only.

You don't want to take a chance on leaving any loose ends to be resolved by someone else after you move on to your next project.

Completing quality control

Because you've been performing quality control on your software project throughout the course of the project — checking that your project results consistently conform to your project standards, and making modifications as required — the idea of project quality control should not be completely new to you.

At the beginning, during the quality planning portion of the software project, you identify the quality standards you expect to meet, and decide how you will meet these standards. Later, you use these standards to conduct quality assurance testing. Quality assurance follows the methods that you decide upon to make sure that the project used necessary processes to meet the quality requirements that you defined.

Quality assurance and quality control aren't the same thing. Quality assurance is testing that occurs during the main part of the project. Quality control monitors and tracks the project results to make sure that the product meets quality standards, making final rectifications when necessary.

If part of the project or the product does not meet the quality standards, you make the improvements that are necessary to meet the quality standards set forth.

As a part of your quality control process, you might create a *quality checklist* to ensure that you and your team members have performed all of the required steps required to adhere to your set quality standards. Quality checklists are great tools for your testing staff so that they can document that they're following the correct processes. See Table 16-1 for an example of typical fields you may use for your quality checklist.

Knowing your scope verification from your quality control

The difference between scope verification and quality control is that quality control has to do with making sure that your product is up to the quality standards that your client has set forth for this project. Scope verification, on the other hand, has more to do with the stakeholders formally accepting the deliverables of the project. When the stakeholders formally accept the completed project scope and all of the resulting deliverables, they are verifying the project scope.

You can create one quality checklist for the project to ensure your project team is adhering to project quality requirements, and create a quality checklist for the product to make sure that the software is made in accordance with industry standards for quality.

Table 16-1	Project Quality Checklist	
Project Quality Activity	*Responsible Person*	*Complete*
The project work plan has all predecessor and successor tasks identified	Project Manager	Yes
The project work plan includes the appropriate change control activities	Project Manager	Yes
All firm-wide standards and regulations have been distributed to appropriate team members	Communications Manager	In Process
System documentation is complete and accurate	Documentation	Due 05/02
Turnover meetings with help desk manager have been scheduled	Project Manager	Due 05/07
Turnover meetings with operational staff have been scheduled	Project Manager	Yes

You can perform quality control testing before scope verification (see the following section "Completing scope verification") or you can perform quality control at the same time as scope verification.

Completing scope verification

During the planning phase of every project management process, project managers the world over create a scope management plan; this plan details how you define your software project scope and declares how the project scope should be controlled to prevent scope creep. In your scope management plan, you must also record how you will verify your scope. Indeed, in the quality planning stage, you describe how the software would be formally accepted by the appropriate stakeholders. Your firm may already have a set process on how the scope will be verified. If not, some options for methods of acceptance of the product/project (scope verification) are

✔ **A sign-off sheet for formal acceptance of all project deliverables.** This would be signed by you along with all appropriate stakeholders. See Table 16-2 for an example of some of the items to capture on this formal deliverables acceptance spreadsheet.

✔ **A letter or e-mail from the client.** A less formal solution, the letter should state that the client accepts the software product or system in its current state and that the client is satisfied with the results.

✔ **A formal project closure meeting.** During the meeting, you do a short presentation on the final product and the clients agree that you and your team have successfully created what they asked you to create.

Table 16-2	Scope Verification Sign-Off Sheet Example		
Deliverable	*Client Sign-Off*	*Responsible Team Member*	*Sign-Off Date*
System Documentation	Client Stakeholder	Project Manager	05/01
Training Manual	Systems Training Manager	Training Coordinator	05/01
Support Material	Help Desk Manager	Cut Over Manager	05/05
Testing Results	Testing Manager	Project Manager	04/17

No matter which method of scope verification you choose, you should always get something formal in writing from the clients stating that they are satisfied with the final deliverables of the software project. Even if the client is your best friend (or perhaps especially if the client is your best friend), the necessary formality of having something in writing is vital to the process, and will benefit you if the client later requests a change to the software. You can also use the documentation as part of your portfolio later, or frame it and create an appealing geometric tile pattern on the wall of your cube.

Closing Out Vendor Contracts

The closing process group includes all activities associated with bringing your software project to a close; this process includes finalizing all proceedings with your vendors.

In some instances the software project manager is the vendor; in other instances, the software project manager performs closing activities with other vendors. There's also a possibility that you could simultaneously wear both hats; depending on the hats, that may, at times, look silly. This process of closing vendor contracts indicates that the client is satisfied with the project deliverables (or that you are satisfied with the deliverables provided by one of your vendors).

The following sections go over some of the activities related to closing out the vendor contracts.

Auditing vendors' work and deliverables

Would you ever consider walking into the showroom at your neighborhood car dealership and buying a car without at least looking at it? Most of us probably wouldn't even consider turning over any cash without taking the car for a test drive, kicking a tire or two, and pretending to catch a glimpse at what's under the hood.

The same concept applies in the case of paying vendors for their work and deliverables; you should perform an audit to verify that the work meets all the documented requirements of the software project.

Of course, you wouldn't want to wait until the final phases of your project to ensure the vendor understands the project requirements and is conforming to them. Throughout the project you should conduct meetings with your vendors to ensure the work is progressing appropriately. You should also create and distribute documentation, such as performance reports, after these meetings.

Before a vendor can send you a payment request, you must ensure that the vendor has completed all of the stated requirements on the testing. Check out Chapter 12, in which we provide a detailed example in which the software project manager contracts with a vendor to perform each phase of the system testing on a software project. For such a vendor relationship, where the responsibilities include creating quality testing software, the audits would include making sure that a vendor

- ✓ Performs all appropriate testing phases
- ✓ Documents all issues discovered during testing
- ✓ Assigns each issue a priority — low, medium, high, critical
- ✓ Completes and distributes all required performance reports to the appropriate stakeholders
- ✓ Creates and distributes the appropriate reports from the testing issues database

This list of audits will vary depending on what kind of vendor you're working with and the specific tasks the vendor has been given.

You may also conduct periodic inspections and audits of a vendor's work so that you know whether there is a problem long before the project is completed. These inspections and audits could be either scheduled or random — or both. You will also be viewing performance reports outlined in your communication plan.

No matter how you perform audits throughout the process, you must still perform a final audit at project closure before you formally accept the vendor's final deliverables. If you're the vendor, expect the client to perform an audit on your work.

The vendor audit could be something as simple as a checklist or as elaborate as a formal meeting with a presentation of all appropriate deliverables. See Table 16-3 for an example of data that you should capture in a vendor audit. This checklist is for a vendor company that's been hired to perform all phases of the testing for the software you've been hired to create.

Table 16-3	Vendor Audit of Software Testing for Vendor Testy McTesty	
Deliverable	*Date Completed*	*Notes*
Unit Testing	02/01	Two outstanding low-priority issues to be resolved by Technical Team by May 2.
Functional Testing	03/02	No outstanding unresolved issues.
Integrated Testing	04/02	One outstanding medium-priority issue to be resolved by Interface Team by May 15.
Volume Testing	04/04	Conforms to stakeholder requirements.
Testing Summary and Documentation	05/20	All documentation completed in appropriate format.
Testing Sign-off Sheets	05/22	All sign-off sheets completed by appropriate stakeholders

In this example, the vendor has several unresolved issues discovered during the software testing. Unresolved issues may be acceptable to you if you hired the vendor to expose issues so that your team could resolve them. If you hired the vendor to expose and then resolve issues, you may not want to sign off on the project. Your expectations would certainly have been outlined and agreed upon at the beginning of the project when you signed your contract.

Paying the bills

If you work for a large firm, they probably already have processes in place for paying vendors. This process usually occurs in the accounts payable department. It is your responsibility to make sure you understand the processes so you will know whether you have accountabilities in this area.

Regardless of whether you work for a large firm, a small company, or work as an independent contractor who outsources some work to other independent contractors, you have a payment system in place.

Before you pay your vendors, be sure the appropriate audits, inspections, and performance reports have been successfully completed and distributed to the appropriate stakeholders. As with all other aspects of project management, be proactive. Set the expectations at the beginning of the project and follow your well-documented communication plan to ensure all appropriate stakeholders have been communicated with regarding all deliverables that must be successfully completed before payments can be made.

Completing the Project (Or at Least Transferring It to Someone Else)

So far you've been mired in the sometimes overwhelming details of creating and modifying project plans, completing tasks, setting milestones, facilitating stakeholder meetings, and meeting your tight deadlines. You and your software project team have gotten used to the daily grind of writing code, testing that code, rewriting the code, retesting, and so on, with the ultimate goal of completing the system on schedule. Of course, you have worked hard to consistently exceed stakeholder expectations, and now you can see that you've reached your goal: This project is almost over. It's finally time to turn the software over to the operational team. You always knew this time would come; you obviously didn't expect to be stuck in project mode forever did you? We hope not.

As with everything else with project management, you should be proactive in your approach to turning over your project.

The activities leading up to your system activation (or *go-live*) include the necessary steps to prepare your operational team or production team for the transition. These steps may include

- **Getting the help desk up to speed:** Begin involving the help desk associates in informational meetings toward the end of your project so that they can be prepared to support the system.

- **Engaging the help desk personnel in the system activation support:** These associates can get great information from your project team, end users, and other stakeholders as they provide end-user support during the go-live process. For example, they log user problems, answer user questions, resolve issues, and more.

- **Getting the operational staff off and running:** You need to ensure that the operational staff understands what kind of training they will need in order to provide ongoing support for the software. You won't necessarily need to provide this training, but you need to provide input on this vital subject.

- **Facilitating at least one turnover meeting with some of your key team members, the help desk staff, the appropriate members of the organization's operational team, and any other pertinent stakeholders:** During turnover meetings, you and other stakeholders have the opportunity to review the system documentation and answer questions.

- **Making sure that your system documentation is complete, concise, and correct:** You and your team have built the system and someone on your team should have been assigned the task of completing system documentation.

Don't forget that someone also needs to be assigned the ongoing task of keeping the system documentation up to date. That most likely will not be someone from your project team, but just remember to remind the operational staff that it needs to be done.

This is not an exhaustive list of system turnover activities. Your organization may have mandatory steps you should take when turning over the software to those who will be supporting it.

Be sure to know what your organization or client expects of you and your team when you hand over the system to the operational team. Be proactive. You should gather this information during the planning process. The actions you take at the end of your project will be what people will most remember about you and your leadership. You don't want to come to the end of your project and get caught saying, "Duh, was I supposed to do that?"

Celebrating!

Although celebrating is something that often gets put aside because of new priorities and team members moving on to other software projects, some of your team members (and some professional project managers, ahem!) may insist that this is the most important portion of the project.

You've all worked hard to accomplish your goals and exceed stakeholder expectations. Take the time to show everyone — your team members and other stakeholders — how much you appreciate them. Project team members will be grateful and will remember that you are the type of project manager who values your team, which is an important impression to leave because you will undoubtedly form new project teams for your future projects. No one wants to work for a software project manager who doesn't show appreciation for the team.

Celebrate your success, not just because it's good for the team, and your image as a leader, but because it gives you an opportunity to let other project managers and executives know what your project was all about — and what a fantastic job you did. Under the auspices of tooting your team members' horns, you can legitimately toot your own horn — which is never a bad political move if you do it without being a brag.

Planning your celebration

You don't have to rent a ballroom and have a formal dance-off or anything. Just do something to show appreciation, such as:

✔ Take your project team for a scheduled lunch at the local pizza parlor.

✔ Have a massage therapist come in for an afternoon to provide free massages (this is also a great reward at the stressful times during the project; you can't imagine what this can do for your team morale!).

✔ Schedule an outing at a local park and allow team members to bring their families. This is also a great opportunity to show families how much you appreciate their spouses, parents, and kids.

✔ Have a team appreciation day where you prepare a meal for your project team members. You and other key stakeholders could actually serve the meal.

✔ Rent out a movie theater for a day and allow team members to bring their families to all watch a movie together.

The possibilities are endless and will vary with the scope and success of your software project (as well as the limitations of your budget), but you should do *something* to show you appreciate your team and celebrate their success, commitment, and hard work. The more thoughtful your expression is the better.

Releasing project team members from the project team

Well, you and your software project team members have spent an exorbitant number of hours working together these last few weeks, months, or years. You've overcome seemingly insurmountable obstacles and created software that's so outstanding that you even surprised yourselves. You've completed your lessons learned documentation (see Chapter 17) that you began at the start of your project, and you've shared it with all your team members and appropriate stakeholders. You've expressed to your project team members how much you appreciate their efforts, and your team has celebrated its success together. Now it's time for your project team to disperse.

As with all other aspects and phases of project management, be proactive in disbanding your team. Don't wait until you're at the project closing festivities and say, "Hey, by the way, you can sleep in tomorrow."

Because you started out with such a well-defined project plan that included all phases of your software project and you communicated this plan to your team, everyone knew at the start of the project when they would be released (or rolled off). To be proactive, you should review roll-off dates with your team members on a regular basis; sometimes project end dates fluctuate, and you don't want anyone to be surprised. For example, initially you may have agreed that an individual would be on your team for eight months, but if the project is extended, you would certainly want that team member to stay until the project is completed.

Nobody likes surprises (except little kids), so be sure project team members know the dates they'll be needed right from the start. Before they're released from this software project they will probably already be planning their next steps, especially if they're contractors without the security of a health plan and a set salary. Being aware of their project roll-off date well in advance will enable your project team members to

- ✔ Begin reviewing other software project opportunities if they are private consultants or contractors.

- ✔ Start ramping up for their next project if they work for an organization that has another project ready to begin.

- ✔ Continue working with you on the next project you manage because they really liked the way you showed your appreciation at the project closing celebration! Of course, they want to work with you because you are a model software project manager.

- ✔ Begin managing their own software projects after learning superior project management skills and techniques from such a superb teacher — that's you.

Be sure each team member understands the time expectations of this project so that they can be proactive in planning their next opportunities.

Writing evaluations

You may be expected to write employee evaluations on all project team members. Make sure you know these expectations right from the start so that, again, you can be prepared for this by keeping employee documentation throughout the project. In some instances, you won't be expected to write the employee review, but you will need to provide input to the team member's functional manager for the evaluation. Follow the rules of your organization when conducting employee evaluations.

Employee evaluations can be an unbelievably time-consuming pastime. If you have a large team and you have to do evaluations for all of them, develop a system, and don't procrastinate.

Receiving evaluations

You may find it beneficial to ask the team to evaluate your performance as the software project manager. After all, these people know your work characteristics better than anyone else, and if you're evaluating them, they should be able to evaluate you. Plus, it really helps drive home the sense that you are interested in their opinion.

Evaluations provide you with the input that will help you to improve your skills as a software project manager. When you improve your project management and leadership skills, you benefit, and so do your future clients.

Writing evaluation questions that give you results

You may want to write evaluations that ask employees to rate you on a five-point scale. Better yet, provide a combination of questions that require written/typed response and objective ratings.

Here's a list of questions, along with a better way of asking the question so that you can get more detailed feedback and avoid the dreaded yes-or-no answer:

- ✔ **Good question:** Did the project manager communicate project changes in a timely manner?

    Better question: Rate the project manager's timeliness when communicating project changes (1 = not applicable; 2 = not timely; 3 = often, but not always, timely; 4 = usually timely; 5 = always timely).

- ✔ **Good question:** Did the project manager achieve the project scope?

    Better question: Using a five-point scale, rate how well the project manager achieved the project scope (1= not applicable; 2 = the scope was not met at all; 3 = the scope was mostly met, but there was some scope creep; 4 = the scope was met, but there was some minor scope creep; 5 = the scope was achieved in all areas flawless).

✔ **Good question:** Did the project manager make the most of resource skills? How could this have been improved?

Better question: Rate the project manager's management and allocation of resource skills. How could this have been improved?

✔ **Good question:** Was the project manager a good communicator?

✔ **Better question:** What suggestions can you offer the project manager that would help him improve his communication

- To the project team?

- Across functional teams?

- With appropriate stakeholders?

✔ **Good question:** Was the project manager a good leader?

✔ **Better question:** How would you suggest that the project manager improve her leadership skills?

✔ **Good question:** Were meetings effective?

✔ **Better question:** Using a five-point scale, rate the project manager's meeting facilitating skills. What suggestion do you have on how these skills could be improved?

✔ **Good question:** Did the project manager seem to know what he was doing?

✔ **Better question:** Overall, how would you rate this project manager's project management skills and expertise? What suggestions would you offer to improve overall project management skills of this project manager?

✔ **Good question:** Was the project manager responsible?

✔ **Better question:** Rate the project manager's willingness to take responsibility for his own actions and mistakes.

✔ **Good question:** Did the project manager give credit to team members for their successes?

✔ **Better question:** How did this project manager perform at giving credit to others for their successes?

The primary goal of this should be to include questions that will provide your team members with the opportunity to provide honest and helpful feedback that will allow you to grow as a project manager.

Remember, even if one of your team members makes a negative comment, that's still positive if you learn from that comment.

Your team members may suggest that you allow them to give you feedback anonymously. You may do whatever feels right, but in our experience, if you're trying to build a sense of accountability, your team should feel empowered to offer all reasonable and constructive feedback with their name attached. We're all accountable for our actions and our words, and we should all be willing to own what we say. Welcome the feedback — positive or negative — as long as a name is attached to it.

Case Study: Completing a Project Post Mortem

You are a software project manager for KT Consulting, Inc., a medium-size consulting firm specializing in software project management. You've been with the company since it was founded six years ago and are one of the most respected project managers in the firm. That's why senior management asked you to lead a project for a sometimes difficult client — Barbwire Helmets, Inc. — which wants to create Web-based tutorials for its production staff.

The client is a manufacturing firm creating much sought after barbwire helmets, and is having some difficulty with worker safety because some employees have not been following proper safety procedures. The executives have determined, through root cause analysis, that the employees aren't following the appropriate procedures because they don't always understand what those procedures are.

The client held several meetings with you to define the business purpose and objectives of the project. These are as follows:

✔ **Business purpose:** Decrease the number of worker accidents, which will result in

- Fewer fines by the associated government agencies

- Increased worker productivity due to less time off work because of injuries

- Increased employee morale

- Decrease in money spent on broken equipment

- Decrease in health and accidental death/dismemberment insurance

✔ **Project objectives:** Create a Web-based tutorial for production workers that will instruct employees on appropriate safety procedures for manufacturing barbwire helmets:

- Software should provide a database where employee scores are kept

- Tutorial should provide hints when an employee enters an incorrect answer

- System reports should be automatically distributed to employees' supervisors, and they should include final scores and number of attempts before passing

- System should require 80 percent for passing score

- Software should allow training department to schedule classes online

- System should send online reports to managers if an employee registers for a class but does not show up on the specified day

- Full system documentation, including instructions on how to troubleshoot most common errors, should be included with the system

You're energized about starting such an interesting software project, and have been anxious about working with Barbwire Helmets, Inc. You hope that this will be as exciting as your last project, working with Fire-Filled Pants, Inc. You're ready to get rolling. You've gathered the appropriate project team members, met with the client to understand the project requirements, and started the project planning process.

Your client, Mr. Safedee, is impressed with the amount of detail that you've put into the scope documents, project plan, quality management plan, and risk management plan. He's also impressed that you understand the importance of involving the appropriate stakeholders right from the beginning. You reviewed the work breakdown structure (WBS) with the client and the team and everyone understands that if a task is not in the WBS, it will not be done — no exceptions. Your software project team is thrilled that you've set the correct expectations with the client. They know that you will have fewer problems in the future by performing this level of detail in the planning now.

Your client is satisfied with the project schedule plan, cost management plan, and risk management plan. Your project team understands the roles and responsibilities matrix and the staffing management plan. Everything is going so well that you're wondering why your boss warned you about working with this difficult client. What's so hard about all this, you wonder?

Then you look at the schedule and realize that with the small size of your team and the tight schedule required of you, you will not be able to complete the entire project in time. You and Mr. Safedee agree that you should outsource part of your project. You decide that you will contract out the software testing phase of your project. You contact Testy McTesty, the world-renowned software testing agency, and your contact agrees to provide the following services for your WBT project:

- Unit software testing

- Functional software testing

- Integrated software testing

- Volume testing

- ✔ Issue identification
- ✔ Issue resolution
- ✔ Testing documentation

You and the Testy McTesty representatives agree to a fixed-price contract with an incentive for completing by a predetermined date. This is important to you because you need to have time to perform other activities after the software is completely tested and you don't want to take a chance on getting behind schedule.

You've documented all of the details in your procurement management plan and contract management plan and included constraints, assumptions, deadlines, performance reporting requirements, evaluation criteria, payment methods, and change control.

You understand from your client, Barbwire Helmets, Inc., what is expected of you as the vendor; Testy McTesty, your vendor, understands what is expected of you, their client. All is right with the world.

Being the exceptional software project manager that you are and working with your brilliant hand-selected project team, you complete the Web-based tutorials on time and within budget. Testy McTesty completes its portion of the project but have a few testing issues from the integrated software testing phase. These issues are still unresolved. You don't worry too much about it, though, because these issues are deemed a low priority.

At project closure, your client, Barbwire Helmets, Inc., performs the following actions:

- ✔ Quality audits
- ✔ Scope verification
- ✔ Close vendor contracts
- ✔ Receive your invoices
- ✔ Performance review on your work as the project manager

You and your client sign the scope verification documents and all project closure documents and you perform the following actions:

- ✔ Document performance reviews on your team members
- ✔ Provide surveys to your project team members to solicit their input on your performance as a project manager

✔ Complete your lessons learned document (the one that you started at the beginning of your project)

✔ Review lessons learned documentation with your team members and distribute it to the appropriate stakeholders

✔ Celebrate your team's success by writing an article about your project team in your company's newsletter; distributing gift certificates to each team member; holding a team lunch where you prepare and serve the meal; providing hot air balloon rides for your team members and their families

✔ Perform audits of Testy McTesty's work

✔ Receive Testy McTesty's invoices and pay your bills

✔ Close out all contracts

✔ Turn over all system documentation and review it with your client

When you submit your performance reports to your superiors, they realize that this wasn't a difficult client after all. You explain to your superiors that because you were proactive and followed the appropriate software project management processes throughout the project, you gained the trust and respect of the client and attained a higher level of continuous success. You also explain that because you make a habit of documenting what you learn from each project, you have continued to hone your skills. You attribute the fact that you have the respect and admiration of your team to your positive attitude and generosity when the hard work is complete.

Your superiors agree, you get promoted, and you are engaged to teach other KT Consulting project managers the proper methods of project management — particularly the activities around project closure.

Chapter 17

Documenting Your Software Project

· ·

In This Chapter

▶ Writing the lessons learned document

▶ Documenting a project

▶ Documenting your documentation

▶ Creating the help manual

· ·

*A*ll too often, project managers look at writing the documentation for their projects with the same vim and vigor with which they used to apply to writing thank you cards to their grandmothers. But the truth is, a project worth doing is a project worth documenting. Documenting your plans for a project is essential, but it's just as important to document what actually happened during the project. This documentation is future historical information: What you write today will help you and others tomorrow.

Documentation makes a historical record of the experiences — mistakes and successes — from which you've learned in your software project. What seems crystal clear in your mind now may not be so clear two years later when it is time to update the software and start the project anew. Think of how much information will be lost if members of your team quit, retire, or transfer to other departments.

Using Teamwork When Writing Documentation

The project was not a solo project; if it was, you couldn't really call yourself a manager. Because many hands worked on the project, many hands should also work on the documentation. Developers can write sections about development lessons learned, to be read by future developers, far better than you can. Your focus should be on the project manager's section, as well as rounding up the whole document to make sure it has as consistent a *look and feel* as possible.

Some project managers add a technical writer to the team from the beginning with the purpose of them heading up the creation of a *look-and-feel document* (to direct the formatting and tone of written work from a corporate perspective) or *style guide* (to handle standards for spelling, grammar, and other particulars), as well as accompanying documentation for your project. In fact, many companies have set procedures for formatting and writing important documents. If your budget allows you to hire a technical writer, you'll find that this is money well spent.

Here are a couple of important tips to keep in mind:

- ✔ **Have meetings:** When you finish the *lessons learned document*, the document should be something that everyone on the team is familiar and comfortable with. That does not mean they have to agree with all of it — many times we would like to not see specific problems put in writing in the hopes that they will be more quickly forgotten — but it does mean that you should hold meetings to discuss issues and work through them.

- ✔ **Set milestones:** Just as timelines exist for other parts of the project, they should exist for the documentation as well. You will find yourself needing to provide motivation to keep it moving along. Treat this part of the project as if it is as important as the creation of any module or component (it is as important!), and make sure that it gets done.

You may meet resistance from your team when it comes to documenting lessons learned. Reluctance to create this documentation can often be a result of fear. A developer may wonder, "If everyone else knows what I know, I won't be needed." When you encounter this belief, you need to confront it head on and assure the individual that this document can serve to illustrate to everyone just how much they do know and make them even more relevant and valuable — not the reverse.

Three factors to consider when you write

Whenever you write anything, whether it's lessons learned documentation, training materials, or system test plans, there are always three factors that you should take into account:

✔ **The method of documentation (printed or electronic):** If it is electronic, can the document exist within another document, or must it be a stand-alone document? If it is printed, is it a subset of a large document or a stand-alone entity?

✔ **The scope of the documentation:** Should the document only address a change that was made, or should it be all-inclusive? Any time you make a major change to the

operation of a site, you need to document exactly what was done. Needless to say, you should also only make one major change at a time to fully realize the ramifications of that change before making any others.

✔ **The target audience:** Is the document to be used to jog your memory six months from now, or is it something to distribute to all users? If it is only for you, you can get by with a few lines of terse notes. If it is for distribution to users, you need to be specific and offer as much background information as necessary without going overboard.

Completing the Lessons Learned Documentation

The input to any project should be the *lessons learned document* from previous projects. The output from any project should be the lessons learned document for future projects. In other words, you use previous lessons learned documents when you start your project. When your project is complete, you should be able to produce a lessons learned document as one of your deliverables.

You should always start your lessons learned document at the beginning of your project to ensure you capture lessons learned right from the start. See Chapter 2 for information about initiating, planning, and beginning a project.

Arguably, the lessons learned document can become the single most important document that a software project manager is ever involved in. It is your chance to pass on information to other project managers and to maintain records for yourself. Lessons learned can save untold time and money.

Maintaining the lessons learned documentation throughout the entire project helps to keep things in perspective; you can show your software project team that it's acceptable to make mistakes (everyone does it) as long as you learn from mistakes and use the knowledge you gained to make better project decisions in the future. You can empower your staff to take calculated risks if they know that all mistakes offer opportunities to learn.

The lessons learned document is the written history that the project existed and the story of how it came to be and what you learned from the project. Without this document, the project runs the risk of being forgotten over time. Although the project may or may not prove to be important in the long run, the lessons learned from it will always have immeasurable value. You should document lessons learned for every project — even if the project is cancelled at an early stage — because every project can teach you something.

Getting your historical information together at the beginning of a project

Whenever you start a new project, you should always seek out all existing lessons learned documents from similar projects that have come before and use them to help prepare for your upcoming venture. And when you write your own lessons learned document, you should bear in mind that others will be reading this document in the future, so you should write to that audience.

Your best input for project planning is historical information, which can include

- Lessons learned documents
- Past project files
- Procurement information
- Interviews with previous project team members
- Rumors, gossip, and hearsay — kidding! (This kind of "data" is never reliable.)

See Chapters 2 and 3 and all of Part II if you're not sure how to go about planning your project.

Creating a lessons learned spreadsheet at the beginning of the project

At the very beginning of your project, before you can even imagine an ending, you ought to create a spreadsheet to document mistakes and successes. Better yet, why not create a template for the spreadsheet so that major project areas are covered. Share the template with your team and make documenting lessons learned a regular agenda item for your team meetings, asking the question, "What did we learn from this?" If you enforce this level of critical thinking, team members will take ownership of this process, and they will be as proud of their successes as they are glad they learned from their mistakes. The final product — the lessons learned documentation — is a great historical document that shows the cumulative results of their contributions.

Look at the example of a lessons learned spreadsheet in Table 17-1 to inspire you about how to use this valuable tool in your own software projects. Remember, the column headings should vary depending on the particular type of software project that you're managing. You'll be amazed at how quickly this spreadsheet becomes a regularly expected part of your regularly scheduled project team meetings, and your team will take pride in making contributions to it.

Table 17-1 Lessons Learned Spreadsheet for Future Documentation

Topic	Project Area	Lesson Learned	Team Owner
Testing	Workflow Testing	Prior to starting the testing phase, we need to set the expectation that testers don't stop to resolve issues — they just need to document each issue.	Testing Manager
Testing	Workflow Testing	During workflow testing, we need to encourage end users to perform their normal job functions.	Testing Manager
Training	End-User Training	During the planning phase, we need to set the expectation that 90% of end users must be trained in order to ensure successful system implementation.	Client
Reports	End-User Reports	Start gathering information on needed end-user reports at the beginning of the project to compensate for the learning curve for stored procedures.	Client
Print Testing	Testing	Ensure that all appropriate project team members understand the complexities of testing the print capabilities of the project.	Project Manager

Organizing Your Lessons Learned Document

While you may want to impress others with a long discourse, only professors love long essays. Future project managers — your audience — value lists of practical tips. You should record only the vital information that'll likely be needed later for reference.

A quick online search will yield dozens of lessons learned document templates. Every organization has its own methods and includes different information. Also, some info is of greater or lesser importance depending on the type of software project. That said, every lessons learned document should include the following information:

- ✔ A summary or foreword section
- ✔ Lessons learned by major stakeholders involved in the development of the software
- ✔ Acknowledgments, references, and resources

Every lessons learned document should evaluate the overall project successes and failures, as well offer an assessment on what the better approach should be. The document should not just be a list of problems that lacks evidence of reflection and discovery.

Organizing the summary of your document

The lessons learned document should begin with a summary section identifying why it exists, what type of project this was, and what the timeframe for completion was. For example, you might write something like this:

> *The Corona project was a project in which we built a Web-based program that allowed the residents of Corona, California, to pay traffic tickets online. Originally expected to last six months, the project lasted roughly eight months, between January 2 and August 15, 2006.*

This section can be called the Foreword, the Summary, or any similar title, but its purpose is to allow the reader to quickly identify whether the rest of the document is worth reading. The foreword should not be more than one page and may include a specific list of functions the software was originally contracted to include.

Many introductory sections also include acknowledgements and lists of those involved in the project. It helps to have this information readily available at the beginning of the document so that future readers can seek out you or another member of the team as questions arise.

Organizing the meat of the document

Following this introductory section is the actual documentation of lessons learned. You can take one of several approaches to writing this portion of the document — from listing activities in chronological order to alphabetizing under topics. No matter which approach you take, we highly recommend that this material be divided into sections.

One of the easiest divisions you can choose is to break the content down into lessons learned by various key stakeholders, with each group getting its own section. Prioritize the order of the groups based on who is most likely to need the information. For example:

✔ Lessons learned by developers (this should be the first section because developers have a higher chance of needing the information than others).

✔ Lessons learned by project managers (second in importance).

✔ Lessons learned by users (third in importance).

✔ Lessons learned for other participants.

In every part, you list problems and solutions. You should be as specific as possible about the problems; problems have a tendency to follow patterns, so your specific description of a problem (and its coordinating solution) may mirror something a future reader is facing. The best thing you can do with a lessons learned document is give future readers an "A-ha" moment when they stumble across your text in the two-years-from-now time capsule and realize that you just helped them immensely.

Organizing your references, contributors, and resources

After the meat of the document, the lessons learned document should end with a section of references, resources, and contributors. The acknowledgements section at the beginning of the document tends to list everyone who worked on the *project,* while the contributors section often lists those who contributed to the *document*. Although you may like to believe that those two lists were identical, some people have the gift of writing and organization, and some don't. You may discover that pulling coherent, usable documentation from some team members is next to impossible.

Some members are a part of the team because their skill and expertise is needed in an area other than documentation. As much as you may not want to, you'll have to accept the fact that the writing is not something they are good at. Of course, accepting this fact may be a whole lot easier if the team members are crack coders!

Documenting the project's successes

Success is sweet.

It feels good to accomplish something and know that you pulled off a task that was very difficult. It makes you feel all warm inside and beam with pride. But you know this already, right?

Many people tend to downplay success and pass it off with, "Ah, shucks, it was nothing," or, "Just got lucky." Inside we may know that we did the impossible, but are afraid that saying so out loud will sound like bravado. After all, no one likes a braggart.

Regardless of how you feel inside, you cannot be afraid to commit the successes to paper as part of your lessons learned documentation. Be honest about what was accomplished and don't be afraid to toot your own horn if necessary. The success came because you figured out what worked and directed your team to get the job done, and that is something that someone else can benefit from on their next project.

Commit it to paper, be honest about it, and feel good about it!

Documenting the project's failures

Along the path, you experienced failures as well as successes. You went in one direction believing that it was the best path to follow, then were blindsided by an issue that you never gave much forethought to. This is natural with almost every project. These are the unknown unknowns that whack you in the head and wreck your project.

That experience of failure needs to be a part of your lessons learned documentation. You document your failures so that future projects will not run the risk of being similarly blindsided and so that readers can see what worked for you and move down those venues instead. This is your opportunity to save others from a whack in the head by incorporating these successes and failures into your lessons learned document.

Not everything works. It's the way of life. It's the way of projects.

Thomas Edison patented 1,093 inventions — that's 1,093 successes he had with projects. Now imagine how many things didn't work out. Each one of those failed projects represented an opportunity to learn and refine skills. Some of Edison's inventions even came as the result of trying to do one thing and ending up with a completely different result. This story is repeated time and time again in history. The invention of Sticky Notes came about as a result of trying to create glue. The invention backfired, and the glue only sort of stuck.

What was tried and did not work is just as important as what was tried that did work. If you document, in your lessons learned documentation, the route that led to failure, you'll create a map that keeps someone else from going down that same road, wasting money and time racing to a dead end.

Sometimes an entire project ends in failure. When that happens, the project truly becomes nothing more than a *feasibility study*. Documenting the causes of the failure can really help out in the long term. You can say whether you think future projects of this type can ever be feasible and offer specific recommendations that ultimately improve your company's strategic approach.

Documenting the better approach

It's a question we all hate: If you could change any one thing, what would it be? If you could go back in time, knowing then what you know now, what would you do differently? What would have been a better approach than the one you took?

While the exercise may seem unoriginal, or even passé, it is judicious and more than just an exercise in analytical reasoning. Keep in mind that you are creating a document to be read for future projects. Telling a better approach to take, even if only in the theoretical sense, can give the next project a better starting place than the one you used.

Offering advice for future project managers

Having just completed a project, you know what worked and what didn't. You know what you would do differently, and you know what subtle changes you would make if you had the chance to do it all over again.

You also know that sometimes your advice isn't heeded, just as you sometimes discount the advice of others who offer it to you. Even if you feel as if no one cares about your advice, you need to write down every bit of the advice you have. Pretend that the audience consists only of you. Write this section to yourself and no one else. Put it in the report, and know that those who read it have the chance to gain from it.

As long as you write this section with the frame of mind that you can learn from it the next time you read it, you will be doing better than 99 percent of the project managers who complete this section.

You may be tempted to add advice like, "Never work with that rotten programmer from ABC Programming, Inc. He's arrogant and lazy, and he never does what you ask him to do." Of course we know we don't need to tell you this, but we're going to tell you anyway. Do not put anything in writing that expresses a negative, emotional opinion to other people. Even if you feel like your project was unsuccessful because of the actions of individuals, express these concerns neutrally and in general terms, such as, "A high level of programming skill was needed in this project. I advise future project managers to give unknown candidate programmers a brief skills test and conduct thorough interviews when filling the positions. Make sure someone in HR calls outsource candidates' references."

Creating the User Manual and Help System

Every piece of software needs a user manual and a help system associated with it, even if the piece of software is a subcomponent of a much larger software product. If you're building a subcomponent, the documentation for this smaller piece may simply need to be incorporated into an already-existing framework; alternatively, it may need to have stand-alone documentation and help files. If you're creating a stand-alone product or a component with stand-alone help and documentation, you have a real onus to create the best documentation available.

Your technical writer or assigned team member should start creating the user manual and user help documents at the start of the project. This is an important deliverable to your software project, and should not be withheld until the end of the project.

We've all heard the usual gripes that users don't read the documentation, and that they just want someone to do it for them. Developers often like to ask, "How hard can it be to press the Help key?" Before you give these complaints any merit, let us ask a question: When was the last time you read the manual accompanying the software you bought, whether it be a development package, a word processor, or something else?

Odds are that you didn't read it any more than the user wants to read what you write. Why? Because you think the documentation that accompanied your purchase is worthless, too long, and was written by someone who doesn't speak your native language, is inaccurate, wrong, confusing. . . . You get the idea. We'll let you in on a secret: The *For Dummies* empire was built to fill a gap between the needs of software users and the worthless documentation they received from manufacturers.

You want the documentation you read to give you the answer to the question you have in a way you can understand it. Then you want to move on with your life. Amazingly, that is what the user of your software wants from the documentation you create, as well.

This is another area where it can often pay huge dividends if you can afford to have a technical writer as part of the team. Having an experienced person in this field can lessen the burden on the team.

The following sections offer broad areas of advice for creating documentation for your software product. Read *The Practical Guide to Project Management Documentation* by John Rakos, Karen Dhanraj, Scott Kennedy, Laverne Fleck, Steve Jackson, and James Harris (Wiley) for more information on creating project documentation. Your company probably has specific guidelines that you should follow, as well.

Using the project scope as a reference

The starting point of anything the user is to see should be the project scope. Why did this software get created in the first place? What purpose does it fulfill? The user is using the software for that very purpose, and the only thing they want to know is how to accomplish this specific task.

Begin with the scope, and then work through the operations, always focusing on the fact that the user hopes to reach the end point as quickly (and painlessly) as possible.

Establishing operational transfer

Operational transfer, the movement from the project implementation phase to the support phase, is about more than just the user coming to understand your new application to the point of being productive. It also represents the availability of the project team and the supporting IT staff to help users. You need to coordinate, that is, really communicate, the interaction of the folks that'll be using your software, the department that will support your software, and the project team that created the software.

Keeping in mind that the end user is trying to successfully complete a specific task (whether that is generating a report about drinking water in the Amazon, formatting a disk while making giggling squeals, or something else that your software does), you need to focus on walking those users through that process.

Here are some basic steps to follow when it comes to documenting operational transfer:

1. **Start with the assumption that users have never used your software before.**

   They are not familiar with your train of thought, and do not know how to do the task that they realize they need to do.

   Good documentation starts with logical programmers who create programs that allow users to perform tasks using a variety of simple, uniform methods. If you've had good programmers working on your project and good quality assurance and testing, you already know where things are working and where things may require extra explanation. You also know which scenarios are most likely and which scenarios are least likely (you can guess that someone won't be trying to use the spell checker in software meant to record complex statistical data) so that you can focus on the areas that users are most likely to need help in.

2. **Walk users through a very quick, common operation from start to finish.**

   Don't go into any options or special features. Walk through the most basic operation imaginable and document each step.

   Don't make too many assumptions about the level of technological abilities of users. We hope you figured out the users' abilities when you talked with the client and set up the product scope. But just because a program performs a simple task doesn't mean that the user is technologically unsophisticated — and vice-versa. Maybe a piece of software does something pretty advanced. That doesn't mean that the user has the same skills as your programmers.

3. **Discuss how someone may need to deviate from that basic operation if users need to do other things.**

   Explain why someone would want to read from another file, format the output a specific way, or whatever else your software can do.

4. **Begin walking through the operations again.**

   This time, incorporate the option(s) that will make the changes. Again, assume the reader has no experience with your software and was not part of the team that created it. You don't want to talk down to users, but you do want to avoid racing through the material as if you were talking to a new developer joining the team.

Death by documentation

All too often, we tend to think of documentation as an add-on component to a project rather than as an actual part of the project. The truth of the matter is that documentation can make all the difference between whether a project is a success or a failure.

Time after time, companies have created good products and then not invested the necessary resources into their documentation. Many of these products failed in the marketplace, not because they were bad products, but because people didn't know how to use them.

There once was a large software company (which no longer exists) that used to make a very good development package. Version 3 of this company's software was very well liked and stood a great chance of becoming the dominant development platform in a specific field.

Wanting to gain that market domination, the company put all of its resources into coming out with version 4 — something that would blow the socks off everything else on the market. The company changed the user interface in version 4. It changed the options. It changed the calls. It changed so much about the product that users could barely tell by looking at version 4 of the product that it was the same product as version 3.

In fact, the company had created a development product that was well ahead of its time, and should have moved programming forward dramatically. What happened, however, is that the whole thing backfired and the software was dismissed. Meanwhile, another company came along and released the development software that became the *de facto* standard.

What went wrong? How did this company fail so miserably?

The company sold the product for two prices. The first price gave you only the software media. The second price (roughly twice as much) gave users the software media and thousands of pages of bound manuals on how to use it.

Most programmers thought that moving from version 3 to version 4 would be an evolutionary move (as opposed to a revolutionary move), and didn't buy the manuals (or couldn't convince their managers that it was worth paying twice as much for the product to get the books). Without the manuals, developers fumbled around and couldn't figure out how to do what they needed to do. Frustrated and angry, developers abandoned the package.

Those who did get the manuals were overwhelmed — literally — by thousands of pages spread out through five books that cross-referenced one another so much that users had to have all the books open at once in order to figure out how to do what you wanted to do. Those who spent the extra money also abandoned the new platform.

Eventually the platform died; not because it was not good, but because the documentation killed it. Properly written documentation, properly packaged with a superb product, could have propelled the company to a position of envy.

When you design your documentation, keep this tale in the back of your mind and make certain that your products don't fall prey to the same fate. This catastrophe is easy enough to prevent, but you must make a conscientious effort to do so.

Avoiding helpless help systems

Here are some important questions:

- Have you ever called an automated help system and been put on hold and transferred from one extension to another, never talking to a human being, and getting hung up on after an hour of frustration?

- Have you ever asked someone a question and been more confused by the answer than you were when you started?

- Have you ever tried to read a reference book (not this one, of course) and wondered what language it was written in?

- Have you every worked with a program whose help system crashed?

- Have you every worked with a program whose help system contradicted itself?

Those are situations most of us can identify with and they share the same end result: frustration. When you want an answer, you want an answer that you understand, and you want it now. Here's what users don't want:

- They don't want to be sent somewhere else.

- They don't want to have to think about and process what was said.

- They don't want to have learned more than they need to know at this minute.

When you design a help system, whether it lives online or in a print format, you need to keep users in mind and KISS.

The best rule is to place yourself in the position of the end user you are creating the material for. As long as you keep these basic tenets in mind, you'll create documentation and help systems better than most that are currently out there.

Part VI
The Part of Tens

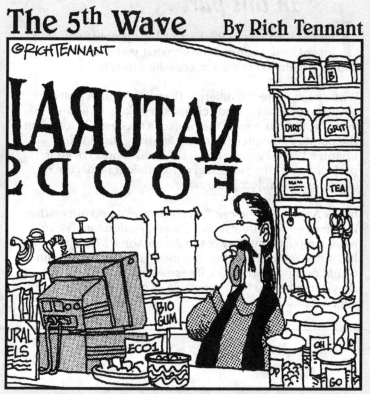

The 5th Wave   By Rich Tennant

"I asked for software that would biodegrade after it was thrown out, not while it was running."

In this part . . .

The two chapters in the Part of Tens provide you with lots of useful information on what you should and should not do to ensure a successful project.

While each project is different than every other software project, some items or disciplines are likely to always increase the chances of the project's success. By avoiding the points in Chapter 18 and by applying the tips in Chapter 19, you greatly enhance the likelihood of your project being successful and of maintaining a degree of sanity as the project progresses.

In the Appendix, you can find some useful and interesting information regarding resources and professional development support, courtesy of the Professional Management Institute. You can also find out more about the PMP and CAPM certification exams. These exams are tough, but they can take you to the pinnacle of project management success.

Chapter 18

Ten Ways to Make Your Software Project Crash and Burn

You can make your software project crash and burn in so many ways that limiting this chapter to just ten is difficult. Some of the forces that could terminate your project are beyond your control: Say the CIO resolves to pull the project for financial reasons; or perhaps your project sponsor decides not to sponsor the project because of political considerations. Maybe the alignment of the planets just does not make the project feasible.

In this chapter we focus on just ten ways that you — and you alone, without the intervention of the Head Honcho, project sponsor, or astrological omens — can kill a software project.

Failing to Plan

Failing to plan ahead is the most obvious way to fail. If you're looking for the quickest way to end your project, don't spend the majority of the total project time on planning. In fact, why not just avoid planning altogether? That ought to ensure that the project never takes off.

Planning is the most time-intensive part of the project management process because it involves all of the project management knowledge areas. Planning includes creating project plans, gathering requirements, crafting communication plans, forming risk management plans, and developing quality management plans.

Because creating project plans is an iterative process, it can get pretty tedious. You develop a project plan, something happens, and then you have to adjust the plan and communicate these changes to the appropriate stakeholders. It's really quite boring to do things right (especially if you have to do them right more than once), so we suggest not concerning yourself with any types of planning.

Where planning is concerned, here are the two things you should definitely *not do* if you really want to blow your software project out of the water:

- **Don't create a communication plan.** The stakeholders and sponsor will eventually hear the status of the project anyway, so why bother developing the communication plans? An added bonus is that you can spend the time you save looking for a new job.

- **Don't bother with resource management planning.** Most project managers believe it's worthwhile to create a resource management plan that outlines the requirements for people, equipment, supplies, and so on. Planning resources is highly overrated. Instead of planning for and documenting your resource needs so that you can be prepared for each phase of your software project, it is much easier to just figure everything out as you go.

Ignoring Risk Management

As we discuss in Chapter 5, there are risks inherent in every project. Actually, there are risks in everything you do. You took a risk when you picked up this book — you could have dropped the book on the big toe of your left foot and ended up in the emergency room. But you determined that the rewards you would get from reading this book were well worth the risks. And of course you were right.

If you consistently ignore risks, you consistently miss opportunities associated with taking a chance on an anticipated outcome. Risks do not always have a negative outcome. Julius Caesar would never have become emperor had he not crossed the Rubicon. People who plan for risks often win.

Risks are categorized into two categories, *pure* and *business*. You can't do much about a pure risk. If Caesar had contracted malaria while crossing the

Rubicon River and died, well, that's a pure risk he would've taken and lost. Business risks, on the other hand, can be anticipated and planned for. As the project manager, you may have to cross the metaphorical Rubicon when you accelerate a project in order to decrease time to market, or gamble that an inexperienced programmer will write in good code, free of errors, so that you can decrease costs. If these gambles succeed, you may have managed to swim the English Channel, never mind the Rubicon (which is a rather poor excuse for a river to begin with).

Projects are more likely to fail at the beginning and succeed at the end. They fail at the beginning because of the huge quantity of unknowns that you must plan for. You have to think about scope creep, technology advances, and the unrealistic expectations of the stakeholders. There are so many risks associated with software project management that it would take too long to plan for all of them — even if you could identify all of them.

So why bother creating a risk management plan, performing qualitative and quantitative analyses, and worrying about risk assessments when you already know that all projects have a ton of risks? What's the point of documenting and planning for risks when you already know they are going to occur? Either play the odds or just hope for the best; things will work out some way. If you really want your project to crash and burn, take a risk and don't create a risk management plan.

It takes much longer to fix problems that occur because of a lack of risk management planning than to avoid them in the first place. But because we're talking about ways to kill a project, failing to adequately plan for as many risks as possible will assure that your path to project success will be blocked by the project Rubicon.

Letting Your Ego Lead the Project

This may be a complete shock to you, but you really don't know everything, and even if you did (which you don't), you can't do everything. You need to rely on others to help complete your software project. Everyone on your team and all of your stakeholders have something to offer to the success of the project. Trying to perform all project tasks on your own or without soliciting input from your subject matter experts is a brilliant step if you want to sabotage your project.

Trying to do everything on your own is easy enough, but to really kill your project right, be sure to also deny that you will make mistakes along the way. Remember the story from Chapter 17 regarding the invention of sticky notes? In the process of trying to create one thing, someone made a mistake and created something completely different. If that inventor's ego had been too large to admit the mistake, we may not have sticky notes today. Think of the consequences:

- A gentle breeze could scatter all of your reminders into oblivion.

- You might be forced to stick reminders to your walls with the sharp edge of a pistachio shell, staples, or a miniature hammer and nails coordinated to match your cubicle's personalized design scheme.

- You would have to throw all your notes on the floor and hope for the best.

Documenting your mistakes enables others to benefit from your errors. Don't worry about it; most of these mistakes have been made by other project managers at one time or another. Of course, if you don't want others to learn from your mistakes, but you *do* want to show off your enormous ego, never admit your mistakes. Whatever you do, don't ask stakeholders or team members for their input on any area of the project. The project is sure to sink, but not before giving you an ulcer.

Letting Your Iron Triangle Melt

No, the Iron Triangle doesn't refer to a large sandwich with three types of cheeses and plenty of sautéed onions on lightly toasted rye. As we explain in Chapter 1, the *Iron Triangle* refers to the universal project constraints of time, cost, and scope.

If you make a change to one constraint in the Iron Triangle, you must also change the other constraints in order to maintain balance.

Of course, you could melt this Iron Triangle and thus make the software project crash and burn by

- **Agreeing to move up a deadline without securing other resources.** This tactic is great because you have the potential for blowing your deadline *and* increasing costs.

- **Agreeing to enhance or add to major product features without increasing the timeline.** Way to kill your staff! Of course, if you want to add bling, you have two choices: pay overtime (blowing your budget) *or* blow your deadline.

- **Allowing resources to leave the project early without adding time to the project's deadlines or hiring a replacement.** If you make a change to any of the sides of the Iron Triangle, you need to change the shape and balance of the entire triangle so that the project timeline, cost, and scope remain in balance.

Hiding from the Project Team

There are times, especially when deadlines approach and things are particularly frantic, that you will be tempted to hide in the nearest broom closet, retreat to a bathroom stall with your feet propped up, or become a chameleon and blend into the wallpaper. Even the most experienced project managers have been tempted to hide out a time or two.

Becoming invisible to your project team creates some very interesting scenarios:

  ✔ **One of your programmers could inadvertently redefine a project requirement.** Oh, who cares — requirements are for the weak anyway.

  ✔ **The team may resort to turf wars.** Will they settle the tiff with a dance-off or with fisticuffs?

  ✔ **Your sponsor may realize that the software project can be completed without its project manager.** While you're hiding, we hope you're circulating your resume.

You are the project manager; it's your responsibility to manage the project. You've got to be visible to motivate the team, resolve conflicts, distribute project information, and help to create a cooperative and compatible project team. If you want to crash your project, go ahead and check out. Your team, sponsor, and stakeholders may miss you, but they'll get over it. And you'll find a new job eventually.

Hovering over the Project Team

Smothering your project team can be just as detrimental to your project management success as hiding from your project team. If you want to kill your chances for managing a successful software project

  ✔ **Don't worry about teaching leadership; it's not really your job, anyway.** Some project managers like to strike a balance between offering guidance and support and allowing team members to learn from their mistakes. Others, like you, just micromanage every detail.

  ✔ **Don't concern yourself with affording your team members with the opportunity to demonstrate their creative problem-solving skills.** Enabling team members to use their knowledge, education, and experience to complete their assigned tasks would be good for their personal and professional development. Which would be good for the project. Which you don't want.

- ✔ **Cripple your staff's ability to do anything, large or small, without your approval.** Don't show team members that you trust their judgment to make important decisions. Whatever you do, don't let them act on those decisions without your approval.

- ✔ **When in doubt, hover.** Breathe down their necks and look over their shoulders. These actions afford you with the chance to gaze at all their family photos and the knickknacks on their desks.

When you hover over your project team, all kinds of great things start to happen. Team members will begin to come to you every time they have a simple question, such as:

- ✔ What color should I make the heading of this section?

- ✔ Should I have three lines of comments in this section or two?

- ✔ Does this look better with four radio buttons or should I remove one?

- ✔ Can you make Bob stop looking at me funny at meetings?

Remember that you have a dual role as a manager and a leader. If you are doing a superb job of leading your team (motivating, inspiring, and directing them), then you can focus more time on managing the project. Team members will recognize that you have the confidence in them to do their work successfully.

On the other hand, if you hover over your team, you take a chance on:

- ✔ Frustrating team members.

- ✔ Creating an atmosphere of mistrust.

- ✔ Encouraging team members to come to you for even the simplest questions.

- ✔ Forcing your team members to become robots who never have to think on their own because they have someone else to do that for them.

Creating Unrealistic Schedules

Remember, there will be times when the CIO or some other fancy pants will vaguely relate the objectives of a software project and casually ask you how long it will take to complete a project before you have the information necessary to answer that question with a shred of accuracy. Sometimes, you can stall by telling the CIO that you will get back to her with an answer as soon as you receive more specific information, but other times she will insist on an immediate answer. As we discuss in Chapter 8, you need to consider so many variables before answering scheduling questions:

- What is the scope of the project?
- How many experienced programmers can you hire?
- What is the budget?
- What are the requirements of the project; what functions should the user be able to perform with the software?
- What is the business question that this project will answer?
- What are the assumptions and constraints (flip to Chapters 2 and 3 for more information)?
- Who are the stakeholders?
- What are the activities that need to be completed, and in what sequence must they be performed?
- What is the risk tolerance (check out Chapter 5) of the department or organization?
- What are the risks of the project?
- How will project success be determined?

You have to consider all of these questions (and more) to answer that one simple question: How long will it take? Surely (we hope you don't mind being called Surely), you can go ahead and trivialize the entire project management process by giving a quick answer to that question. Then again, you could always go ahead and put together unrealistic schedules. Your team will thank you for all the free time they'll have if you stretch out the schedule too much. Or, you can take the time necessary to effectively create the time estimates and provide a realistic and accurate project schedule.

Consistently Being Inconsistent

Consistency is the most crucial consideration. No it isn't. Yes it is. It could be, maybe. The point is that when you are the project manager, people are going to rely on you to consistently provide accurate and timely project communications; you also have to make key project decisions that will have significant consequences to many stakeholders.

Team members are going to ask about their schedules as well as about their roles and responsibilities. Your sponsor and other stakeholders are going to require information regarding project status, risks, timelines, and trouble issues. Kind of scary isn't it?

Maybe you'll get lucky and be able to work with a team that doesn't appreciate consistency because it's so boring and predictable. The feeling of uncertainty may provide your team with a sense of excitement, because they know that at any moment you will change your mind about a decision you made yesterday or change their on-site work schedule. Your team's morale is sure to increase as members band together to try to figure out how to sabotage you. Just be careful about eating that homemade brownie they bring you.

Your stakeholders may be thankful for the opportunity to try to figure out what you really mean when you talk to them, and jump at the chance to second guess everything you say. Sponsors will understand if you change your mind every time you talk to them, right? Yeah right.

After you gain a reputation for being inconsistent — either in determining schedules or taking a particular stand or dealing with conflicts — this reputation sticks with you and people quit relying on you. Consistently being inconsistent can deep-six your project, but the long-term impact is that you will be labeled a flake every time you're given a project to manage in the future.

Doing Nothing

How hard can it be to do nothing? Just don't respond to any requests for information and don't take any initiative toward planning your project or resolving issues. For example, don't do these things:

- ✔ **Give your sponsor regular status updates.** What a pain it would be to manufacture reports of your ongoing process.

- ✔ **Create a thorough project plan.** You don't really need to gather requirements — not when you could get a manicure instead.

- ✔ **Create a risk management plan.** You're not doing anything at all, which means you're not taking any risks. So why bother managing risks that don't exist?

- ✔ **Come up with budget, time estimates, and a definition of scope.** These things take way too much time, anyway.

- ✔ **Come up with a quality management plan.** Let the product come out as the programmers originally intended, even if it doesn't work.

You may think it's easy to do nothing and to refrain from being proactive in resolving issues and conflicts, and it is — at first. You need to make sure that the project is completed successfully, on time, and within budget. Of course, it is your prerogative to do nothing, and result in terminating your project.

Being a Wimp

Here are some facts for you: As the project manager, you're required to make some tough decisions; sometimes you have to say no to either your team members or to stakeholders; you won't always be liked or popular; and you will have to answer some tough questions from your sponsor if anything goes amiss with the project. You can't always be the most popular person in the room, but you can earn respect if you do the right things for right reasons and expect the same from the rest of the team.

If you want to aid the crash and burn of your project, be a wimp. Specifically, here's what you must do:

✔ **Be sure to give your team members everything they want.** Sometimes teams need incentives, but a hot tub in the break room is out of the question.

If you give everyone everything they want, you can be the most popular project manager on the block. You can join all the other popular project managers in the unemployment line and you can share stories about the glory days when you were a wimpy project manager.

You shouldn't withhold from your team the things they really need, however, like tools, training, and resources.

✔ **If your team members want to schedule vacations during critical due dates, let them.** Your lead programmer shouldn't miss his own wedding, but you should find out whether team members have vacation conflicts before you hire them.

✔ **If your stakeholders decide they must have time-consuming feature changes without changing the timeline or cost of the project, go ahead and agree to those changes.** After all, saying no or negotiating is just too hard.

✔ **Never take a definitive stand on any tough issues.** A project manager never seems less trustworthy than when he or she appears to be weaseling out of giving a straight answer.

Wimpy project managers don't last long in that career. It is absolutely impossible to be an effective software project manager (or any kind of project manager) and be a wimp. The personality trait and the job description don't work together. They can't work together.

To be an effective project manager who can gain the respect of your sponsor, team members, and key stakeholders, you will be called upon to make tough decisions on a regular basis. You need to know when to take a stand and when to negotiate. Being a strong leader doesn't mean you have to be Machiavellian or rigid; you can still earn respect by being flexible and fair and by giving staff some things while holding back on others. Although you need to have firm guidelines in place so that others know what to expect of you, you also need to make some decisions on an individual basis. If you would prefer to be a wimp, then you should look into another profession — such as being a professional big baby.

Chapter 19

Ten Ways to Make Any Software Project Better

*Y*ou've done your homework, read this book, received advice from other software project managers, and created a terrific software project plan. That's wonderful! Congratulations. Now let us help you make that terrific project plan even better. There may be just a few things that you can do to make your software project even more brilliant.

Asking the Right Questions

Universities and colleges should offer classes in how to ask questions. In fact, Asking Questions 101 should be a required course for all project managers because it is such an important skill and is so often underrated.

When you're gathering requirements for your project, you must ask questions of many people, particularly other software project managers.

You need to talk to project managers who have completed similar projects so that you can get their input on what lessons they learned from their projects. Many new project managers ask experienced project managers about mistakes made or lessons learned from previous projects, but don't forget to also ask what went well on the project so that you can modify those activities to fit your particular software project.

Don't forget that other more experienced project managers can be a terrific resource for you.

One of the most important questions you can ask of your sponsor and appropriate stakeholders is, "How will we know that this project is successful?" Make sure you know what success is supposed to look like for this particular software project.

Of course, after you have asked all of the appropriate questions of the appropriate stakeholders, be sure to document and distribute these answers and requirements so that if you have made a mistake or an omission, stakeholders have an early opportunity to communicate this back to you.

Being a Good Communicator

Don't underestimate the power and importance of communication.

Stakeholders can tolerate a lot of things, but they will not tolerate being unaware of something that they should have already known.

You might discover that you are going to encounter some cost overruns. That's bad news by anyone's standards. You may have just found out through software testing that you have a huge bug in your program and that's going to extend your already tight schedule. That's not exactly something to call home about or a cause for celebration.

But both of these issues, as well as others, would be a lot more palatable if you communicate them to the appropriate stakeholders as soon as they come to light. If you don't, you run the risk that your stakeholders will hear about these issues through the grapevine. You do not want that to happen.

Communicating effectively doesn't just entail conveying negative information. To communicate successfully, you must relate all project information to appropriate stakeholders.

Take the time at the start of the project to develop thorough communication plans. Document the method of communication, the receiver of each communication, and the time period for each communication. Then, stick to it. You won't regret taking the time to implement a communication plan, and we guarantee that sooner or later communicating effectively will be one of your saving graces.

Showing Your Leadership Skills

A project manager must have visible leadership skills. You will be making tough decisions, sometimes communicating painful information, dealing with difficult people, and managing important risks. You must have impressive leadership skills to prevail in difficult circumstances like these.

Keep in mind that someone can be an effective manager and a so-so leader at the same time. A good manager can track issues and changes, manage resources, and write a great project plan. A leader can keep the project's vision in mind, get others to agree about its direction and goals, and inspire and motivate the software project team to accomplish those goals.

Creating the Right Project Plan

Okay, you're ready to start developing your project plan. Have you

- ✔ Spoken with the appropriate stakeholders?
- ✔ Met with experienced project managers who have already completed similar projects?
- ✔ Collaborated with your project team members to understand their strengths, weaknesses, and experiences?
- ✔ Understood how each team member can contribute to project success?
- ✔ Discussed expectations with your project sponsor so that you both can develop a clear understanding of what project success will look like?
- ✔ Documented your software project's assumptions and constraints so that you know how they affect your software project?
- ✔ Developed a solid change control system so that you can prevent scope creep?
- ✔ Documented and distributed a clear, concise communication plan?
- ✔ Created the project charter (or ensured that someone else created it) and received sign-off by the project sponsor?

Creating a project plan isn't something that you do at the beginning of the project and then put away in a drawer somewhere only to be removed when you hit a snag or need scrap paper. Creating project plans is an iterative process that occurs throughout the life of the project. You may modify the plans depending on situations or problems that occur throughout the project.

Keep in mind that one of the purposes of the project plans is to document and communicate exactly what you hope to accomplish when you create the software. You must document the resources required to accomplish project tasks, start and end dates of each task, and predecessors and successors of each task (what has to happen first and what has to happen next). Before you document all of this information, be sure to

✔ Talk with the appropriate stakeholders

✔ Gather all of the requirements

✔ Meet with your sponsor

✔ Talk to other project managers who have gone before you

If you thoroughly do all of these things, you will most likely create a thorough and accurate project plan.

Finding the Correct Sponsor

The sponsor for your software project has the authority to assign resources and offer guidance in resolving issues. These are not responsibilities for just any doofus; you must pick the right doofus. Just kidding.

It is imperative that you find the correct sponsor because this person can apply muscle on your behalf when necessary and, because of his or her executive position in the firm, can help you enforce project decisions.

The project sponsor also has the customer's needs in mind, understands the business objectives of the software project, can help resolve issues, has a role in developing the project's strategic objectives, and is your main point of contact for all executive-level decisions.

Because the sponsor for your software project is the one you have to rely on at crunch time, you want a sponsor who is actively engaged in the project. Avoid a sponsor who has so many other irons in the fire that she won't have the time to focus on project issues.

Also, the project sponsor will be the one who announces to the world that you are the Big Wig Project Manager for this software project. Ideally, you should have a positive and constructive relationship with this person.

You may not always enjoy the luxury of choosing a project sponsor. Many times you are merely told who the sponsor is. If all this information is moot because you have no say in who your project sponsor is, here's what you can do: Make your sponsor look really, really good. Take on all the best attributes you can and then give credit to the sponsor. And smile.

Recognizing Failure Before It Arrives

How can you recognize something before it even arrives? It's possible, and you don't have to be clairvoyant, either. If you know how to look for the signs of impending failure before the failure actually occurs, in fact, you'll have a significant advantage in the software project management game.

The other crucial element (perhaps more crucial than simply recognizing signs of failure) is being proactive in dealing with potential issues before failure bears its ugly head. You know that if you see or smell smoke, there's probably a fire nearby, right? Great, but recognition makes no difference if you don't run for the fire extinguisher.

Remember that projects are more likely to fail at the beginning than at the end. So do everything in your power to prevent failure at the beginning. Spend a sufficient amount of time planning your software project, gathering requirements from your customers, and developing a strong, solid communication plan (and adhering to it), then use those exceptional leadership skills of yours to build a strong, motivated, software project team.

Here are a few signs of potential project failure:

✔ Have you or anyone from your project team started to let a few deadlines slip? That's bad. What's worse is if no one's even a bit surprised anymore when deadlines do slip.

✔ Has your project changed so much you don't recognize it anymore? If too much scope creep has, um, crept in, your project is in danger.

✔ Are you starting to have a high turnover from your team? If people are dropping like flies (for whatever reason), they are taking knowledge with them. That's bad. But what's worse is if they're leaving because morale is low or because they don't respect their project manager.

✔ Speaking of low morale, are you seeing signs of it? Are team members bickering more often than usual, losing interest in the project, or putting silly words in the middle of their software code just to see if anyone notices? Are programmers sleeping at their desks, coming in late, leaving early, or taking marathon lunches?

✔ Has your sponsor been missing meetings with you? Does he or she appear disconnected from the project?

✔ Have your stakeholders started getting a vacuous look in their eyes whenever you mention deliverables and risks?

✔ Has the sponsor started to micromanage you? Do you lack the autonomy you need to bring the project to a successful completion?

After you know what these signs are, deal with them as soon as you spot them. Be proactive; don't wait for your Invitation to Project Failure to show up in your interoffice mail box.

The key to turning around an imperiled project is communication. This means not just *talking* with your sponsor and team members, but *listening*, too. Then you must act.

Planning, Planning, and a Little More Planning

There are five process groups involved in project management. These process groups are

- Initiation
- Planning
- Executing
- Monitoring and controlling
- Closing

You will spend most of your time in the planning phase, and this is completely logical when you think of all the activities that you and your software project team will accomplish during the planning process. You will be

- Developing project management plans
- Developing project schedules
- Defining project scope
- Estimating duration of activities
- Estimating costs and budgets
- Documenting communication plans
- Creating risk management and quality management plans
- Planning the scope
- Creating the work breakdown structure
- Determining the project sequence of activities
- Estimating the types and quantities of project resources

Planning is not a one-time deal. That's why they call it an *iterative* process.

Documenting Your Project Even if You Don't Want To

But then again, why wouldn't you want to document your software project? As we say in Chapter 17, a project worth doing is a project worth documenting. Your project is worth doing, right? Not only should you be documenting your software project plans as well as all of the subsidiary plans, but you also need to document your lessons learned.

Here are some tips for documenting lessons learned:

- **Start early:** Most people start their lessons learned documents at the end of a project, but they should start this documentation at the beginning of a project. Create a spreadsheet that has placeholders for each area of your project and then add to this document as the project progresses. By the time you close the project, you will already have a nearly complete lessons learned document that you and others can use for your future software projects.

- **Make it a group thing:** You could even make lessons learned an agenda item for each of your project team meetings. After team members become accustomed to seeing this lessons learned document and watching it grow as the project progresses, they will start feeling ownership of the document. The project team will also get used to thinking in terms of every issue or problem resulting in a lesson learned instead of just considering problems as something to overcome.

- **Spread it around:** When your software project is complete, you can distribute the lessons learned document to your project team and then complete it with the team during the post project review meeting. Your team, your sponsor, and all the stakeholders over all the land will be in awe of your superior project management powers.

Hosting a Successful Project Meeting

Have you ever attended a meeting that reminded you of a three-ring circus? There was no agenda, one guy was talking on his cellphone, several people were having side conversations, you weren't sure of the purpose of the meeting, and not only that, but the donuts were stale? Don't let this happen to you. Hosting a successful project meeting is not that difficult, and requires just a little planning and thoughtfulness.

First, and maybe most importantly, send out an agenda to all invitees prior to the meeting. In the agenda, document the purpose of the meeting. So far, this doesn't sound too difficult, right? Well, it doesn't get any more difficult than that. On the agenda, document each agenda item, along with the responsible person and the time span for each agenda item. When attendees walk into a conference room, they should have absolutely no doubt as to the purpose of the meeting. Here is an example of a well-prepared meeting agenda:

Meeting Agenda for Review of Training Methodology

Meeting Date:	Tuesday, November 12
Meeting Time:	1:00–2:00 p.m.
Meeting Location:	Room 123A
Facilitator:	Mary
Recorder:	Tony
Meeting Invitees:	Bob, Tom, Sue, Mary, Tony, Glenda, Gladys, Roger
Meeting Purpose:	The purpose of this meeting is to review the training methodology for the software that will be implemented on June 10 of next year.
Agenda Item 1:	Discuss the three basic training methodologies (1:00–1:30 p.m. [Tony])
Agenda Item 2:	Review the CBT (1:30–1:45 p.m. [Glenda])
Agenda Item 3:	Questions and Next Steps (1:45–2:00 p.m. [Tony])
Next Meeting:	Tuesday, November 19
Next Meeting Location:	Room 123B

Be sure the agenda is distributed prior to the meeting. When attendees walk in the room for the meeting, they should already understand the purpose of the meeting.

Here are some helpful hints for making the meeting more efficient:

- ✔ **Start the meeting on time.** The best way to get people to be at a meeting on time is to gain a reputation for always starting a meeting on time.

- ✔ **Stay on topic.** When someone brings up a topic that is not on your agenda, offer to place that item on the *parking lot,* which is a document where you keep items to be discussed at a later time.

- ✔ **Play the librarian.** When two or more people begin to have a side discussion, calmly remind them that everyone needs to stay focused and stay away from side topics. Is that subtle enough? After you say that once, you're unlikely to say it again.

- ✔ **Always talk about follow-ups.** The last agenda item should include next steps or follow up. Before they leave the meeting, all attendees should have a clear understanding as to what will happen next and when it should happen.

- ✔ **Don't let the minutes pass you by.** Always, without fail, every time, forever and ever, follow up each meeting with meeting minutes. Distribute them as soon after the meeting as possible and be sure to ask for corrections or additions to the minutes. If someone sends you changes to your minutes, send out the corrected minutes as soon as possible. Be sure to include all appropriate stakeholders in the meeting minutes, whether or not they attended the meeting.

Post the minutes on either a team Web page or a shared drive somewhere on the network. Stakeholders should have easy access to all meeting minutes and they should be stored in an organized fashion.

Establishing Project Rules Before the Project Begins

It's so easy to follow rules when you know what they are. It's pretty much a no-brainer to follow an established, well-known rule.

If you want project team members to adhere to project rules, make sure they know what the rules are before the project begins. Better yet, ask your team members to contribute to the list of project rules. Take advantage of the expertise and intelligence of the smart people you hired. People are always more likely to follow rules if they helped develop them.

After you establish guidelines, cover them in the project kick-off meeting. Go over each rule and ask if anyone needs clarification. Don't forget to follow up with documentation.

Communicating Good and Bad News

Remember when you were little and you broke your neighbor's window with your curve ball, or received a bad grade in citizenship, or "accidentally" cut your brother's hair? You were probably a little apprehensive about telling your parents the bad news. That attitude gets carried over into adulthood. People may not be eager to communicate bad news, but they have no problem communicating good news.

It may not be easy, but you need to communicate both good and bad news in a timely manner. Stakeholders have to know what's going on, and it's your responsibility to communicate with them. This is really easy advice to understand, but surprisingly difficult to follow.

It's best to communicate bad news as soon as you have the information.

Believe me, your stakeholders will react more positively if they hear news in a timely manner than if you wait and tell them something when it's too late.

If the schedule may slip, or your costs may be overrun, or you think you might be losing a key team member, promptly communicate that. You never know, someone to whom you're communicating may just be able to help you with the problem or issue. At the least, give them that opportunity.

Appendix

Formal Project Management Training and Certification

As with any other professional field, there are organizations, certifications, and career development opportunities that you should be aware of. Accountants have their CPA (Certified Professional Accountant) designation; engineers can take tests to become PEs (Professional Engineers); and project managers can look forward to obtaining their PMP (Project Management Professional) status through the Project Management Institute.

PMI supports all areas of project management, not just software project management.

Getting Up Close and Personal with the Project Management Institute

The Project Management Institute (PMI), founded in 1969, is an increasingly influential and prominent organization that focuses on enhancing and encouraging the career development of project management professionals, while offering opportunities for professional development and knowledge sharing. PMI serves as a project management resource. Membership benefits include

✔ Access to project management professional publications that exhibit examples of successful project management ventures. The PMI's publications are immensely helpful in providing peer learning opportunities and mentorship.

- ✔ Opportunities to join special interest groups and local chapters in the PMI network. You can teach others and receive information from other professionals who work in the same field as you, or in other fields.

- ✔ Access to knowledge areas, project management career information, and training information and opportunities.

- ✔ Memberships in PMI colleges, where members share a common interest and expertise in a particular project management knowledge area.

- ✔ Numerous opportunities for professional development and networking.

Visit the PMI Web site at www.pmi.org for more information and to discover a plethora of other reasons for joining this prestigious organization.

PMI has over 200,000 members (and it continues to grow) from over 100 countries. The current annual membership fee of $119 for an individual membership or $30 for a student membership is a bargain.

Finding Out Whether the Project Management Professional Certification Is for You

If you're already a project manager or work on project teams as a developer or in some other capacity, you probably know several project managers. Conduct an informal poll: Of all the project managers with whom you are familiar, how many have their PMP certification? Probably not many. The PMP certification isn't an easy qualification to obtain. This certification is the top of the line because it's so difficult to obtain, and it is very highly regarded.

Earning the Project Management Professional (PMP) certification is a challenging and arduous feat. First, before you can even start the certification process, you have to have worked as a project manager for a predefined number of hours. The conventional wisdom is that as you continue to work as a project manager and gain experience in the field, you will become better at being a project management professional. After all, most people learn best through experience, so you should become better at project management the longer you do it, right?

When you become a PMP, you also pledge to abide by the PMI code of professional conduct. You can find out more about the PMI code of conduct from the PMI Web site and from almost every PMP certification study guide on the market.

Some of the other requirements for obtaining PMP certification are

✔ High school diploma or a comparable certification.

✔ At least 35 hours of project management education.

✔ A minimum of 7,500 hours working in a leadership role and providing direction for particular types of tasks.

✔ At least 60 months of project management experience.

PMI randomly audits applications, so be sure to keep all of your documentation.

✔ You must pass the PMP certification exam, which consists of 200 multiple-choice questions. The questions you get are random, so if you and your best buddy take the exam at the same time in the same location, you won't be asked the same questions.

If you have a baccalaureate degree (otherwise known as a bachelor's degree), you only have to work 4,500 hours in a leadership role. And instead of 60 months of project management experience, you'll only need 36 months.

Understanding what a PMP certification says to others

The esteemed PMP certification demonstrates to potential employers, stake-holders, your project team, and others with an understanding of the difficulty of attaining PMP status, that you have completed the arduous requirements necessitated of this standing. This accomplishment also shows that you have a solid understanding of project management concepts and principles. When you earn the PMP certification, it shows that you are willing to work hard and that you take your choice of careers and professional field seriously. Obtaining your PMP certification validates that you understand the principles and accepted practices of the project management field. It also proves that you are willing to go the extra mile to attain professionalism in the field of project management. The PMP certification is recognized all over the world.

Understanding what the PMP certification gets you

Obtaining your status as a PMP is likely to increase your chances of a higher salary, advancement in the project management field, and the respect of your peers. Your skin will glow, there will be an aura about you, and your teeth will be whiter. Plus, it's cool to have another set of initials after your name.

Getting started

If you are thinking of working toward your PMP certification, first of all, great decision. Secondly, here is a checklist of things you should be doing now:

- ✔ Study project management books for the certification (look for books with PMP and Certification in the title).

- ✔ Accept the fact that passing the PMP certification exam relies on you thoroughly understanding the Project Management Body of Knowledge (PMBOK) and that although you may answer a question one way if you answer based just on your own professional experience, you need to consider the answer based on the PMBOK.

- ✔ Take as many practice tests as you can get your hands on.

- ✔ Read, reread, and then read again the most recent version of the PMBOK, paying particular attention to

  - Project Management Processes

  - Project Management Knowledge Areas

  - Inputs, Outputs, and Tools/Techniques of each knowledge area

  - Professional Responsibility (this is something you will be expected to know and to embrace)

- ✔ Know every mathematical formula *ever* written.

To pass the four-hour PMP certification exam, you need to achieve a score of approximately 69 percent. Don't be surprised or disappointed if you don't pass the PMP certification exam on your first attempt. It's not an easy examination; if it was, it wouldn't be as prestigious or influential. Many people do not pass the test on their first attempt, and this is nothing to be ashamed of. You can take the test three times within a year; if the third time isn't a charm, you must wait one year to reapply to take the certification exam.

If you earn a 72 percent on the exam and someone else earns a 99 percent, you still receive the same certification and it doesn't indicate on the certificate that you received a particular score; it just says that you passed. So, don't sweat it; you just need to pass the test.

When studying the PMBOK and other reference materials, make sure you know how to apply the concepts. Don't just memorize definitions or formulas, or you will be in trouble when you attempt to take the PMP certification exam. The exam asks you to apply the concepts and formulas to specific scenarios.

After you earn your PMP certification, you're required to obtain 60 *professional development units* (PDUs) every three years to maintain your professional status. If you fail to do this, you have to take another test in order to regain your PMP certification.

You can earn PDUs by:

✔ Taking courses

✔ Writing papers

✔ Participating in various self-directed learning activities

✔ Taking part in professional activities

✔ Volunteering for community or professional groups

What Is the CAPM Certification?

The PMP certification is not the only credential offered by the Project Management Institute. Another professional certification offered by PMI is the Certified Associate in Project Management (CAPM) certification. The CAPM is a professional designation geared toward members of project teams, as well as those who are just starting out in the field of project management. If you're not quite ready or willing to take the PMP certification, the CAPM certification is a great opportunity for you to find out more about and contribute to the field of project management.

The CAPM certification is also sought out by professionals in many fields who want to show that they are knowledgeable and willing to invest their time and energy to the field of project management.

Earning the PMI CAPM certification is also a prestigious and valuable recognition of your interest in and knowledge of project management principles.

Just as with the Project Management Professional certification, you must meet some requirements to earn the designation. These prerequisites are

✔ High school diploma or a comparable certification

✔ A minimum of 1,500 hours working on a project team

✔ 23 hours of formal project management training

Deciding between the PMP and the CAPM

You can visit the PMI Web site to find out how to register for both certification exams. Here are some specifics if you can't wait that long:

- **PMI members:** The computer-based PMP exam is $405. The computer-based CAPM test is $225.

- **PMI nonmembers:** The computer-based PMP is $555. The CAPM is $300.

Maybe both the CAPM and the PMP are right for you — at different points in your career. The CAPM might be right for you now and the PMP certification could be appropriate for you in the future. One way or the other, both Project Management Institute professional certifications are impressive credentials to obtain and both will demonstrate that you are knowledgeable of project management practices and processes.

If you're already a PMP, you can't take the CAPM exam.

While the PMP certification is valid for three years, the CAPM certification is valid for five years. At the end of five years, you can take the CAPM certification exam again, or, if you meet the requirements, you can register to take the PMP certification exam.

Both of these certifications can assist you in developing your career in the field of project management, and either may be right for you at different points in your career.

Index